WANNABE A WRITER WE'VE HEARD OF?

WANNABE A WRITER WE'VE HEARD OF?

JANE WENHAM-JONES

ACCENT PRESS LTD

Published by Accent Press Ltd – 2010

ISBN 9781906373979

Printed and bound by Thomson Litho, East Kilbride, Scotland

Cover Design by Red Dot Design
Cover Photo: Bill Harris L.R.P.S.
Illustrations: Jane Wenham-Jones except pages 99 and 126, by Shirley Webb

PRAISE FOR WANNABE A WRITER?

"The ultimate how-to book"
Writing Magazine

"Practical and funny... packed with information and advice"
Gaynor Davies, Fiction Editor, *Woman's Weekly*

"A brilliant read."
Freya North

"Helpful, warm and generous. If I were starting out now, I'd find it invaluable."
Isabel Wolff

"Excellent. A must-have book for every budding writer."
The New Writer

"... beautifully amusing... In the world of serious and frequently daunting advice for writers,
Wannabe a Writer? is as refreshing as a fizzing Alka-Seltzer after a big night out."
National Association of Writers' Groups

"I don't think I'd have taken so long to write a
publishable novel if I'd had this book to hand!"
Katie Fforde

"Brilliant!"
Sue Cook

I bought *Wannabe A Writer?* on a whim, having dabbled with writing since school. Following Jane Wenham-Jones' practical and witty advice, it didn't take long to sell my first short story. It was as if someone had just flipped a switch and I knew how to do it. Two years later, I have publishing contracts for eight books and owe Ms Wenham-Jones a very large drink.

Tamsyn Murray, children's and teen author of *My So-Called Afterlife* (Piccadilly Press) and the *Stunt Bunny* series (Simon & Schuster) www.tamsynmurray.co.uk,

Wannabe Writer? brought me out of the closet. Having read it, I felt full of regret for my lost years scribbling away in secret and then hiding my work from prying eyes. Now three years on, I have written four novels and been signed up by an agent. Being the author of a published novel, one day, is now a real goal rather than just a wistful, secret daydream.

Annie Ireson

'When I read Wannabe A Writer, I felt as if Jane Wenham-Jones was sitting next to me on the sofa explaining how I too could get published. Her honesty in owning up to mistakes and her sense of humour along with her invaluable knowledge of the whole industry, inspired me. I followed her advice to the letter, wrote a proposal to How to Books, and they offered me a contract. I'd *never* have done it without Wannabe a Writer.'

Fiona Mackenzie
Author of *How to Start and Run a Petsitting Business*. (How to Books)

Wannabe a Writer? will keep you entertained from beginning to end, as well as providing you with invaluable information about writing and getting published. After suffering a few rejections, *Wannabe a Writer?* gave me a much-needed boost and it really helped me focus on my goal and make sure I wasn't repeating old mistakes. Shortly afterwards, I got a two book deal with Headline review and I am currently writing my third novel. *Add Wannabe a Writer?* to your list of 'must have books' and get writing!'

Sasha Wagstaff, author of *Changing Grooms* and *Wicked Games* (Headline)

For my parents – Felicity and Roy.
Without whom I'd never have been heard of at all ☺

ACKNOWLEDGEMENTS

I always look forward to writing these because it means I've finished the book and always stress in case I forget someone. Am so sorry if, this time, it happens to be you!

There are too many names to list them all so I will simply say I am massively grateful to every single person mentioned in this book. I am constantly touched and humbled by the generosity of other writers and I appreciate your time answering my questions, your patience when I hassled and chased, and your collective wit, wisdom and expertise.

Thank you too to all my fabulous twitter friends – it would have been finished a lot sooner without you but wouldn't have been half the fun.

Rave reviews also to: Emma Leatt who did such a sterling job on the index (and whoever came up with the concept of "work experience"), Bill Harris who took my photographs with great fortitude, Shirley Webb who stepped in when I couldn't draw dogs, my agent Teresa Chris for all her (fierce ☺) support, the wonderful Lunching & Chatting group from the Wannabe website for their friendship and enthusiasm and everyone at Accent Press. (I am banned from mentioning my son Tom in print on the grounds that I am an embarrassment but he is, of course, still my little soldier whose support I treasure and whom I love to bits xx).

They say it's not what you know, but who you know, and in that I've been very lucky. To all the fantastic authors, editors, producers, fellow-hacks and assorted greats of the literary and media world who have helped me, not only with this book but so many things along the way since I started writing, I am indebted. Love yer all. Thank you. And it must be my round…

ACKNOWLEDGMENTS

FOREWORD

I still remember my early days as an author when my main experience of publicising my novels was to do everything I could to avoid it! I was terrified of giving talks and dreaded the thought of people sitting at home, listening to me on the radio. I wish I'd been able to read this book back then. *Wannabe a Writer We've Heard Of?* is fantastically informative in ways I would never have imagined. I've published more than 20 novels now but, reading this, I've still learned many tips and tricks about promotion and PR I didn't know before and, more to the point, I shall be employing them.

This guide covers not only getting into print, but how to get your book "out there" to be appreciated by as many people as possible. The advice is invaluable and thanks to JWJ I'm now working on my first ever elevator pitch. (Watch out Stephen Spielberg – that means YOU!)

Jane writes so entertainingly, and with such verve and wit, that anyone would enjoy this book, even those who don't want to be published and have never written anything longer than a shopping list – it's that much fun to read.

To sum up I really, really recommend this guide – read it, learn from it and be braver than you think you are. Seriously, it could change your life.

And to all you writers out there, good luck!
Jill Mansell

CONTENTS

INTRODUCTION	1
A BOOK TO PUSH	3
So you've got yourself a book deal? (Or not ☹)	3
Tell me about it	4
Getting out there, getting known	5
Quiz – Could you be a Media Tart?	5
In the meantime…	10
The paperwork and other boring bits	10
The role of the agent	11
For my male readers	13
COUNT DOWN TO P DAY	14
What happens next	14
The author photo	15
Covers	23
Blurbs	25
Bits & biogs	26
Cover quotes	28
Give-aways & promotions	29
AI sheets	30
Make friends and influence people	30
Postcards & bookmarks	33
Other sales aids & gimmicks	34
The power of email	36
Time it right	37
Deadlines and lead times	39
What's my angle?	45
The Perfect press release	49
Quick quotes & sound bites	57
How to have a launch party	60

HITTING THE SHELVES 73

We have lift-off   73
The lure of bookshops   74
Make friends with your bookstore   77
What if I'm not in stock?   80
Love your book-buyer too   81
And if I'm self-published?   82
Rave reviews – or not   84
Amazon – a double edged sword   89
On-line stores in general   93
Get over yourself   93

ON THE CAMPAIGN TRAIL 96

Book signings   96
Bookshop events   104
Newspapers & magazines   108
The interview   116
Radio   121
Photos part two   128
TV   135
Public speaking   157
Literary festivals   166
Writing conferences   168
One thing leads to another   171
If you don't ask, you don't get   171

PUTTING IT ABOUT – THE ART OF EXPOSING YOURSELF 174

Keeping up the momentum   174
A media presence   174
Cultivating your local paper   180
Expanding your repertoire   183
Notable dates   186
Plugs & stunts   187
Game shows   188
Being charitable   193
Raffles & auctions   194

Being nice   195
Serendipity   197
Being determined   197

NETWORK! NETWORK! NETWORK!   202
Make friends and influence people Part Two   203
Keeping a database   203
Following up   204
Where to go, what to join   205
Parties & dos   205
Working the room   205
Wear the badge, Madge   206
The danger of canapés   207
Hangover cures   208
Being a party animal…   209
…Or not.   210
Building a readership   212

BURNING QUESTIONS & COMMON CONCERNS   215
What shall I wear?   215
Beauty tips and tricks   217
Do I need a facelift?   219
Hair today, gone tomorrow   221
Losing weight   221
The internal combustion engine   222
Reverse parking   222

THE INTERNET – PROS AND PROS   223
Websites   224
Newsletters   226
To blog or not to blog   227
Anonymous blogging   230
Going on a blog tour   233
Facebook   236
Twitter   239
YouTube   241
Other things you can do online   243

Alerts   245
Being professional   245
Never explain, never complain   245
Tomorrow's chip wrapping? Unfortunately not...   249

NO SUCH THING AS BAD PUBLICITY? 250

Never say no   250
Never say die   251
Good lines when things go wrong   252
Learning to say no   254
Taste and discernment   256
Nutters & weirdos   257

SHALL I JUST HIRE A PR? 262

JOIN MY WAITING LIST 265

WANNABE A WRITER WE'VE HEARD OF? 266
WHAT THE EXPERTS SAY...

USEFUL INFO 283

INDEX OF CONTRIBUTORS
(PLUS NAMES DROPPED OR MENTIONED)   289

COMPETITION 301

WEBSITE 303

CONTACTS 305

NOTES 307

INTRODUCTION

Some writers are shy, retiring creatures who like nothing better than to remain in their dusty attics hunched over their latest masterpiece, shunning the limelight. Forced to stumble, blinking, into the real, commercial world, they mumble in self-effacing fashion when interviewed about their literary endeavours and scuttle back to their desks the moment all that nasty centre-of-attention stuff is over.

I am not one of those.

And if you've just got your first book deal, are working at getting a book deal one day, are thinking of self-publishing and want to shift a few of the books when you do, or have been published for a while but aren't selling as many books as you'd like to, then it would be as well if you weren't either.

Some books fly off shelves and websites all on their own, just by word-of-mouth, without a single bit of advertising, marketing or the author ever being interviewed anywhere. But it's unusual.

Someone knocking on your front door and saying: Have you got any short stories to sell? Or: Would you like to have your own newspaper column? is extremely unlikely. Being chosen at random to appear on television to plug your latest novel only happens in the sort of dreams one gets after too much garlic bread (the cheese business is a myth – it's overdosing on bruschetta that gets me every time).

The difficult truth is that there are thousands of new books published every month and tens of thousands more writers wanting their own work to get recognition too. Competition for shelf space and readers is fierce. And, sadly, writing a damn good book, while still essential of course, may not be enough. We live in an age of celebrity and X Factor, publicists and five minutes of fame. If you want to get anywhere these days, staying in your garret is no longer an option.

If you hanker after writing jobs, need better sales figures, or long to be noticed among a veritable sea of new scribes, you need to Get Yourself Out There. Your publisher will encourage this, your readers will like it, you might be downright terrified by the very thought but, hey, it's got to be done.

Actually, you know, it can be a lot of fun. And, thankfully, it's never been easier.

There are more radio stations, TV channels, magazines, websites and online stores out there than you can shake a stick at and more opportunities to thrust yourself forward and grab an audience than ever before. Don't worry about a lack of contacts or the fact that nobody's ever heard of you or that you're 'shy'. These are trifles.

When I started writing, I was the somewhat knackered, washed-out mother of a toddler who'd lost the art of conversation and whose only brush with fame was when Reg Varney from *On the Buses* came to open the school fete.

I had never been in a newspaper save being photographed in the local rag clutching a riding cup, aged 11. I knew no journalists, had never met a TV producer, and wouldn't have recognised a PR opportunity if it had got up and made me an egg sandwich.

All I had was a publishing ambition and a gob on me. Since then, I have, in my quest to sell books, been on radio and TV, appeared in numerous newspapers and magazines, held dozens of signings, given hundreds of talks, offered myself for auction and even stood on a box at Speakers' Corner (not for the faint-hearted).

I have met Terry Wogan, kissed Michael Parkinson (I have to say this was unsolicited and he looked fairly revolted throughout) and spent an hour on stage with Julian Clary (plus Valerie the dog – bless).

If I can do it, so can you. Don't worry that you don't yet know what to say on the radio, or how you'd go about setting up a book-signing, what to wear when you give a talk or how to deal with the legions of fans camping outside your front door (we can but dream). You soon will if you read on.

I know what you're thinking. Huh, you're saying, as you're flicking through this in the bookshop, wondering if you really want to spend a tenner to listen to me witter on about self-publicity or whether you'd be better off with the latest Jilly Cooper or Ian Rankin, which is what you came in for.

Jane Wenham-Jones? I hear you snort. *I* haven't heard of her.

Maybe not. But, dear reader, look at it this way: You have now...

A BOOK TO PUSH

So you've got yourself a book deal? (Or not ☹)

If you've just sold your first book, massive congratulations. I hope you have celebrated long and hard while you can, not only because this is a fantastic achievement (just finishing a book is a momentous feat. I have at the time of this sentence only written 7,000 words of this one and am coming out in a light sweat every time I hear the word deadline), but because from now on you're going to be very busy and there won't be too much time to sit around quaffing champagne until you get to the launch party (more of that later).

If you're still writing your magnum opus or touting it about, your turn will come (think positive ☺). This is for you too, because there's nothing like being prepared (I wish I had known all I know now when my first book came out – it would have saved a lot of time and some far-reaching mistakes) and you may decide to self-publish, or upload an e book in the meantime. In the latter case, ALL the promotional effort will be down to you so take a deep breath and start bracing yourself now.

And if you've been published for ages and are still skulking in your study afraid to face your potentially adoring public, it's time to get a grip.

There are plenty of damning statistics to say that while more books are being published – either in traditional print, print-on-demand or as e books – than ever before, the big sales are concentrated around an ever smaller number of key titles or authors.

There's lots of evidence to show that if you're not in a three-for-two deal or flagged up at the airports and piled high in the supermarkets then it's very difficult to sell in shedloads.

But there are other factors that affect EPOS (Electronic Point of Sale) figures and 'difficult' should not be confused with 'impossible'.

When it comes to promotion, every little helps and whatever stage of the game you're at, having a grasp of how the publicity machine works will go down well with agents and publishers.

"An author who has a good grasp of PR, and is prepared to do pretty much anything to get themselves and their book noticed, is a bonus." says publisher Patrick Janson-Smith, who has worked with some of the biggest names in the business. "Book-plugging is a chore, no question, but in this visual, touchy-feely age it has to be done."

Literary agent Carole Blake agrees. "Not being media savvy at the outset wouldn't stop me taking someone on," she says, "but it would mean I'd have to coach them strongly once they were a client. Much as I hate to admit how big a part it plays, being media savvy makes a huge difference now."

It really does. You might not be able to force your way into a promotion for publication day or persuade your publisher to flog out for an ad on the tube just yet, but chip away and get your book read and talked about and the buying-public asking for it, and all this might come later.

The first – and ultimate – trick, of course, is to write a really terrific book that everyone wants to read, but the second is to let those potential readers know it's out there. So:

Tell me about it!

I am frequently amazed by the published authors I meet who shake their heads sadly at the mention of sales figures, yet have never appeared on the radio, or been interviewed in a magazine or given a talk.

Why not? I ask myself. Or occasionally, them.

"Nobody's asked me," they reply. Or "I'm not very good at that sort of thing."

Or, once: "I don't have your chutzpah." But believe me, I didn't always have it either.

Front can be learned and cultivated like anything else. If it helps, remember it's a two-way process. Magazines have pages to fill, radio stations many hours of airtime. Editors and producers need interesting people who will write and say fascinating things just as much as we need those vehicles to plug us.

Nobody's going to buy a book that they don't know exists. And nobody is going to call you up and offer you a platform to talk about it from, if they don't know *you* do!

Getting out there, getting known

In order for a stranger to know who you are, they've got to have done one of these things:

Heard someone else mention you, listened to you on the radio, read about you in a newspaper or magazine, seen a picture of you, watched you on TV, come across you on the internet, seen one of your books in a bookshop or bought one of your books and actually read it.

You might think, being a writer, that the last two options were the most obvious routes to fame and fortune but unfortunately, as already mentioned, being piled high in the bookstores is no longer a given.

With more and more publishers scrabbling for shelf space for their titles, having your book selected for sale in the supermarkets or on stations and at airports is a cause for celebration rather than to be expected and even if you are stocked in quantity and displayed prominently, the competition for sales is still tough.

So there are two routes you can take. You can sit back and hope that at least a few people will get hold of a copy of your work and will be so bowled over that they tell all their friends who in turn tell theirs, that the news will spread like a rash, that internet orders will rocket, shops will be forced to order it in or increase their stock, and you will hit the best-seller lists by that holiest of grails – word of mouth. (If this happens to you, then hurrah and gosh and I can't tell you how jealous I am.)

Or you can hedge your bets and give the whole process a bit of a nudge.

Let's see what you're made of first...

Quiz – Could you be a Media Tart?

1. **You are happiest when you are:**
    a) Alone at home, curled up on the sofa with a good book.
    b) Out in the fresh air, walking the dog or playing sport.
    c) Having an informal dinner with your family or a small group of close friends.
    d) Partying till the early hours when you treat the assembled company to a rendition of *I Will Survive*, sung into an empty champagne bottle.

2. **As an auditory experience, which gives you the most pleasure?**
   a) Listening to Radio Four.
   b) Birdsong, wind through leaves, the tinkling of water running over stones.
   c) Your favourite piece of music.
   d) The sound of your own voice.

3. **Thinking about your interaction with others, which most closely describes your social life?**
   a) I do not open up easily but once I have, I am loyal and committed. I stick mostly to a small, trusted circle I have known for a long time.
   b) I enjoy a get-together when I have time and have a variety of pals from school days, work or through my children. I'm just too busy to keep up with them all!
   c) I am outgoing and sociable and love meeting new people. I send hundreds of Christmas cards, remember birthdays and am always ready for a night out.
   d) I have 2356 friends on Facebook and not a clue who any of them are.

4. **And what do your friends and colleagues say about YOU?**
   a) He is utterly dependable, always on time and would never break a confidence.
   b) We don't see much of her these days, but she's always good value when we do.
   c) He tells a good joke and is the life and soul of the party.
   d) For God's sake keep her off the sherry.

5. **What are your views on television programmes such as *Britain's Got Talent*?**
   a) I find it uncomfortable and embarrassing and don't understand how people can lay themselves open to such humiliation.
   b) I admire the entrants with genuine talent but, on the whole, wish we didn't live in a culture where being famous is seen as an end in itself.
   c) I feel envious – I wish I could sing, dance or play a musical instrument.

d) I'm developing an auto-erotic burlesque act with songs from the musicals that will demonstrate my ability to play the spoons between my knees while climbing out of a body stocking. Simon Cowell won't know what's hit him.

6. **You come home to find your partner in bed with a local dignitary. Do you:**
    a) Shout, scream and throw things while sobbing uncontrollably and wailing about betrayal.
    b) Go downstairs and fetch the bread knife and a pair of nutcrackers.
    c) Stand your ground and calmly announce your intention to tell the interloper's spouse, children and colleagues at the town hall unless your council tax is waived for the next decade.
    d) Hurl both sets of clothes out of the window, whip out your camera phone and start preparing your story for the *News of the World*.

7. **You are in a swish restaurant when you realise that there in the corner is a well-known reviewer of books for one of the national papers. Do you:**
    a) Do nothing. Everyone is entitled to a little privacy and it would be inappropriate and undignified to approach someone when they're outside work.
    b) Watch said reviewer like a hawk until she goes to the loo then drop everything and beetle after her, hoping to be able to engineer a casual conversation while you're both washing your hands
    c) Wait until he has finished his meal. Walk nonchalantly past his table and place a copy of your novel and business card on it, murmuring, "I'm your biggest fan – how lovely to meet you" on your way to the door.
    d) Rush up to the table immediately, elbow any superfluous companions out of the way and position yourself on your target's lap, breathing huskily, "I'm the latest literary sensation and this is your lucky day."

8. **How internet savvy are you?**

a) I don't have a computer. I still think it's nice to write letters by hand and see nothing wrong with using the telephone and holding a proper conversation.

b) I take an interest in technological advances, I have a computer and an email account and know how to use Google. I am considering employing someone to design me a website.

c) I have a website, a blog, and a database of contacts. I carry my laptop with me on the train and am starting a Facebook group to help further my networking opportunities.

d) I am on Facebook, My Space, Spacebook, My Face and My ArseAndElbow. I write three blogs under four names with interconnecting RSS feeds. I belong to 17 networking sites, 15 chat rooms and have three online address books. I have built seven of my own websites, my laptop and desktop computers self synchronise on the hour and I sleep with my mobile strapped to my arm and the alarm set to go off every forty minutes so I can post regular tweets on Twitter.

9. **You are asked to give a speech at a family wedding. Do you**

a) Lie awake for weeks beforehand having palpitations and gasping "why me?" until forced to go to the doctors for beta blockers. You still pretend you've gone down with laryngitis.

b) Feel very nervous but also flattered and touched to be asked. You are determined to do your best and decide to keep it short, sweet and complimentary. You practise endlessly in front of the mirror until you are word perfect.

c) Rather look forward to it. You plan a couple of dirty jokes and the story about the time the bridegroom was arrested for wearing no trousers. You knock back the bubbly, figuring that it won't matter if you forget the punch line because everyone will be drunk by then anyway.

d) Buy a choice of outfits and book in for a hair cut, manicure and fake tan. You get the music to go with your slide presentation arranged professionally and have a lighting engineer on hand to make sure you're lit on your good side. You've invested in a radio mike so you can exploit your full range of hand gestures and you employ just the right number of well-judged and witty props. You take questions from the audience afterwards and get the entire performance up on YouTube well ahead of any boring old footage of the bride and groom.

10. **A popular TV channel is holding a competition to write the opening to a best-selling novel. The winner will be invited to pitch their book to a panel of agents and publishers on a much-hyped and innovative new books programme with a celebrity host, and may get a lucrative publishing contract. Do you:**
   a) Decide not to enter. You know you'd be so terrified to be on TV that you'd twitch, hyperventilate, sweat buckets and be totally unable to speak, let alone pitch anything. You're already having flashbacks to what happened in the school nativity.
   b) Think you may as well have a go. You know you'd get stage fright but you'll worry about that if and when the time comes. You probably won't win anyway.
   c) Write and rewrite your opening chapter. Seek expert advice on your synopsis, get a proper author photograph taken and have some postcards printed. Google the industry professionals involved, read up on all their authors and join the online fan club of the celebrity host. At least if you get chosen, you'll be fully prepared.
   d) Chain yourself naked to the steps of the TV studio.

Now add up your score

Mostly As Taking part in a publicity campaign might seem traumatic at first but take it slowly. Begin by striking up conversations at the bus stop or in the doctor's waiting room (and possibly get some more beta-blockers while you're there). Practise saying "I've written a book, you know!" In the meantime, hold up a card that says it, instead.

Mostly Bs You show promise but need to think big and bold. Start by dyeing your hair purple and taking up karaoke. It's all about being noticed. Consider a torrid affair with a member of the cabinet, or a well-placed tattoo.

Mostly Cs You display a good understanding of what it takes to thrust yourself into the public eye. Now work on your individuality and unique selling point. Could you learn sword-swallowing or get arrested for taking your kit off in the middle of the cup final?

Mostly Ds You're a natural and I can't teach you a thing. (Only that those who buy the *News of the World* don't always read books…)

In the meantime…

If you've just got your first book deal, then you'll have all sorts of things to think about before you can start trying to wheedle your way onto the sofa of your favourite chat show.

For traditional print, there is typically around a year between that heady moment when you get offered a contract and your book being on sale – though this may vary – and a whole lot of stuff has to take place over that 12 months, which you will be involved in to a greater or lesser extent.

There'll be general editing notes to go through, a line edit, a copy edit and page proofs to check. You'll be asked about your acknowledgements and any dedication, shown cover designs and your AI (Advance Information) sheet and any advertising material planned. You'll probably need to supply an author photograph and may be asked to help write the blurb for the back of the book.

I won't get us bogged down in every last detail of all of these but will talk about the ones that are going to impact on your publicity efforts. So for published authors simply in need of a boot up the backside (kicking butt my speciality), you skip to the bit about getting a fab photo taken (it's a good start) and I'll just run through a few things you know already.

The paperwork and other boring bits

Aside from exactly how you are going to take the world by storm there are a couple of other things to think about when you've just got a deal. I wasn't going to get into them for two good reasons.

Firstly, I knew I'd find it tedious and second, literary agent Carole Blake has pretty much covered all the bases in her excellent and comprehensive guide: *From Pitch to Publication. Everything You Need to Know to Get Your Novel Published* (Macmillan) and I wouldn't even attempt to compete.

But I do feel duty-bound to issue just one word of warning: what the contract says DOES matter. Even if you think the money isn't important now, it will be later, and however excited you are, you really mustn't sign anything at all without getting some proper, expert advice.

I know how you may be feeling – when I got my first publishing contract I was so elated I'd have taken five quid and a half-share in a hamster – but you need to take a deep breath and a little time to make sure you're getting the best possible deal. And that you fully understand what you're agreeing to.

If you already have an agent then no problem – he or she will be on the case. If you haven't, then it's a good idea to try to get one. This is a subject I go into in some depth in *Wannabe a Writer?* so I won't bang on about it again now, except to simply say it's not so tricky once you've got an offer under your belt, and the Society of Authors (SOA) is an excellent organisation to join in the meantime.

They will vet your contract and that alone justifies the joining fee. I didn't have an agent when I started out and the fourteen page contract didn't mean an awful lot to me. I was lucky in that it was with Transworld, who, being a big, reputable publisher who adhere to the SOA's recommended standard terms of contract, made me a fair offer.

But I still got it checked out by the SOA who made a couple of small suggestions for changes in my favour which Transworld agreed to.

Once you are a member of the SOA you will be entitled to all sorts of legal and technical advice at no extra cost and will have access to free guides on a variety of topics, that you can download from their website.

So even if you have got an agent, I should join anyway. You may well enjoy the events and the networking and it's a place to turn to if you need help quickly. Think of them as the authors' union. There in case of any crises along the way. And ready to fight your corner if necessary.

The role of the agent

Which pretty much sums up what a good agent will do for you, too. He or she is the one who will haggle about money, take up the cudgels on your behalf should things get tricky with the publishers and who will – if she's anything like my own dear representative, The Fearsome One – bark down the phone if she thinks you're not putting your back into it.

Some authors regard their agent as a good friend. Others regard the relationship purely as business. One well-known novelist claims to be so terrified of her agent that she's begged not to be named.

Novelist Emma Darwin likens her agent to "a firm (not strict) aunt" while author and columnist Lucy Mangan describes hers as "the one person on whom I feel I can offload my doubts and neuroses and ask to dispel my profound ignorance in all business and practical matters without being embarrassed. I think this locates him, slightly worryingly, as something between a therapist and priest."

The Fearsome One – forget any sort of shrink or man of the cloth and think Penelope Keith meets Attila the Hun – likes to bond with her authors via retail. They shop – in the sort of outlet where they spend vast wedges of cash and she is offered a chair, a chocolate and a small glass of champagne – while TFO drops pearls of publishing wisdom you ignore at your peril.

Agent Carole Blake views her clients "as professional colleagues I'm working for." It is a bonus, she says, if they become friends too. Many of them are.

But whatever your relationship with your agent, do not expect him or her to be your publicist. This is your job (and if you are fortunate, you will be assisted by a publicist from your publishers too). But in the same way as you should keep those at your publishing house fully informed of whatever you are up to, so it is best to keep your agent in the loop as well.

Because, although he or she probably won't personally set up events for you, they can help the process along. "Everything I know about, I can build on," says Carole Blake. "For instance, I know many review editors and festival organisers, so I can help with introductions, or by tipping off an editor or organiser that a nice author is on the way to them."

Agents may come across opportunities too which they'll pass on if they know you're a willing candidate for a spot of self-promotion. The Fearsome One has been instrumental in my being asked to speak at events and when she was asked to provide tips for BBC Radio Scotland's *Write Here, Write Now*, she suggested they contact me too.

The more agents understand what a whiz you are on the publicity trail the better they can sing your praises to publishers too. And, if all the authors an agent has on the books are equally forthcoming, this can help everyone. "Every tip and contact I learn from one author's career is put into the pot to help all the others I represent," says Carole. "It only makes sense to share info."

For my male readers

When I wrote *Wannabe a Writer?* I intended it to be helpful to both sexes. I was still charged by some, (despite going to the great trouble of giving my views on the rules of football) as having been "a bit girly".

This is probably because I am – er – a girl (albeit a middle-aged-old-bag-type one) and am bound, therefore, to look at things from a largely female perspective.

However, I have taken the comments on board and have strived through the writing of this book to keep my male readers in mind at all times. Therefore may I say, before we go any further, that even if you want to ignore the bits about wearing big knickers and using concealer – everything I have to impart is for you too. (And do see page 222.)

COUNT DOWN TO P DAY

What happens next

While the paperwork's being signed and the editing process is getting underway, other departments at your publishers will be swinging into action too, as they decide how to best package and present both you and your book.

There'll be cover designs to consider, catalogue entries to prepare, marketing material to be thought about. Those in charge of all this will be in touch when there's something for you to see and will soon shout when they need some input from you.

But there's one thing I'd suggest you do even before you are asked and that's get a good author photo taken. Because even if this isn't required on the book jacket, you're going to need one. For your website, for the online profiles you're going to set up, for Twitter, for Facebook, to accompany any blogging you may do (we will get to all this later). For now, suffice to say that if you do your publicity properly this picture is going to pop up all over the place, so you want to leave yourself plenty of leeway to get it right.

This is not the occasion to get your mate to take a quick snap on his or her camera phone and say "that'll do," and you may need to build in time for the unexpected.

Like your agent giving it the thumbs down. Novelist Claire Seeber, who shares with me the dubious pleasure of having The Fearsome One as an agent, followed instructions to the letter, dressing as she'd been told to and finding a photographer friend, who was also an ex-model, to take her pictures.

"Being hugely unphotogenic, I was quite pleased with a few of them," says Claire, "I looked almost half-decent." She duly sent off a selection to TFO and waited for the phone to ring. There was a long silence at the other end and then TFO delivered her verdict. "This photo of you in white, leaning against the wall?" she said. "You look like a street-walker."

When I was first asked for an author photo, I didn't have an agent but I did have a vast spot on my chin. It was so huge, people spoke to it instead of me and I had to delay the photo session until the last possible moment.

So get yours in early.

But read this first.

The author photo

Everything I have to say about the minefield that is the author photo can be summed up in four short words: Thank God for Photoshop.

These days, this magical piece of software would have zapped my spot with one decisive mouse click, but back then it took four inches of slap and some clever lighting to just about bleach it out. It was generally agreed the end result was quite fetching. Or as one of my friends put it, "What a lovely photograph – it doesn't look a bit like you!"

A state of affairs I could have done with at the ensuing launch party where pictures in the local paper showed me signing books with an arm like a sumo wrestler's thigh and the wider consensus of opinion was that I looked six months pregnant.

PhotoShop could have dealt with the extra stomach too so if you're not familiar with this life-saving software, that can blur wrinkles, erase chins and smooth out blotches, it's time to make its acquaintance.

However, unless you are a whiz with intricate software and have many hours to devote to mastering its complexities, don't rush out and buy it yet. The full version of Adobe PhotoShop is expensive (although there is a much cheaper basic version called PhotoShop Elements) and you could lose your life getting to grips with how it works.

Much better to cultivate a nerdy friend who has already mastered its finer points. Personally I wouldn't know how to do any of the filtering and cloning necessary to attend to my crows' feet but luckily I know a man who does. And I keep him on speed-dial.

If you have enough dosh of course, you can hire a professional to take your pictures and this is a sound investment. Although, personally, I would advise against one of those make-over/glamour photo companies that promise to totally transform you.

I am used to writers looking nothing like their mug shots and have learnt to keep my face impassive when introduced to yet another Grande Dame, long familiar as a soft-focussed beauty from the inside of a book jacket, who turns out to be an old crone with no lips; but others may gasp.

You don't want to see shocked expressions when eager fans/potential promoters meet you in the flesh, so it's prudent to use a photograph that is reasonably up to date and try for one that is still recognisable as you – but a you at your best.

Unless you have lots of money and fancy it anyway, you don't, at this stage, need a flash portfolio of yourself draped over the furniture in a dozen different poses. For now, a single fabulous picture should suffice.

It's true that you usually have to take about a hundred shots to get that one good one, and, if you can afford it, a professional photographer, who understands about lighting and angles will probably get there quicker.

But if a friend with a good digital camera can be persuaded to take a few dozen snaps of you dolled up to the nines, you're still bound to end up with a couple of decent ones in there somewhere. You can even utilise the self-timer function and have a go yourself and probably get a perfectly good picture.

Particularly if you bear in mind that it's the lighting that makes all the difference.

If you decide to have some shots taken outside, choose an overcast day or pose in the shade. This is a must for me anyway as my eyes are so sensitive to sunlight that I end up squinting terribly if I don't wear dark glasses. And while I would be thrilled if I were always photographed in a huge pair of shades – they immediately add glamour and can hide a multitude of sins – they tend to be a big no-no to picture editors, who take the view that they're OK on celebrities but make us ordinary mortals look dodgy.

So for a picture you can send out anywhere, sunglasses are best avoided. (Or any glasses, come to that, as they cause all sorts of problems with reflection). A softer light also works wonders on skin tone and will be much more flattering than direct sun.

Indoors, try to use natural light from a window. If you have to use flash, don't stand against a wall because you'll get harsh shadows. (My photographer chum tells me the more advanced camera user can get round this to a certain extent by bouncing the flash off the ceiling.)

A small lamp at your feet or a sheet of white card on your lap can roll back the years as the light/reflection will bleach out wrinkles and imperfections. (And conversely a harsh top light will enhance every crack and crevice till you look like your grandmother.) **NB** it's really worth keeping a note of what worked well and what didn't – where you were/what time of day it was/ whether the curtains were drawn right back, etc. – because it saves an awful lot of time when you come to do it all again.

Wherever you are, go for the plainest background you can find, check for anything distracting – trees that appear to be growing out of your head for example – or anything you wouldn't want visible, like your underwear drying on the radiator.

Do think about what clothes you want to wear (the experts advise against wearing black or white clothes because it can play havoc with the exposure) have your hair done, spend time on your make-up and experiment to find out which is your best side. (I have only recently discovered, after dozens of photo sessions, that my profile looks totally different – there's a decade and a possible nose job in it – if taken from the left.)

Think about how you are standing too. If you are a woman, this is where a female photographer can come in.

The arm photo from that first book-signing came back to haunt me. A woman's magazine reprinted it to use in an article about me later and it was even worse in colour. The offending limb had taken on a sort of mottled effect and filled most of the page.

After a further shot of my abdomen appeared, looking like the BEFORE in those ads for exercise machines, I began to understand why the famous get precious about who takes their picture and why Barbara Cartland was rumoured to carry her own up-lighter.

As it turns out, the late queen of romance went further than that. Steve Arkell, who now runs the TV production company Retina, was once a Senior Producer on ITN's News at Ten and tells a great tale about trying to get Dame Barbara on camera, which is worth digressing for.

It was during the 1990s, when the rocky relationship between Prince Charles and Diana was hot news. Dame Barbara, then in the 90s herself, was often in demand to be interviewed on the topic, not only for her traditional views on romance but because she was the mother of Raine Spencer, Diana's step-mother.

One night when a fresh story broke, a couple of hours before the programme, Steve phoned her estate in Hertfordshire and was told she'd be happy to do a live interview for the bulletin. "I scrambled a camera crew and satellite truck and we all dashed the 30 miles from central London to her country house. We arrived en masse to be greeted by her butler and shown to the pantry, where we were each offered a glass of sherry. By then it was approaching 10 o'clock." As the minutes ticked by, Steve was getting "a bit jittery" but he "observed the pleasantries", and was relieved when, after pouring the sherry, her butler picked up the internal telephone, and put Steve on to Dame Barbara herself. She would, she told him, be "delighted" to give the interview, enquiring when he would like her to do it.

"In the next ten minutes would be good," Steve replied, only to find the conversation rapidly over. "Oh no, I couldn't possibly," said the multi-million-selling author. "Please put my butler back on the line".

Her butler subsequently explained that Dame Barbara couldn't under any circumstances do an interview before lunchtime the following day. "Despite all my persuasive journalistic skills," says Steve, "he wouldn't budge. And no, I couldn't see her in person to try and talk her into it."

It transpired that staff needed time to order the flowers, get the hairdresser and make-up artist in, and there were "all sorts of other preparations" to be made. It became clear that Steve had come for a chat about the possibility of doing an interview, not the interview itself.

"I braced myself and rang the newsdesk, who were, not surprisingly, miffed. But at least I could tell them they'd have the interview for the following day's Lunchtime News."

The next day Steve and the crew were wheeled into the drawing room (after refusing an early sherry), and there was Dame Barbara seated and "beaming radiantly". Surrounded by several huge bunches of pink flowers, she looked, Steve says, "not a day over 80."

She was "sweetness and light personified" he recalls. "Her only stipulation was that we lit her with pink light from beneath. I refrained from asking her if she wanted Vaseline smeared on the lens as well."

Dame Barbara Cartland was a woman, Steve tells me, who "knew all the tricks of the trade." And a few extra ones, it seems.

"Although we didn't discuss it, I'm absolutely certain she also knew what wouldn't show on camera. Which – in those days before High

Definition – was the tape which had been strategically placed on her hairline to hold her face up."

Good for her, I say. Had I known where to get a pink up-lighter I'd have got one too, but not being famous or even vaguely sought-after, I simply vowed to carry my own bin liner and put it over my head next time anyone came near me with a Nikon. And to keep my limbs out of sight.

Fortunately, however, when the next book came out, a wonderful woman called Valerie Cameron came along to take my photo and she taught me what to do about arms. I now remember to hold them away from my body while keeping my chin down and my diaphragm in. Which can make one resemble a constipated chicken, but produces a picture that doesn't bring on suicidal thoughts.

The editor of the local paper I write for now sighs whenever a new photograph of me arrives. "Hmm," she'll say, squinting at it without enthusiasm. "You're doing that arms thing again, aren't you?"

You may consider that all this is just sheer vanity and prefer to take the view that nobody buys a book on the strength of an author photo, but remember it's not just about your book jacket.

Think about all the magazine editors, journalists and TV producers you might encounter as you tramp the publicity trail. All of whom will, unfortunately, be interested in appearances. This may not feel fair but realistically it's always easier to promote someone who looks intriguing, whether that's because they are arrestingly beautiful, breathtakingly ugly, or are wearing an outrageous hat.

Remember also that such people see thousands of author photos so an eye-catching picture can only help. Quirky touches are good. For my third novel, *One Glass is Never Enough*, I was photographed clutching a large white wine.

If you've written *The Definitive Guide to the History of the Teapot* you may like to hold a cup of PG Tips. If your book is all about dogs you could cuddle up to the family mutt, and so on.

I received a letter at *Writing Magazine* once from one Jo Reed, an author of dark fantasy, wanting to know if she should don full goth make-up for the photo in the front of her forthcoming novel.

I loved the idea but, out of interest, I asked my local Waterstone's Manager, Neil Batten, if he thought an author photo made much difference to those who might buy the book. His view, after entertaining me with tales of little old pensioners writing erotica who hired buxom young beauties to pose for their author pics, and burly policemen writing as women who made sure they were never photographed at all, was that it does make a difference sometimes.

Neil cited examples I hadn't thought about – pointing out that for any sort of aspirational book, for example, the potential reader would probably be very interested in what the author looked like; and I can see this makes sense.

One would want to see that the author of *Give up smoking, drinking, eating cakes and everything else that gives you any pleasure at all and look terrific for ever* (No Hope Press) was actually glowing with health and vitality and not just as lined, stressed, spotty and toxic-looking as the rest of us.

And that the person behind the cuddly childcare book looked as though you could trust her with your baby and not that she might be tempted to eat him.

So Neil was enthusiastic about the Goth make-up idea. "Yes, why not," he said. "Readers of that genre may well pick up the book and think, she looks like my sort of person!"

And I must say this is a logic I can vouch for myself. You would be surprised at how many emails I've had from readers feeling we'd get on well now they've seen me with a glass stuck to my face.

How to get a great pic

1) **Take your time.** Try to relax. If you're under pressure, and watching the clock you'll look stressed and harassed. If you're uptight because you don't like having your photo taken, have a massage or a glass of wine first.

2) **Prepare yourself.** Depending on gender or preference: spend time on your make-up, wield the hair gel, put on great jewellery, have a shave – or not.

3) **Wear the right clothes.** Choose a simple shirt or plain top and avoid stripes, spots, loud patterns and huge bows that will distract from your face. (Unless you have a boil on your chin.)

4) **Experiment.** Try different expressions and poses (but look into the lens). Keep checking at the back of the camera to see what works.

5) **Remember lighting is all** – a professional will know how to light you to advantage but if you're doing it yourself, try brighter and darker spots till you get it right. Get it wrong and you'll look haggard and a hundred, while the perfect light can knock off years. (If you get desperate, so can a facelift.)

6) **If you're a woman think posture.** Stand up straight, do not hold your arms against your sides and if you have a chest, use it. As a friend of mine whose boyfriend is a photographer for the tabloids, was once advised after a particularly gruesome photo of her appeared in print: "Stomach in and tits out, darling – not the other way round!"

FAQS

What if I'm using a pen name?

I'm too egocentric to have ever used a pen name but lots of writers do, for a variety of reasons. And if you're using more than one – say your own name for one genre and a pseudonym for another – and want never the twain to meet, then the matter of providing photographs involves a little more effort, but is by no means insurmountable.

One writer I know – an attractive redhead – who has two personas, one for her erotica, one for the 'straight' stuff, has a long black glossy wig she uses for the sexy photo shoots, and a female friend who occasionally writes under a male name, uses a picture of her brother.

Quite honestly, as long as you use different photos nobody will probably notice it's the same person anyway – even without a disguise. I never look the same in any two photos I have taken and you can always let your hair fall over your eyes, wear a false moustache or be photographed from an unusual angle.

When novelist Madeleine Wickham was first published as Sophie Kinsella with her earliest Shopaholic book, the author photo of a woman carrying shopping bags, was taken from the back. And most effective it looked too.

What if I'm no good at make-up?

Go to your local department store and get a make-over with one of those dispiritingly perfect-skinned young girls or women-of-a-certain-age with an orange face. Yes you'll feel embarrassed as you scuttle back to the car park looking like Bette Davis in *Whatever Happened to Baby Jane?* But heavy make-up can be surprisingly effective in front of the camera – especially if the photo is going to be in black and white. (You can always tone it down with a wet flannel later.)

What if I'm a bloke and don't do hair and make-up?
Google 'metrosexual' and for God's sake keep up.

What if I'm a bloke and feel a berk posing for the camera?
Get a grip – do you want to make it or not?

What if I'm genuinely ugly or totally un-photogenic?
Hire a stand-in or make your personal gimmick the fact that you always appear with a paper bag on your head.

YOUR best author photo
Make a note here of what worked well for you. The name and phone number of the professional you used or the factors that gave you a great photo taken by a friend. Record where the photo was taken, what time of day it was, and what lighting was used – daylight/artificial lighting/flash, etc. If you discovered which side you look best from – put this down here too. You may think you'll remember but, believe me, in a year's time you probably won't.

My author photo

Covers

Before I was published myself, I never gave the cover of a book a second thought.

In the good old days when you found authors alphabetically rather than according to which offer of the week they were in (or not!) my kind of browsing for something new to read went a bit like this: wander slowly up and down the shelves looking for an interesting title. Read the blurb on the back and the first paragraph and, if both pass muster, head for the till. The cover was just something that held all the pages together. Not any more!

One of the first things I learned – about five minutes after getting a book deal – is that The Cover Is All. Scary rumours abounded about big multiples ordering solely on the strength of the book jacket and taking precisely four seconds per book to give it the thumbs up or down.

Writers spoke sorrowfully of the work that should have won the Booker/taken the Costa or reached the sofas of millions through *Richard & Judy*, if only their publishers had "got the cover right" and every book rep seemed attuned to the best-selling properties of a jacket-design you can see from the far side of the shop. It was all news to me. And the whole cover business – why some covers work and some don't – still largely remains a mystery.

Which is fine because publishers will generally have the last word on what the cover of your book looks like and it will say this in your contract. They will usually, out of courtesy and interest, show you the designs being considered and will listen to your comments. This can be a good thing and then again, sometimes it isn't.

I loved the cover of my first novel, *Raising the Roof*, with a passion (tho' frankly if they'd wrapped it in kitchen roll, I'd still have spent weeks hugging it). It was turquoise and mauve in pretty pastel shades (I was so taken, I had my hair dyed the same colours) with a little row of houses along the bottom and a jolly, curly script for the title.

I did make one small suggestion when I was first showed the artwork – to make the house in the row that was clearly a bit dilapidated, more so – and this was taken up, but it was all pretty much perfect from the start.

I thought it was the last word in eye-catching and soon learned to spot a turquoise-and-mauve cover at twenty paces. The only problem was, it often wasn't mine. That year, the shops were awash with mauve, the shelves a turquoise sea. Columnist Mick Hume, (the rotter ☺) wrote in *The Times* that my book was "impossible to spot among all the other paperback chick-lit."

However, it is worth noting that he wouldn't have even known it existed had I not had the gall to invite him along to the presentation of the Real Writers Awards which, as a past prize-winner, I was helping to promote at the time. To my pleasure and surprise, he pitched up and I got my mention on those hallowed pages. So, perhaps no such thing as bad publicity, but we shall debate this later!

Moving on, I loved the design of my second novel with a passion too. *Perfect Alibis*, my editor Sadie Mayne, told me, had one of the best covers Transworld had ever produced. I thought so too. It featured a glam-looking bird in a tight black dress with a six-inch waist. Sadie had also thought of a good shout line – *Have you ever been in lust with someone you shouldn't?*

Unfortunately, by then I thought I knew a bit about covers and publicity too (though quite clearly not enough!) and came up with what I thought was a better one. *How to have an affair and get away with it.* This, I said, would be attention-grabbing when we were doing the media campaign. The publishers went with my idea.

Which actually was a slight mistake. While this shout line certainly got attention, it wasn't always the right kind. Yes the press picked up on it – I was featured in *The Sun*, invited to go on *Kilroy* and *Trisha*, and photographed supine in a feather boa on the centre pages of the *Daily Star* but that sort of coverage didn't necessarily translate into mega sales. And I soon found, when doing signings, that there would be a lot of interest but not quite so much flocking to the till.

Women would pick the book up and put it rapidly down again the moment they'd examined the text on the front.

"Oooh no," they'd giggle. "I couldn't take that home, Henry wouldn't like it ..."

Which was OK if I was there in person to explain the moral message in chapter 24, but not so great if I wasn't.

Journalists, too, mistook it for a manual for adulterers, which might have got me screamed at on daytime TV, but didn't get me on the best-seller lists.

I don't regret it a) because I got to do a whole heap of TV and radio and other fun things I probably wouldn't have been asked to do otherwise, which led onto other writing jobs, not least the commission for this book, and b) it was a valuable lesson. Namely that shock value is only OK if it's the right sort of shock targeted at the right sort of audience and not every public appearance is going to help sell books (see later chapter on taste and discernment!).

By the time my third novel came out, I thought I'd learned from this and had it sorted. What was wanted this time, I decided, was a cover to sum up the symbolic, literary and psychological implications of *One Glass is Never Enough*. I was so convinced by my concept and had such a clear image engraved upon my mind I begged to be allowed to personally organise a photo shoot and come up with some visuals.

We set the shot in a local bar: a glass of red in the foreground, a couple entwined in soft focus behind, and had the result (I posed as the woman myself) photo-shopped to within an inch of its life. I thought it was pretty classy. It said: romance, the heady properties of fine wine, the triumph of mature love …

"Looks like an advert for age concern," said The Fearsome One, crossly. "Hmmm," added my publisher. "The middle-east market won't have booze on the front and the sales team think it's a book for alcoholics."

I withdrew. The current cover is in girly pink with an illustration of a female barely out of her teens (the heroine of this novel is 38). Booksellers like it. It's been in several promotions. I still stick my oar in about covers if I'm asked – I wanted this one to look very similar to my other Wannabe book for example, and I wrote the copy for the front – but I don't shout too loudly.

When it comes to sales and what does or doesn't grab the booksellers and the great book-buying public, I no longer assume I could ever know best.

And the same goes for:

Blurbs

You may be asked to write the cover blurb for your book, someone at the publisher's may do it or it may be a collaboration between you and your editor.

If you are asked to supply this copy then take it very seriously, spend as much time as you can on it, and don't just dash off the first thing that comes into your mind.

Bear in mind that this back-cover copy will not only be the sell that will decide whether a potential buyer puts your book back on the shelf or takes it to the till, but it will appear in a whole lot of other places too. On the site of every on-line book store, in catalogues, in reviews, on the advance information sheet and any publicity material. It needs to capture the imagination, to intrigue, to leave whoever scans it longing to read more.

Best-selling novelist Lisa Jewell, who is a whiz at this – I always long to get into every one of her books the moment I read the back cover – recommends imagining the blurb as a voice-over on a trailer for a movie "though possibly without the American accent". She says:

It might seem daunting to condense an entire 100k word novel into a snappy paragraph but all you really need to do is mention the names of main characters, their state of being, a suggestion of a mystery/terrible dilemma/shocking event/deep dark secret and then finish with a question that makes the reader want to know what happens next. E.g. "Sally was happy. Then x happened and she wasn't happy. Then John walked into her life and y happened. Will Sally ever be able to get over x? And will John be the one to solve the mystery of y?"

The final version of your own blurb may well be a blend of what you think works and what your editor wants. Do your best but if the publishers want to change it, be prepared to smile sweetly and not to get too precious about the exact phrasing. Remember that your publishers deal with blurbs all the time, and they get feedback from their sales team and the book buyers all of whom are going to know better than you what works.

If you want to see a blurb that does, look up the one for Lisa's novel *The Truth About Melody Brown* (Century) – I defy you not to want to read the book when you have!

Bits & biogs

You will also be asked if you want to include a dedication and acknowledgements at the front of your book and to supply an author biography.

You've probably been writing this stuff in your head for years but now you're doing it for real, again, do think really carefully about what you want to say.

You're going to be cuddling that book for a long time and with luck it will be in print for years to come. It is therefore worth checking anything that's going to be between its covers for cringe factor before whizzing off the copy.

Thank you Kevin 'scrumptious bottom' Pratt for being there, reading the 345 drafts of my manuscript and spoon-feeding me baked beans in bed when my typing elbow was at its worst… might be a precise summing up of your predilections now, but could make your toes curl when you've very sensibly dumped Kevin and are married to Brian.

The author bio deserves careful thought too. This will not only be used for the inside of your book to give readers an overview of your background, lifestyle and literary achievements, but needs to be interesting enough to persuade a few jaundiced hacks and radio producers that out of the 8000 authors of the 8000 new books hitting the market this month, the one they really want to interview is YOU.

Once you are a few books down the line, you can pad it out with lists of previous titles peppering them lavishly with descriptions like "best-selling" and "acclaimed" even if they sold three copies apiece and the only review you got was from your mother on Amazon, who, not having a an overly-masterful grasp of the universally accessible quality of the internet, ended with "love Mum" before reminding you it was Auntie June's seventieth next Thursday.

But early on? When nobody has ever heard of you and your only achievement to date is forcing some poor sod to marry you?

Jane is a more than averagely deranged person who, having failed to scrape a living in any meaningful way, has written a book. She lives with her unfortunate husband and badly-brought-up children on the Kent coast, where she spends her time worrying about how she is going to fulfil her contract to produce the second one.

What do you do then?

Some authors, I have noticed, always begin with their age. Jemima Bloggs was born in 1947 and has since written 369 novels.

I studiously avoid reference to my own birth date unless push comes to shove when I lie with gusto. When my first novel was published I appeared variously in three different women's magazines as 36, 37 and 38. I was 39 at the time and if you ask me how long ago that was, don't believe the answer.

Non-fiction author Peter Brookesmith, who was once referred to as a "gun-toting lecher" by *Private Eye*, says the trick is to appear to be "an expert" on whatever subject one happens to be writing about.

Peter, who also has the distinction of being one of the more eccentric of my uncles (and believe me, in my family, that's saying something) has written books on everything from Loving your Horse to the History of the Assassin and his author bios have followed accordingly, with tales of him with firearm in hand one minute and born in the saddle the next.

We are talking, therefore, marketing hook and a bit of back story. If the book is set in the theatre, then you say you were once an actor; if it's the gritty tale of grinding poverty in the back streets then at least claim an impoverished past in which you and your six brothers shared the same pair of shoes.

At the same time, don't forget the old maxim – know your audience. Remember that this description may well precede you wherever you go. And that describing yourself as an ex-stripper with breast enhancements may go down a storm when you speak at the Rugby Club but won't necessarily hit the right note with the Christian Fellowship of the Society for Clean Living.

As an over-optimistic PR once said to me, make it relevant, make it heart-warming and, where possible, show you've overcome adversity.

In other words if you've written a modern day *Watership Down*, make it clear that you've not only rescued an abandoned orphan rabbit and given it a whole new beginning, but later, it savaged you.

Whatever you write, remember that this too, will be around for a long time. Like the blurb, it won't just appear in the book but on all sorts of promotional material and probably be plastered across the internet too. In my first novel the "about the author" begins:

Jane Wenham-Jones lives in Broadstairs where she walks by the sea and dreams of fame…

I can't tell you how many times that has been recycled in the ensuing decade – seeming ever naffer every time I read it.

Unlike anything nice that's ever been said about the contents of any of my books which I never tire of seeing repeated…

Cover quotes

Sometimes publishers will also be keen to have an endorsement on the front from another, well-known, author saying how fascinating and fabulous they found your novel or non-fiction book.

So if you're a big pal of/have had a torrid affair with, any mega best-selling scribes who might be prepared to help you out in this direction, now is the time to invite them to dinner/threaten to tell the press about it.

If not, don't worry – the publishers can probably call in a favour or two. You just read on, and then get out and network, so that by the time your next book comes out, you'll have met loads of exciting people, have plaudits coming out of your ears and be super-famous yourself. (Otherwise start now – either on that affair, or saving up for a decent bribe.)

Give-aways & promotions

When Sarah Duncan's first novel, *Adultery for Beginners* (Coronet Books), was published, the publicity department at Hodder printed pairs of knickers with the title emblazoned across the crotch and sent them out to bookshops.

"I've no idea if it worked or not," Sarah smiles.

I should imagine it certainly did in terms of getting attention. The novel also included a voucher for a free thong from La Senza.

If you'd rather eat than sport the most uncomfortable garment known to woman, it was Pringles on offer for Lynne Barrett-Lee's novel, *Julia Gets A Life*. The sales reps at Transworld distributed specially printed packets of the well-known snack – Julia's nibble of choice – as part of the promotional campaign.

Two of my own books have featured a competition – Transworld held a draw to win £500 to spend on your home for readers of *Raising the Roof* and in the first edition of *Wannabe a Writer?* we ran a novel-writing competition to win a place at Writers' Holiday and the attention of The Fearsome One (not a prize for the fainthearted but Penelope Jane Randall, our winner – and now a writer you've heard of! – seemed to survive).

Publishers may not always have the budget, time or inclination to run a contest or organise an incentive, but if you have a good idea for one, you may as well mention it, just in case. (I did! See p301.)

AI sheets

What the publisher definitely will do, is to prepare an AI (advance information) sheet for your book which will be sent out to booksellers, and with any review copies.

This will include a picture of the jacket, the technical details – i.e. hardback or paperback, number of pages, format, ISBN, etc. – a blurb, any review comments or endorsements already gathered and probably some information about you.

If you're not sent a copy of this, ask for one and keep it both printed out and stored safely on your computer – so it's ready and handy should anyone require more information at short notice.

You never know when you might happen to meet a friendly, independent bookseller (yes they do still exist!) or find yourself introduced to a chain store manager at a party.

If you visit any shops to angle for signings, go armed with this sheet and if you send out any review copies of your book off your own bat, always include your AI sheet in the package.

NB I always keep a copy of my books, and any current promotional material in the boot of my car. Because opportunities arise at strange moments and 'Being Prepared' is not just for Scouts.

Dyb, dyb, dyb!

Make friends and influence people

And talking of being prepared –

From the moment you know your publication date, start thinking about who you can tell about it. Start with your Christmas card list. If December 25th is actually looming on the horizon, this is one year not to shrivel at the thought.

No need to go as far as one of those ghastly round robins where you share how Rosie sings like an angel, Rupert's head boy and you've had your veins done – but it's worth taking the time to scribble a few platitudes in each card, adding almost as an afterthought: PS *My first book, **The Joy Of Teapots**, is published In May....*

If it IS your first book, your friends and relatives are likely to buy it out of sheer curiosity and to see if they're in it, and if it's your fifteenth it's still worth reminding them where their loyalties should lie.

Even if they don't read, are too tight to spend money on books or hated your last one, they might buy it as a present for someone else (if you are very pushy, and don't mind what people think of you, you could offer extra-value by enclosing a signed bookplate just in case).

If it's only February, it's a shame you'll have to flog out on extra stamps but the principles above still hold good. I am a great believer in the use of postcards – depicting your fab new cover of course – as they come in handy for all sorts of things.

For those not on email, send one out with a seasonally adjusted message, cheerily wishing the recipient a Happy Easter, Whitsun or Pancake Day and adding that you thought they might like to know…

But don't stop here. Spend some time listing all the people who should get to hear about your forthcoming book and all the places where you can advertise it to a few more.

A basic target list might look like this:

- Christmas card list
- Everyone at work
- Everyone at partner's work
- Parents at child's school
- Staff at child's school (now may be a good moment to offer to talk to year six about the joys of becoming a writer)
- All at the tennis/rugby/golf club and/or your embroidery circle/woodwork class.
- Any email groups or forums you belong to.
- Everyone in your on-line address book
- Everyone in the pub
- Local reading groups/bookclubs
- Local bookshops

Make your own list here now:

Postcards & bookmarks

If you are going to get postcards printed, do shop around as prices can vary hugely. You'll find lots of companies on the internet – don't forget to compare like with like in terms of card weight/quantity/size and to check for extras like delivery or artwork charges. And don't ignore what's on your doorstep. Sometimes local printing firms can be surprisingly competitive and you can do that quaint old-fashioned thing of actually talking to someone about what you want and being able to see a proof first.

Some publishers will provide you with printed bookmarks too or you can decide to get these done yourself – depending on how much cash you want to splash. The same advice applies. Ask other authors where they got theirs done and get several quotes. If you can only afford to do one or the other, I would personally go for postcards (which can double as bookmarks anyway) as I find them more versatile.

Ten ways to use your postcards

1) **Make them into invitations for your launch party.** If you're feeling flush get them over-printed. If you're feeling technical and have the right equipment, overprint them yourself. Otherwise print up some labels with all the details to be stuck on the cards, or, if you don't get out much, go for the personal approach and hand-write each one.

2) **Keep them for correspondence** – every time you have to send a note to anyone, anywhere, either write it on a card or enclose a card with your letter. A friend laughed when he saw me putting one of my postcards into an envelope for the dentist. But why not? Might the receptionist not read books?

3) **Leave them on the bus, the train, the tube or plane.** If you can stick them up somehow, so much the better (I carry my own blue tack).

4) **Leave one on the back seat of every cab you take** – you never know who will get in next.

5) **Pin them on notice boards** – once you start looking, you'll see boards everywhere – at the doctor's, the gym, the waiting room at the chiropodist's. Pop one up when the staff aren't looking (keep a couple of map pins in your pocket) and it may survive for weeks. Even if it quickly gets taken down again – at least one person will have seen it.

6) **Ask to leave a pile on the front desk of establishments you patronise.**
NB the success of this may depend on how much money you spend.
Try asking your hairdresser, local tandoori, garage, computer repair
shop or wherever you get your legs waxed.

7) **Dot them about the library**

8) **Hand them out in queues**

9) **Put one on each chair where you're going to give a talk**

10) **Slide them surreptitiously** between the pages of rival tomes in
bookshops.

Other sales aids & gimmicks

I was an early pioneer of the book-jacket as business card and actually
believed I had come up with the idea myself when I had some dinky little
cards printed with my name, email address and phone number on one side
and the cover of my first novel on the other. But since, these days, every
author and his dog does it, I probably didn't.

In any event, you may as well do it too. It looks nifty and it means that
every time you give out your details your book is getting a name check too.

I will offer just the one word of warning – do think twice if your book has
a title that could be open to misinterpretation: such as *Would you Like to Sleep
with Me?* by I.B Willing or, indeed, *Perfect Alibis – How to have an affair and get
away with it* by Jane Wenham-Jones.

Some years ago, my mobile phone rang at midnight and I was woken by
a gentleman with an exotic-sounding accent who'd found my business card
on the floor of a London cab and thought I was running a service for
philandering husbands. He was bemused (and not a little disappointed) to
discover I wasn't prepared to vouch for where he'd been the night before
and was simply advertising a work of fiction.

Generally it works a treat especially when handing your card to anyone
who doesn't yet know you write. "What an interesting design," they say,
peering at it in confusion, giving you the chance to reply nonchalantly, "Oh
yes, that's the cover of my latest book…" and then pin them to the wall
while you insist they write down the ISBN and full Amazon link, on the
basis that they brought the subject up first.

And if you've really got money to burn no need to draw a halt there either. These days there are no end of possibilities to the merchandise available that can be engraved, embossed or overprinted with a slogan, logo, book title or jacket design. So if you want to go the whole hog – and contribute to the general belief that all writers are barking – also consider T-shirts, carrier bags, balloons, badges, mugs, and a banner across the high street.

But there are cheaper and probably more effective ways to spread the word. And the simplest of them all is right there on your computer.

The power of email

Dearest lovely people...
In a shameless act of self-promotion, the latest title in the Housewife
series – HOUSEWIFE IN TROUBLE – is out now. Do please spread the
word and look out for it at your local bookshop/supermarket, remembering to
remark very loudly to passing shoppers how brilliant it is.
Love and kisses,
Alison
Xxx

This short, effective email was sent to me by Alison Penton Harper, the glamorous and very funny author of the Housewife series of novels, with whom I once drank far too much wine (from such encounters are many a writerly friendship made).

Alison claims to "struggle with the whole publicity thing" but I think this is a good example of how one can cheerily tell hundreds of people about a new book (or column or event) with a few mouse clicks.

Alison attached a jpeg of the cover and added the relevant Amazon link as a PS. I got it OK but as a general rule I'd be a little careful with attachments as some systems immediately swallow the missive whole.

It is often better to include a small image of the cover in the actual body of the email which makes it easier and quicker to see too.

Spend a couple of hours preparing two 'email-shots'. One that is casual and chatty for friends/acquaintances/the bloke who cleared your drains/anyone in your address book, and a second – that should be as eye-catching and informative as possible, while still being simple and to the point – to be directed at the media.

You can start thinking about what both should contain as soon as you like – and I'll make some suggestions later – but do not press SEND yet. Because what ever you do, you need to:

Time it right

In the lead up to publication, timing is everything. Do things too early and you'll lose all the impact, do them too late and you'll miss the boat.

Creating a bit of a buzz about the fact that the book is coming soon is all very well – and I'm all for it – but it needs to be well thought out.

Generally, anything that's intended to send potential customers rushing for the shops, should wait until your book is actually to be found there.

I might be the sort of person who would keep a cutting from a magazine to remind me to buy a book when it's published in six months' time and you may well be too, but lots of other readers won't go to these lengths, so there's no point having a big double page feature about your book now if it's not on sale for another three weeks.

(Unless that's absolutely the only opportunity there is, in which case you'll have to rely on readers using the pre-order facility on Amazon – which some do, I'm pleased to say).

You need to approach the whole question of whom to contact and when, with military precision. But first let's just brain-storm.

Think of every media outlet you can approach with news of your book – in the hope of a review/interview/plug/photograph of you grinning manically and clutching said tome.

Include every possibility you can think of, however unlikely. And particularly search your mind for any publication/radio station/editor/journalist you can claim some sort of link with – however tenuous.

For example, when my first novel came out, I made such a list and in its basic form it included all the women's magazines I had ever written for (I began my writing career on the womag short-story circuit) with particular reference to:

My Weekly – the first national magazine to ever buy one of my stories

Woman's Weekly – the first national magazine to actually print one (that first sale to *My Weekly* didn't appear for another four years!).

NB the above was a very happy state of affairs as by wording things carefully I could claim both as a 'first' and thank them for kick-starting my success and was subsequently featured in both too.

All the local papers – I live here!

The local radio stations – ditto

Various specialist magazines to do with mental health issues/property development/the buy-to-let market (all themes in the book)

Any national papers with sections covering same

Writing Magazine, Writers News, The New Writer – I subscribed to all

Various journalists I'd met/corresponded with who might be able to help with contacts/suggestions if I begged.

Now make your list here – just what comes into your head so far – you can add to it later.

> At the outset you have to call in every single favour you can. If you don't make an impact with your first book, you may never get another chance
>
> **Carole Blake Literary Agent**

Next, spend half a day hanging out in the largest newsagent you can find and see which magazines have a books section and/or the sort of features you could imagine yourself writing or appearing in. Add all these to your list.

Also keep an eye out for any slots that are clearly regulars: My First Pet/My Worst Lover/Ten Things I Keep in My Bathroom Cabinet – you know the kind of thing. Anything you think you could have a stab at. A lot of editors may groan when yet another unknown author wants to spill their guts just to get a book plug at the foot of the column, but a) it's still worth a try and b) you won't always be unknown, will you?

NB Don't forget Ezines either – if you look online you will find directories of these galore and a rainy afternoon trogging round the internet seeing what's out there could reap benefits. I must confess this is a relatively new area for me but I have just sent off my mug shot to appear on the front cover of Words with JAM – an online magazine that's going great guns at the moment – and am most excited.

Deadlines & lead times

At some point when that list is complete we'll turn it into a chart – I can get anal when I have to – but in the meantime there's some research to do. As I've said, just as important as the WHO you approach is the WHEN. Some glossy magazines may have a lead time of four months, others may work on two or three, daily newspapers will obviously be looking at a much shorter time span and radio stations will frequently book guests just a few days ahead.

If you have a publicist assigned to you by your publisher, he or she will know these lead times and be the one sending out the info, but you need to know how it all works too – both in case you have extra ideas or contacts and so that you can keep up the momentum long after your publicist has had to move on to other books (he or she will only be concentrating on yours for a relatively short period of time).

Small publishers may not have the resources to offer much publicity help at all. And if you're self-published then, of course, by definition it's going to be muggins doing all the work.

So for the sake of simplicity, let's imagine that for now you're going to be doing it yourself – which, unless you're with a big publishing house, you'll probably have to.

This preliminary groundwork is going to be painstaking and tedious, I'm afraid. But it has to be done and it will be the start of a database that will save you a great deal of time when your next book comes out or you have something else you want to publicise.

You need to find out, for every publication/radio station on your list, who you should be speaking to/emailing and what time frames they work to.

Sometimes the names you need will be in the magazine itself or on a website. Media directories do exist but remember people move jobs and information quickly goes out of date. There are also online companies you can subscribe to, that will provide all such details and more, but these cost, as Tony Mulliken of Midas PR so eloquently puts it, "a bloody fortune".

A polite phone call is best. Good morning – could you tell me who edits your book page/your features editor is/the producer is for the Blah-blah show please?

Once you have a name and an email address you can then decide whether to ask to be put through now, or phone again later and speak directly to the journalist concerned or whether you'd rather continue electronically.

If you can muster the confidence, you will often learn more in a phone call. Flamboyant PR, Simone Klass, maintains email is "a follow-up resource not an instead-of resource" and firmly believes in a live conversation in the first instance.

"Each individual magazine is different", she explains, "and the book page may work very differently from the other pages. It's your job to find out how. Is it done in-house or by a freelancer? What are their lead times?"

But more importantly, she says, if you are actually talking to someone there are other things you can find out. Simone, who describes herself as a "personal advocate" and whose professional strapline is "Get out of your box" – recommends that an author's ambitions should run beyond simply a mention in the books section of a publication.

Both because the figures are stacked against one – thousands of new books come out each month and only a handful can possibly appear in each magazine – and because "that's what everyone goes for".

If Simone were on the phone for you, she'd also be looking to find out what sort of features were planned over the next few months and how best you could become involved. "You need to look at alternative ways of getting yourself known," she says. "The books page? That's just bread and butter – you need the extra tricks."

Simone's not wrong and we'll look at that whole concept of promoting books from other directions later on. She's also not in the least shy or retiring and does this stuff for a living.

More ordinary beings may find it difficult to start selling themselves to an unknown editor, and I do sympathise. I have taught myself to make cold calls but I do appreciate that, for some people, phoning up the switchboard let alone chatting up strangers, is nerve-wracking (I still leave certain calls until after lunch and make sure I've had a glass of wine with it!) so do what is best for you.

Some authors find it easier to pretend they're someone else as in, "Good afternoon. I'm doing the publicity for A.B. Writewell. Could you tell me please who I need to speak to about …"

Celebrity photographer Paul McMullan tells me Katie Price/Jordan used to do this all the time. When he was working for the *News of the World* they'd get a call 'tipping them off' that Jordan would be riding her horse through the woods in her bikini in an hour's time.

"We knew it was her on the phone," he says, "but she'd always pretend to be someone else. We always went," he adds matter-of-factly, "because she had such enormous breasts."

Other, lesser-chested, mortals may choose to do everything by email. Some take a valium and a large vodka and operate on that 'feel the fear and do it anyway' principle on which I have lived most of my life.

Even if you have no problem at all making phone calls and info gathering comes easily to you, it can still be immensely time-consuming and dispiriting to phone up fifty radio stations, twenty-five magazines and a dozen newspapers when you've got lots of other things to do (possibly including a second book to write).

This is when it can be useful to find an articulate young nephew or niece/impoverished student/intelligent teenage son or daughter of a friend and wave some ten pound notes at them.

(**NB** I do not recommend using your own teenager – in my experience using one's offspring for any sort of simple admin or office-related tasks invariably consists of him addressing three envelopes, requiring a rest and extended tea break in front of the PlayStation, filing four pieces of paper and then putting in a bill for fifty quid.)

My sister once took pity on me when I was up against it and phoned up vast numbers of radio stations to check the same people were still in the same jobs. A lot of them weren't, which is why you may need to repeat this task at yearly intervals. If you can farm it out, it helps. Better to be organised first than prepare a wonderful email-shot and find half the addresses bouncing.

By whatever means you do it, try to establish for each publication of interest:

1) Name of books page editor, plus phone number and email address
2) Name of features editor, ditto
3) Their lead times
4) Any particular slots worth targeting

When you've got all this info together, this is the time to turn it into a nice little chart, put it in a contacts book or on a set of index cards (do this in addition to any records you keep on your computer because we all know what they're like. Your hard drive will combust or there'll be a power cut just as you need to phone the editor of *Cosmo*).

A chart is good so that you can see at a glance when you have to send information where. And it can also be handy for keeping track of who's been sent what. Something like this helps:

Publicity chart

Publication	Contact	Details	Send info	Date sent	Response?	Chased	Result
Teapots Monthly	Fred Smith	fsmith@PM.co.uk	October	4/10	16/10		Doing Review
Teapots FM	Tania Spoon	tsppn@tpfm.com 0207 123 8000	Early Jan	3/1	4/1 will come back with dates	11/1	Interview Teabreak show 15/1

But all the organisation in the world can't legislate against the odd case of bad timing and if an opportunity comes up, at the wrong moment, do what you can with it anyway. Better to get a mention than not at all – though it can be extremely irritating when you can see what you're missing.

Giles Coren wrote an amusing piece about this in his column in *The Times* on 27th February 2010 regarding his book *Anger Management for Beginners* (Hodder) that was due to be published in the May.

It was the week that the story had broken about Gordon Brown allegedly bullying everyone in his office (upon which I myself had a good rant in my own small local column. Bullying?? What sort of feeble creatures are these civil servants, God help us.) Anyway, Giles, quite understandably, was frustrated and dismayed. All those column inches about controlling one's temper and how Gordon should have anger management and there he was, the very author of the very book. He wrote:

> Nooooooo!!! Not yet! Wait! Wait! Please save all this for May when my book's coming out and I can spread myself across the tabloids in sexy underwear with all sorts of advice for Mr Brown on how to deal with his choler, featuring enormous great pictures of my book, which will appear so phenomenally zeitgeisty (or perhaps zeitgeistily phenomenal) that it will be made into a film and a musical and a board game and an iPhone app and a Happy Meal and a menswear range and a perfume, and I can go and live in Barbados, next door to Simon Cowell.

This made me laugh lots, while feeling for him. It was a shame, but at least he was still able to write about it. As a reader, I was then aware of the fact that he had a book coming out and would be even more likely to go and pick it up when I saw it in a bookstore.

In fact because I like Giles's writing very much and he makes me giggle – I actually pre-ordered it. And I suspect I wasn't the only 'fan' who did that. So not a perfect scenario but word still spread.

While it's hot

If this is your first book, you've got a slight edge on the rest of us because you are NEW. And on some levels, unless destined to be the next JK Rowling (and we have to be realistic about these things) you'll never be as hot as you are now.

So grab the moment and do absolutely everything you can to get yourself as widely talked about as possible. Keep adding to both of the lists you've started and leave no opportunity unturned to spread the word a bit further. But before you do, it's important to think about exactly what that word is.

Whether you are still pitching to editors and agents or already lucky enough to be trying to boost book sales, you are going to need some sort of USP (unique selling point). For readers in the former category, this is a real rejection my agent received for one of my novels:

> I enjoyed this novel very much, and think Jane writes with great personality, warmth, charm and humour. Her central characters are likeable and funny, and I

like the way she explores relationships between friends, mothers and sons, and men and women. In the end, however, I felt this novel didn't have any particular hook to set it above the rest in a very competitive field, and this is why I'm afraid I won't be able to take it on…

To me, this is the most frustrating sort of knock-back you can get. It would almost be better if the editor in question said, "the beginning's slow, the middle sags and the end's totally unbelievable. Oh and her writing's crap too." At least one would have something to work on.

Having said that, I know where the editor was coming from. There are thousands of books with warmth, charm and humour that explore relationships. What was so different about mine?

This can happen when you are published too. If you phone up a radio producer and say, "Hey, would you like me to come on your show and plug my novel? It's about this girl who's pretty pissed off with life and then she meets this great bloke and they live happily ever after–" you may well hear a yawn at the other end of the phone.

Similarly, if you've written about a woman who makes a new life for herself after divorce or bereavement, a spy who crosses continents to protect government secrets, a friendly police inspector who solves murders by the dozen, a boy who's really a wizard or any number of scenarios that have all been done before and, let's face it, since there are only supposed to be about seven plots in the whole world, they probably have, it's not going to sound different enough.

All my novels have dealt with infidelity in one form or another but I would never just announce my book is about someone who's having an affair (because that really has been done to death).

The trick is to make your book SOUND different even if it isn't. And to make yourself stand out too. You need a hook, you need some pithy sell-it-in-a-sentence lines to come out with. You need, above all, an angle.

What's my angle?

Unless you live in a remote village containing 17 people and nobody's fallen off their bike lately, "Author writes book" isn't much of a story.

So the first thing you must do before you embark on any sort of publicity trail is to decide what your angle is going to be. To do this, you need to examine your own life and the plot of your novel/content of your non-fiction book in minute detail and see how many things you can find that might make a feature or news story.

For example, if you've written a novel about a single mother with ten children who becomes a lap-dancer to make ends meet, then if you yourself have strings of children and/or have been a lap-dancer, then these obviously are the things to highlight in your press release.

But if you haven't? Then you need to dig a bit deeper. Here are some of the things you could do. Firstly, you could pretend. If it won't upset anyone (i.e. if you are not the local vicar's wife or hoping to stand for parliament – although in some parties of course, a bit of a shady past is a positive bonus/entry requirement) then no-one will know that you weren't really tempted to try your hand at being a bunny girl/male escort /stripper/kissogram when you didn't know where the next packet of Pampers was coming from.

But, if you don't want your mother-in-law having the vapours or the new girlfriend thinking you've been round the block one time too many, then invent a friend who did this instead (how do you think I get away with writing about infidelity all the time?).

Speak warmly about the plucky lap dancer you met along the way, who inspired you to write your book after you witnessed her swinging her tassels till all hours with unrelenting cheer, to put food on the table for her six small children. Just imagine the character in your book and make it up as you go along (it's as well early on in your media tart career to embrace the old adage to never let the facts get in the way of a good story).

Have some uplifting anecdote ready about how she was eventually whisked off her feet by a rich punter who wanted to take her away from it all and bring up the whole string of kids as his own, or a tear-jerking one about how her eight-year old appeared at 3 a.m. pleading with her to "come home Mummy" so she now works in Asda instead.

If it's going to make you uncomfortable straying so far from the beautiful white truth (you'll learn) then take a more technical approach.

Trawl the internet for some statistics on single mothers or the cost of bringing up children and show that there are more of the former and the latter are getting ever more expensive and announce with authority that there is a growing trend for mothers to look for exotic/lucrative night work they can do while the children are asleep. (If someone has recently published a survey on anything at all even vaguely relating to children/mothers/unusual occupations of same, consider this a gift from God)

Explain that you interviewed a string of nightclub workers in the course of writing your book and present yourself as a bit of an expert on the motherhood/childcare/work/life balance and comment on the disturbing influences of the entertainment industry and dichotomy between the female form as both nurturer of infants and titillator of sad old men who have to hang round strip joints to get their rocks off.

But whatever your angle/USP is, make sure you've got one before you tell a soul anything. Think of your book, and yourself, as a product. Be clear in your mind what that product is and what it does. It doesn't, of course, have to be as racy as above!

Jean Fullerton writes Victorian family sagas set in the East End. She very much sees herself as a 'brand' – Jean Fullerton, the East End Saga Writer – and her books as product. "Thanks mainly to Jack the Ripper people all over the world know about East London," she says."That's 5 brownie PR points straight away but it's not enough."

Jean has thought carefully about how to best present herself and her books and has taken a strong marketing approach to the way she does it.

Contrary to what my mirror says some mornings, I wasn't around in 1888 so I can't really link myself or my stories directly to those events, so I have to find another hook to hang the Jean Fullerton East End writer on. So who am I and what makes my stories of the East End worth reading? Bit of a bonus on this one because I was born within the sound of Bow Bells so I am an honest to goodness Cockney, "ows yer father?' and all that. Thanks to my parents, that's another 5 brownie points and it adds onto the authentic voice of my professional marketing persona. Now, just by a happy fluke I still live only 3 miles from where I was born, so again the authenticity of my East End voice is there. East London writer still living near her roots.

Take a look at your book and yourself and have a think about what the themes are/what the main subject matter is/what you could hold forth about. Often there is more than one angle to be extracted from any one novel or even any non-fiction book.

If it's the latter you're promoting, did your interest in the subject stem from a particular experience – something daring or traumatic for example? Does it reveal some new and fascinating theory?

If, say, your book is about collecting teapots, maybe you can dig up some research that says teapot collectors have longer marriages or are considered more sexy.

Or confess that your first wife left you when your collection of 3,500 assorted spouts in the bedroom meant there was no longer any room for the bed.

Think eye-catching headlines and cast your net wide. If you look through *The Writer's Handbook* or *Writers' & Artists' Yearbook* you will see hundreds of specialised magazines. There's bound to be one – let us call it *Teapots Monthly* – that would love to hear from you. And consider publications on associated topics – *The Tea-Drinkers Digest*, *China-Lovers Weekly* or *My Beverages* might also be interested.

If it's a novel you're flogging, again look beyond simply the main themes and subject matter. For example, *Raising the Roof*, my first novel, was essentially a chick-lit drinks-too-much/needs-a-man type romp set around the buy-to-let market.

I wrote a piece for the *Sunday Express* property pages about the perils of becoming a landlady, and was interviewed by Rosie Millard for her *Sunday Times* column on the same topic.

But I also spoke on the radio about mental health issues – the heroine's sister has a severe psychotic episode in chapter 25 – and, by dint of my sending her a book, the nutritionist Amanda Ursell featured my heroine's made-up 'Shelf Diet' in her then column in *Woman's Own*. This was in addition to several features in the women's magazines simply by virtue of it being my first novel, on the subject of turning real life experiences into fiction.

My third novel, *One Glass Is Never Enough*, is, in a sentence, the tale of three women running a wine bar. But my list of 'angles' I wrote down for my publishers, for marketing and publicity purposes, looked like this:

1) **Wine bar**
   - Was co-owner of Harpers Wine Bar in Broadstairs for two and a half years. Can give interviews/write features on the realities behind the middle-class dream in both a serious and humorous fashion

- **NB** Very topical – loads of city types dream of leaving the rat race to run a pub/wine-bar. Can do 'when the dream turns sour…' type article or upbeat comical one full of anecdotes. Ten things you need to know, etc.
- Women in business – how they differ from men
- Going into business with friends – pros and cons.

2) **Depression /mental health**
- One in four people suffer from depression
- I have extensive personal experience of being the relative of those affected. Can write/speak from the point of view of carer instead of the more standard approach from the viewpoint of sufferer. Heroine, Gaynor, says in this novel: "that means three out of four of us have a hell of a lot to put up with" – can use that as starting point.

3) **Infidelity**
- Still on lists as 'expert' on female infidelity after *Perfect Alibis*. More scope for further articles and interviews – bringing this new novel in.

4) **Writing world**
- Offer articles/interviews on writing from real-life experience
- Writing about real people – pros and cons – laws of libel, etc.
- Contribute to Writing websites/forums
- Speak on above – conferences/workshops circuit.

5) **Shhhh!** This was a goodie but telling you about it here will spoil the plot. And you are going to read my novels after this, aren't you? ☺

The perfect press release

I wouldn't claim to know exactly what that is.

I have no special training or any particular PR background other than what I've picked up along the way and taught myself. So I can only tell you how I do it.

What I can say is that I have quite a good hit-rate with the press releases I send out and have been featured in lots of magazines and newspapers and sounded off on dozens of radio stations. It can't all be my natural and captivating charm.

I've got some advice on what to write on your press-release from real, at-the-sharp-end-get-hundreds-of-the-buggers, editors and radio producers to share with you later but these are my golden rules when I want a press release to lead to an interview or article commission:

- Keep it short
- Keep it punchy
- Try to grab attention in the first two lines – that may be all they read.

This was the beginning of a press release sent as an email-shot when *Perfect Alibis* was re-issued with a new cover:

"According to the current infidelity statistics 60% of men and 40% of women are involved in an extramarital affair."

It went on to quote a poll involving 1,100 women conducted by WomanSavers.com which showed that while 62% of women thought that men cheat more than women, a further survey concluded that only 67% of women questioned said they themselves would never cheat on their partner.

And it then continued:

Jane Wenham-Jones' best-selling PERFECT ALIBIS has been re-published with a new cover since women reported being hesitant about taking home the original – subtitled *How To Have An Affair And Get Away With It* – in case their partners suspected them of cheating too! The new edition is out on promotion NOW!

There followed a picture of the cover, a picture of me, some blurb about the book, some of the subjects I could write/talk about – i.e. why women have affairs/ten top ways to discover if your partner is cheating/ten ways not to be caught yourself, etc. – and some contact details

As a result, even though it wasn't a new book and I'd done a whole raft of publicity the first time around, I wrote a piece for *Scarlet Magazine*, took part in a photo shoot and feature for *Psychologies* and did several radio interviews.

Horses for courses

When it comes to the press release, it's not a case of one size fits all. The above was specifically targeted at getting me some column inches or airtime. Had I wanted to speak at a writing conference or take part in a book festival I'd have sent something quite different.

For example, when your book first comes out, the press release may be more comprehensive, but will probably be 'straighter' and will concentrate on the contents of the book and a biography of the author. Here is the original press release, for the same book, sent out my then publicist at Transworld, Marina Vokos, when *Perfect Alibis* was first published.

A Bantam paperback original to be published on 1st May 2003, price £5.99

Jane Wenham-Jones
Perfect Alibis

'Thoroughly enjoyable and full of deft, sparky humour'
Jill Mansell on *Raising the Roof*

Infidelity for women - a survival guide...

" 'Everyone assumes that PAs must stand for Personal Assistants.' She'd laughed and blown out a long stream of smoke. 'All except the clients, of course.'
'And what is it really?' Stephanie had asked, feeling as if she were caught up in a dangerous but heady adventure.
'PAs', said Madeleine, mouth curved into a seductive smile, voice low and slow as syrup, 'is a discreet service for the chronically unfaithful.' Her smile had widened at the expression on Stephanie's face. 'PAs stands for Perfect Alibis.'"

Stephanie – bored housewife and downtrodden mother – wants a job, and Madeleine's recruitment company appears to be the ideal place to go. Except that PAs isn't quite what it seems.

As she becomes embroiled in the world of Perfect Alibis for unfaithful women, Stephanie soon discovers that there are plenty of them about! Founder member Patsy is a serial philanderer and there's even a dark side to her best friend Millie. For the well-heeled ladies of Edenhurst, PAs is a ticket to risk-free adultery.

When the unreliable Troy, Stephanie's first love, returns unexpectedly to town, even she is tempted. Her life is soon in turmoil, and that's before the tabloids get involved...

Jane Wenham-Jones has written for a wide range of women's magazines, had articles published in the national press and writes a regular column for her local paper. She lives in Broadstairs, Kent, with her son and husband. *Raising the Roof*, her acclaimed debut, was based on her own first-hand experiences of property renovation and letting. She is a past winner of the Real Writers/Book Place Short Story Award sponsored by Hammick's, and co-owner of a wine bar.

Jane Wenham-Jones is available for feature, short-story writing and for interview

For further information, please contact Marina Vokos,
Press and PR Manager, Transworld Books, Tel: 020 8231 6735
e-mail: m.vokos@transworld-publishers.co.uk

Bantam

Have a general press release ready at all times and be prepared to adapt it as necessary. Be alert for anything in the news that you can hang your hat on!

When I contributed to the *Help for Heroes Cookbook*, I was alongside a string of luminaries including Gordon Brown, Sir David Jason, Dame Judi Dench and Bruce Forsyth, so you won't be surprised to learn that my name was not highlighted on the original publicity material.

However, we were asked to name our hero or heroine and say what we'd cook for him or her. I went for Ann Widdecombe, on whom I have harboured a small crush for some years, and when her name was put forward to be the Speaker of the House of Commons, I saw my chance to give it a bit of a push.

I called Hazel, the go-getting head of Accent Press, and suggested an idea for an amended press release. Within half an hour the email-shot that follows had been whizzed off to a raft of radio stations. And the responses started coming in.

I have to say that most of them were from producers enquiring if there was any chance of having the actual Ann Widdecombe on their programme rather than me banging on about how I'd like to make her an egg sandwich (I'm not big on cooking despite having managed to blag my way into three separate recipe books and appear on more than one culinary show) but you get the general idea. It raised awareness of the book and the charity and kept my name in front of the various radio bods even if they weren't exactly gagging to speak to me on this occasion.

And the one interview I did give – on BBC Radio Kent – was picked up by regional newspaper *Kent on Sunday* who ran a piece the following weekend – headed **Widdecombe will always be my hero, says author** that mentioned not only the cook book but my own "range of humorous novels" and which has remained on the internet long after the newsprint hit the recycling bin.

So, all was by no means lost.

Hopefully, the *Help for Heroes* charity benefited. And who's to know if someone didn't decide to read me for the first time after seeing the newspaper describe me as "popular" and thinking that they'd give me a try as I came from their neck of the woods.

Down to basics

But to get back to basics, do remember that the lucky recipient of your press release gets hundreds of them. So you need to make your points quickly, clearly and without being irritating.

Very often chunks of the press release will be lifted wholesale for use in an article about you or read out verbatim by a radio presenter. So spend time putting some words together that get all the salient facts in and that you're going to feel proud of.

If it's your local paper you're targeting – and let's remember here that local should be seen as an elastic term meaning any paper from anywhere you can rake up some connection with (you would be surprised by the number of places I went to school/had my first job/spent idyllic childhood holidays that I still remember fondly) – the editor will be particularly pleased if most of the work's already been done for him because he is probably extremely stretched for time and such papers are notoriously understaffed.

Or, as my old mate Mike Pearce who was my first editor at the *Isle of Thanet Gazette* where I still write a bi-weekly column, puts it:

> The sad but seemingly irreversible decline in the fortunes of local newspapers can, paradoxically, be good news for the publicity-hungry author.
>
> Fewer and fewer reporters are being employed and although this maybe good news for the accountants it can be a nightmare for the editor, no matter how talented, who is trying to fill in the spaces between the adverts.
>
> So any crisp, cleanly-written and useable copy will be welcomed and stands a good chance of finding its way into print.
>
> That does not mean any old junk will do. Carelessly-worded, self-glorifying, over-written hype will add to the hapless editor's daily grind. Not only will a quick click of the delete key send it where belongs, you will have made an enemy of someone who needs cultivating as a vital ally.

Mike offers these guidelines:
- Do use a sensible typeface. Italics are the computer equivalent of green ink.
- The editor is busy, and hasn't time to spare to read a long accompanying message. So simply say you are writing with information/an article and picture about your new book and be sure to add full contact details – phone, email and address.
- Submit articles only when there is something worth writing about. Paying to have your first attempt 'accepted' by a vanity publisher is not newsworthy.
- Remember you are writing for a newspaper, so no flowery words, no waffle and keep it tight.
- A feature on a local author getting a first book published is worth around 500 words, tops.

- Work on the principle that newspaper stories get cut from the bottom, so ensure all the important bits are at the top. Don't devote the first 100 words to your schooldays at St Bunter's and mention your new book in the last paragraph, or you may be heartbroken when you see there is no reference to it when the story appears.
- Self-praise is no praise, so don't ascribe to yourself, or to your book, virtues which will be decided by the reader.
- Deal in facts.

You might wonder what exactly Mike means by the last point. He has kindly offered this example for our illumination: This is the sort of intro he likes:

Hightown dog-breeder Hilary Clipper's first novel will be published next month.

Hilary, 52, of Dalmatian Drive, drew inspiration from more than 30 years working with animals which saw her rise from kennel-girl at the local dog-track to breeding three Cruft's winners.

"Two paragraphs, nine facts." Mike says, gratified.

He does not like this kind of thing:

A brilliant first novel is expected to be one of the year's best-sellers.

Hilary Clipper's hilarious romp is based on what goes on behind the scenes in the intriguing world of dog-breeding.

"Two paragraphs, three untested claims, only one fact," he growls.

Personally I don't see anything wrong with dropping in words like 'hilarious' and 'romp' and 'intriguing' because it gives an idea of the genre of the book, and, I hope, suggests there is more to this than a straightforward account of doling out the Pedigree Chum from dawn to dusk. But I know where Mike is coming from.

Don't get so carried away with writing a 'blurb' that you fail to include the nuggets of hard information that will make an article. Newspapers and magazines do seem to like to know one's age (I see nothing wrong in lying) one's marital status and details such as how many children one has.

Your occupation, previous jobs and anything that makes you particularly fascinating – e.g. you hold the Greater Manchester bungee-jumping record or used to design the Queen's handbags – are worth a mention too.

Once, when getting bored with the same old sound of myself, I idly finished a press release with the sentence: "she has a husband, son, fourteen goldfish and a Shetland pony." No, I don't know what possessed me either but I was surprised by how many interviewers picked up on it. Fortunately it was true – see below.

I really did have a Shetland pony Sylvester – who lived into his 30s Miss him still.

But back to Mike who has a few more words of wisdom to impart before we leave him be until the chapter on 'cultivating your local paper'. I will just say that I have certainly cultivated mine – hence he is now 'my mate' Mike rather than a dimly remembered editor I once emailed – over the years, and I must say it has paid dividends. More of that later.

In the meantime, let's see what else the old boy has to say (he's still giving out instructions for sending out to newspapers in case you've gone off to make a cup of tea and have lost the plot).

- Attach a high-quality mug-shot and a second photo with some relevance to your book. Ms Clipper, for instance, could be cuddling a dog
- Include some first-person quotes in the article. For example, "I decided to write a novel when I became house-bound after my first child was born."
- Do not under any circumstances keep pestering the editor to ask when your article will appear
- By all means, after a few days, send a short email checking that the piece arrived and that you hope it might prove suitable for publication
- A good editor will have the courtesy to reply, but should not be expected to field your persistent phone calls
- If your article appears, be sure to send an email or make a swift phone call thanking the editor, who will be surprised and pleased that anyone should say anything nice about a journalist
- Send him a copy of the book. Even if he hates it, he can give it as a Christmas present so will be grateful.

Quick quotes and soundbites

While you're writing your press releases, composing the email you're going to send all your friends, and writing your media lists, start thinking about things to say too.

There are two questions you will be asked over and over again
1) What's it about?
2) How did you become a writer?

When I am asked what any of my books are about I invariably answer "shagging and drinking". Luckily, others take a more intelligent approach.

"Think out a one-sentence answer," says novelist Emma Darwin. "Think elevator pitch – main character, main conflict."

For those of you not up on sales jargon, an elevator pitch is an overview of an idea for a product, service, or project. But the whole idea of it, is that it's SHORT. It's what you would have time to say if you found yourself in the lift with someone influential who was getting out at the fourth floor.

Think about this for a moment: you're not published yet and you find yourself sharing three square feet of nylon carpet with a top literary agent or the head of Harper Collins.

Or you are published and in steps the book buyer for Tesco. Or the producer of the leading Book Club programme on TV. Or the literary editor for the *Sunday Times*.

You seize your moment. "I've written a book," you gush.

He or she looks at you strangely, thinking, *Oh God, here's another one...* but then – we are playing 'let's pretend' here – wearily asks:

"What's it about?"

You need to be ready with your answer. If you start rambling on about it being "a paradoxical examination of Loss with particular reference to the insecurities and anxieties inherent in the middle-aged man attempting to rediscover his essence of self after the ravages of divorce and redundancy..." they're going be off through those doors like a whippet.

Mumbling, "Er it's about this bloke who um er splits up with his wife and then um er gets a new job and his boss gets murdered..." is not going to cut the mustard.

Instead, you adopt a winning smile as you announce with confidence, "It's about a taxidermist called Stanley who finds a severed head in his fridge."

Get it? Don't get bogged down in themes or the details. Distil it down to Who and What. You can give 'em more later. For now:

It's about a girl who swaps lives with her twin sister

It's about a politician who's got a fetish about lampshades

It's about a boy whose mother swaps him for a Big Mac

Stop now and write your own answer here:

Practise saying the above in a tone that is suitably jaunty/grave/mysterious according to genre and don't include any words that you might stumble over when nervous, hesitant or feeling the effects of too much post-publication champagne.

If you feel a bit more ambitious, you can develop this into a bit more of a shout line.

Writer Christine Carmichael, who sounds pleasingly bonkers and runs something called Romance Angels, "a networking/resource group for aspiring and published writers of Romance" describes her novel in progress as "a Secret Baby story with an explosive Pride and Prejudice twist." I think this sounds intriguing.

Christine likes to think of shout lines in terms of classic tales or films and instructed her 'angels' in a recent posting:

"What's at the heart of the story? Is it a *Cinderella* story? *You've Got Mail*? *The Fugitive*? *Sleeping with the Enemy* – but with a twist?" before, rather quirkily, urging them to use "P words" such as "pride, power, purity and passion."

(Could this be where I've been going wrong? Too many W words: wine, women, wet weekend.... doesn't have *quite* the same ring...)

Have a think about this – is your book about:

A modern-day Robin Hood? (power)

James Bond marries Scarlet O' Hara? (passion)

Heathcliffe settles down and has six kids? (purity of purpose)

If you can think of a good one – my imagination has run dry – write your own shout line for your own fine work here:

Now think about the other question. How did you become A Writer? (Sometimes cunningly disguised as "How did you start writing?") Yes we all know the answer: one day you thought you'd have a go and found you were quite good so you kept doing it. Or one day you thought you'd have a go and you were fairly crap but you kept doing it and got a bit better. Neither are particularly riveting.

So have a think now. This is the time to invent a magazine you edited for the neighbours at the age of seven, a screen-play you left on the school bus that got picked up by a Hollywood agent, a famous literary father or a mad aunt who forced you to write out Shakespearean sonnets every time you wouldn't eat your sprouts.

Think sound bite. Think witty, eccentric and original. We will go into more detail when we come to examine the intricacies of The Interview. In the meantime, the above should suffice if the local rag send a spotty junior along to your launch party or even if the editor herself rolls up. If the wine's free – she may well do.

How to have a launch party

Authors tend to get more excited about launch parties than their publishers do.

When I quizzed Richard Charkin, Executive Director of Bloomsbury, on what he thought about them, he replied "not much". While Bloomsbury, he told me, do have launches for authors, he doesn't encourage them. Do they sell books? I enquired. "Not many." Are they worth it? "No."

They were the answers I was expecting. The received wisdom is that publishers regard a launch as basically a chance for the author to drink lots of champagne with his or her friends (and what's wrong with that!! ☺) rather than an event that will make any real difference to sales or PR.

Some authors feel like this too. "Book launches are more of a celebration of a new book with other novelist friends, to my way of thinking," says novelist Trisha Ashley, "and any extra publicity is a bonus."

That's probably a good way to look at it – I'm all for a dose of realism – but I also believe the launch CAN be a useful promotional vehicle for publicity, if you go about it the right way.

Trisha, in fact, would agree. The heroine of her novel *Wedding Tiers*

(Avon), makes weird and wacky wedding cakes. For the launch, Trisha made one of those featured – an Elizabethan Pomander cake. You can see a picture of it on her website.

"I baked it in a huge round Christmas pudding tin, like a cannon ball, and covered it in icing roses – it took ages to make. We cut it at my book launch at a nearby hotel and I also did wedding favours of wedding cake-shaped bottles of bubble mixture, balloons and heart-shaped candles."

That all sounds delightful but better still, Trisha wrote a story featuring the cake for *My Weekly* and the magazine sent a photographer and make-up artist to the launch and ran an interview with the story, which, as Trisha says "made it all very special".

It made it very worthwhile, I would say. Because it probably got her quite a few readers too.

A bit of a theme makes the party memorable and potentially newsworthy. If you've written that book about lap-dancers and have a few of them strutting their stuff throughout the evening I can guarantee you'll get some column inches (calm yourselves chaps – I am talking newspapers!).

If it's the tome about teapots we're launching upon an unsuspecting public, then a traditionally-dressed hostess demonstrating a Japanese tea ceremony (or perhaps a PG Tips-style chimp swinging from the rafters) is something for the local paper to write about.

And any event where the guests get a bit more than they bargained for, will get talked about for a long time afterwards.

I had a fantastic time at Tamara McKinley's launch party for her *Lands Beyond the Sea* (Hodder). The novel is set in 16th century Australia and during the evening in a hotel in Sussex, we were treated to entertainment by fire eaters and poi dancers as well as a didgeridoo player accompanied by tom toms. As Tamara says, "How exotic is that!?"

Too exotic for my budget, you may be thinking, and that is a valid point. Although publishers will often make a contribution to any bash you organise yourself, if it's your first novel you may not have that much money to splash about (this may be true if it's your sixth, seventh or eighth novel too!).

And if you are digging in your own pocket, you may not consider it money well spent in any case. Especially if it just ends up being a drinking spree with your chums or, as one of mine, recently celebrating the publication of her fifth novel put it, "£800 on canapés and all the people that came would have bought a book anyway…"

Having said that, I do take the view that if it's your first publication, some sort of gathering to mark the occasion is *de rigueur*. Finding oneself finally clutching a copy of one's very own book – the stuff dreams have been made on for many years – deserves to be celebrated.

I held my first launch in a wine bar and invited everyone I'd ever met. I didn't know about themes then so I just got the local bookshop to bring along a shedload of books, sported hair extensions the colour of the book jacket and took out a second mortgage on a dress. Most of the evening is now a blur but we did sell lots of copies, the local papers and radio covered it and I finished the evening on a table, treating the assembled gathering to a rendition of Madonna's *Like a Virgin*.

Do try to do something even if it's just going to the pub or telling all your friends to bring a bottle and their own sandwiches. You deserve it. But don't dismiss something grander. With a bit of thought, you can have a good time and reap the rewards of a bit of publicity too, without totally breaking the bank. And at least making the money you do spend, work for you.

Here are a few ideas:

1) **Hold it in a bookshop.** This can be a cheap, cheerful but very effective way of holding a launch. Go and schmooze the manager and see what you can arrange. He or she will often be pleased to have all those extra bodies in the shop for the sales that should ensue. Sometimes they'll provide the wine and crisps too or your publisher might stump up for this, if you've done the rest. The bookshop staff are likely to want to keep it fairly short but you can always repair to the nearest bar once the formal part is over.

2) **Bring in a sponsor or host.** Marina Fiorato is published by Beautiful Books, a small independent publisher who are very proactive about their PR.

Managing Director Simon Petherick, refreshingly, does like parties.

I like launch parties, mainly because I quite like parties. They're almost totally useless as a way of promoting a book, but they are very good for making everyone feel cheerful, which is an important thing in business as in life. We do our best to get them funded by sponsors, and occasionally we'll put some money up if we feel everyone needs a party. We only really go for launch parties with authors who are likely to attract at least 70-odd people. And bear in mind that no journalists will come, or if they do come, they will just sit at the bar and get drunk and embittered, so you'll just wish they hadn't come. Always remember that it's just a party, so if you want a party, then have it! It won't sell any more books, but the books you sell on a good night can pay for the booze, so that's a good thing!

Marina's first novel, *The Glassblower of Murano* is about a 17th century Venetian glassblower who goes to France to sell his secrets to Louis XIV and help him to build the hall of mirrors at Versailles.

Beautiful Books sealed a promotional deal with prestige French glassmakers Lalique – who not only sponsored a UK tour, but specially made the glass heart pendant which appears throughout the book and on the cover and is what Marina refers to as "the touchstone of the whole story".

Marina was given one of the pendants. "It was really an amazing thing that 'the word was made glass'," she says. Because of their involvement, Lalique also agreed to hold the launch in their flagship Bond Street store which was, Marina recalls, "very swanky indeed. I spent the whole evening trying not to bump into an enormous glass horse's head which cost £30,000. It became increasingly challenging as the champagne flowed!"

3) **Hold it in an unusual place**
Everyone does bars, hotels, shops and restaurants. Not so many go for boats. But that's where I had the pleasure of spending a wine-soaked afternoon when I went to a launch party aboard the beautiful Dutch barge owned by the family Fforde.

It wasn't for the lovely Katie, as you might expect, but her husband Desmond, who had recently bravely entered the publishing fray himself with *A Seaman's Book of Sea Stories* (Accent Press) – a compilation of old seafaring tales he put together to raise money for The Prostate Cancer Charity.

An excellent cause of course, but I wonder if it was the charming venue that swung it for the couple of hacks who turned out from the nationals. A location with a difference immediately gives one something to say. I got more than one piece out of the afternoon myself – writing about it for both my local paper and *Booktime* magazine. And of course I plugged the book at the bottom of both of them.

4) **Give it an unusual angle or theme**

Back to Beautiful Books where Managing Simon Petherick is a positive fund of innovations to get his titles noticed. Marina Fiorato's second book *The Madonna of the Almonds,* is the story of a 16th century Italian widow who makes her almond groves pay by creating Amaretto di Saronno. This time Beautiful Books teamed up with Royal Warrant perfumiers Floris, who agreed to make a limited edition scent. Marina, who describes herself as "enormously privileged" was involved in the process.

I was lucky enough to be admitted into the sacred back room in the lovely Jermyn Street premises, to help chief perfumer Shelagh Foyle develop the fragrance from scratch. I had dozens of tiny crystal bottles ranked in front of me, and Shelagh handed me a series of little paper dipsticks dipped in essences that took me right to the Mediterranean. Rather like making a bouquet from a selection of single flowers, we put together a collection of scents to make up the fragrance. The finished product smells wonderful – like Italy in a bottle.

Marina is now the proud owner of a crystal bottle of Madonna of the Almonds perfume. And Floris subsequently not only featured the book in their window display in St James, but held the book launch at the store.

5) **Have a celebrity guest**. If you know anyone even vaguely famous, now is the moment to invite/cajole/plead with them to attend. This will add a dash of glamour to the proceedings. And if you put the word around, all sorts of people will turn up just to get a look. You can also give the press an anonymous tip-off that the name in question will be there.

If it's a slow week for news, they'll often send someone along. If the name's big enough they definitely will. (**NB** This may not work in Central London where celebs are three to the pound but it does get them going in small towns like mine where someone losing their dog makes the front page.) Don't, however, be put out if the press are then more interested in the VIP than you.

At my second launch, the actress Juliette Kaplan (best known for playing Pearl in *Last of the Summer Wine*) came along. The local reporter, who up till then had been perfectly happy to listen to my fervent account of how the plot came to me in a dream, immediately dropped me like a hot brick and rushed off to talk to her instead. Which was fine. We both made the paper and she bought a book. Result!

6) **Pretend you have a celebrity guest.** Proceed as above but with a story about how they were unexpectedly struck down by the flu/beri beri disease/a passing bus at the last minute. By that time the crowds and press will be in place. You can always lock the doors to prevent them getting out again

So what happens then?

If this is your first book and you have never been to anyone else's launch party, you might like a brief rundown of what actually ensues. It usually goes a bit like this:

There's a table on which your books are piled high (in a pleasing shape if you're lucky – some booksellers are very inventive about this) which someone will be selling.

There is wine – either finely chilled in good crystal or warm in white plastic cups, according to venue – and nibbles of some kind.

These can range from upmarket canapés handed out by neatly uniformed waitresses or smooth-looking young men in tight black trousers, to a paper plate of bendy crisps. **NB**: personally I believe in upholding standards and would recommend Kettle Chips in proper bowls as an absolute minimum (why I haven't got a product placement deal with them yet is anyone's guess).

There's you – looking suitably fetching and thrilled. With a pen in your hand.

There is a motley crew of guests ranging from your editor and publicist to the woman from next door who doesn't read but who's come along just to see what happens. (You could avoid having to shell out for wine for her by photocopying the following page and shoving it though her letterbox). She goes to funerals on the same basis, when she's tired of watching Jeremy Kyle.

There may or may not be members of the press.

NB When it comes to 'press' think beyond simply a news story and the local rag.

Linda Mitchelmore is a prolific writer of short stories for the women's magazine market but has also appeared in four anthologies and has held launch events in her local independent bookshop for all of them. She recommends investigating your county magazine and says:

Get someone who has a decent camera, and who doesn't have a tendency to chop heads off when they take photos, to come along to your book-signing and keep them away from the gratis wine until they have taken copious shots of you smiling and signing for England. Along with a small write-up on what the event was about, the photos can be sent to the 'Life' magazine of your area for the Social Pages. Devon Life has been wonderful to me.

I also like Linda's approach to getting the numbers up:

I've shamelessly looked at what women are taking out in libraries and, if it is romantic fiction I give them an invite, telling them if they can't make the event itself, then not to worry, there will be signed copies available at the bookshop afterwards.

But if they do come? First there's a bit of milling. The super-keen – and those who want to get home to watch *EastEnders* – may buy a book now. The rest will wander about drinking wine and congratulating you, until someone – generally from your publisher's – calls for attention. They then say how marvellous you are, how marvellous the book is and thank everyone for coming.

You then stand up and give a short speech (yes I'm afraid you do!) saying how marvellous the publishers are (if you're having an Oscars moment you can also thank your mother, brother, children, spouse, the entire local football team and the primary school teacher who first inspired you), followed by a short reading – if you want to – and thank everyone for coming.

You then drink far too much wine in sheer relief that that bit is over, everyone else drinks far too much wine as well and – if they have any manners or a shred of common decency – queue up to buy a book which they then bring to you to sign.

Any entertainment you've laid on happens now. At my third launch party, for no particular reason other than I thought it might be fun, some thespian friends acted out a scene from my novel and some others sang for us. (I also had a chocolate fountain for those who don't like theatre or singing but just wanted to stuff their faces.)

Otherwise you stagger about the room until it's time to go home (being careful not to drink SO much you become the entertainment yourself).

Other dos and don'ts
DO:

1) **Include a picture of the book jacket on the invitation**. It could be stuck up on kitchen notice boards for weeks. "Oooh what's that?" friends of friends may ask…

2) **Invite all the local press and key people from the local radio stations**. Even if they don't come this time, it's a way of getting your name in front of them and they might interview you in the future.

3) **Invite the local Great and Good**. Councillors, mayors, the local MP – they're all part of great networks of other G&G's. They've got to talk about something over all those lunches…

4) **Invite anyone who ever smirked when you were getting rejections** Deliver the card personally.

5) **Use signs and posters**. PR Simone Klass reminded me to make this point after she rolled up to a launch in a book shop where there was no signage at all and she almost didn't go in. This is your chance for some extra advertising. Get a sign out on the pavement and posters on the walls (if necessary just get your cover blown up at a local photo-copying place). If you're lucky, they could be left up afterwards.

6) **Think photos**. Not just the press ones. Lots of people may want to take your picture (and do make sure someone gets at least one good one – of you holding a book). Keep smiling, don't scratch or pull silly faces/things out of your nose or decide it would be really amusing to show everyone how you do the cancan. Remember it could be all over Facebook by midnight

7) **Carry a spare pen**. Or ask one of your friends to. There's nothing worse than running out of ink at the wrong moment.

8) **Spend time choosing the right extract to read** e.g. one that is funny/has intrigue/ends on a cliff hanger and doesn't have any words you may mispronounce under pressure (or the influence). Edit as necessary.

9) **Practise reading it**. If it's been shortened you'll need to check the rhythm and that it works out loud

10) **Enjoy yourself.** It's your night – have a ball!

DON'T:
1) **Drink too much before your speech**
2) **Drink too much before the press leave**
3) **Be over-excitable with those who are still trying to get published –** remember how hard it can be to watch others' success when you're depressed about your rejections.
4) **Forget to tell your publishers how much you appreciate them**
5) **Forget to stock up on Nurofen for the morning**

FAQS

What shall I wear?

The short answer to that knotty question is: anything you like.

The wonderful thing about being a writer is that you can never look too eccentric and no-one will know what to expect.

So it is up to you if you want to go for comfort, glamour, shock value or something that holds your stomach in (I gave you the full benefit of my advice on those strange elasticated garments, that render one unable to breathe, in the last book).

I would choose something that makes you feel great and if it's slimming too, so much the better (photographers attached to local papers are not always known for the flattering quality of their shots).

Mainly because the man or woman who feels confident usually looks pretty good too and because if you know you're looking the best you can, your whole evening won't be ruined the first time you see yourself under those horrid strip lights in the loo.

If you like dressing up then this is a night to get your hair done, choose a fabulous dress or a favourite jacket – or whatever makes you blokes feel good – wear eye-catching jewellery, smouldering make-up and a gorgeous pair of shoes.

On the other hand, the comfort factor should not be overlooked entirely. It's going to be hot with all those people in there so either don't wear too much or go for layers. You're going to be on your feet for hours so you might want to think about the wisdom of a pair of heels that you know will leave you crippled by 9 p.m. (Or you could do what I do – wear the heels and when everyone's had a chance to see that you did at least start out looking vaguely elegant, leave them under a table in the corner.)

And you'll be kissing a lot – a launch can be a bit like a wedding without the tears and the sniping relatives – so a lipstick that doesn't end up half way across your face, or one of those lip colour sealants is also useful.

If you decide to go the news-grabbing/crowd-stopping route you might like to think costume rather than outfit and go for something themed.

Browbeat your friends into coming along so you look busy

If you've written a book of pregnancy tips for example you could shove a cushion up your front. If your novel is set during the plague you could sport some oozing, ulcerated sores, and if you've just published a collection of erotica, appearing in a stilettos, corset and a sequinned thong should guarantee some interest.

For the launch of *Perfect Alibis*, it was suggested I dress like the woman on the cover. An ingenious idea but not overly practical, the problem being that she had a sixteen inch waist and I have one … a lot bigger than that. Undaunted, one of my friends made me the matching scarf and handbag, I bought a pair of boots I never did learn to walk in, got some badges made saying PA's in the same type face and I went as the woman-on-the-cover's older, fatter sister who couldn't move far.

Leaving most guests to assume I had bad taste in accessories and was already drunk.

Sometimes an outfit in which to stand out can be dead simple. The launch for *Wannabe a Writer*? was held in Borders on Charing Cross Road. My publishers brought in loads of wine and nibbles, lots of the contributors came – we had all their books piled up too – and we drank the afternoon away.

Having fretted for a week about what I could wear that would be suitably writerly while still distracting attention from the Writer's Bottom everyone would be examining now I'd devoted the longest chapter in the book to it, the answer finally came to me the night before the event.

I ran round the corner to my friendly local printer, got a plain white T shirt emblazoned with the title of the book and teamed it with a pair of sparkly jeans. Hardly glamorous but job done.

Will anyone come?

Yes they will.

Curiosity, love for you, an appreciation of literature and the higher, finer, more cerebral facets of this rich life will bring guests forth. Should it not, take a large felt tip pen to your sign on the pavement and add, FREE BOOZE WITHIN. You'll soon have a crowd.

Do I really have to make a speech?

Yes you do but it can be very short. A heartfelt thank you and "now please buy my book, you tight wads" will suffice.

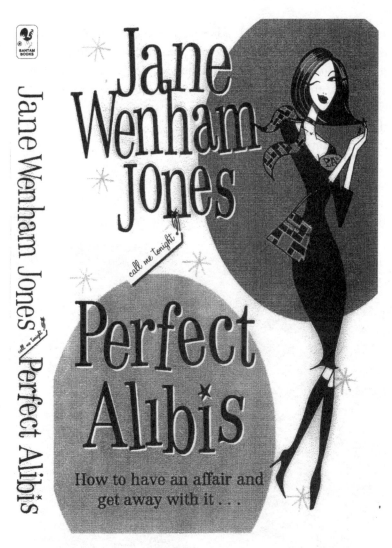

My waist is just a tad bigger than this....

Do I have to read?

Only if you want to. Or your publisher insists. This is probably my problem for having the attention span of a gnat, but unless the author doing the reading is VERY good at it, and the bit chosen is extremely gripping, I tend to glaze over at this part of the proceedings.

Because, generally, I guess, I'd rather read to myself, curled up in a chair.

There are exceptions to this – before you decide not to invite me to anything ever again – and I'm quite sure that hearing you reading would be one of them. So if this is the bit you've been most looking forward to and you want to read, do.

Just don't make it too long and speak up.

I can't abide mumbling.

Have wine, have contributors, will party.
The Wannabe a Writer? Launch. ✗
Borders, Charing Cross Rd. May 2007.

HITTING THE SHELVES

We have lift off

So now your book is Out There – what next? These first few exciting weeks when your book is actually in the shops and/or for sale online are your biggest opportunity to make an impact.

Let's recap on what you've done/are going to do. And add a few more things to the list. We'll explore them in more detail later.

1) **Create a press release and send it to everyone you can think of**. To every editor who ever published anything you've ever written, all the journalists on your list, all the local and regional media.

2) **Get yourself on the radio**. Local radio stations have hours to fill and are always looking for guests. They will give out details of your book on air once they've interviewed you. Sometimes they'll pop it up on their websites too.

3) **Have a go at TV** Regional TV news programmes sometimes use the quirky or unusual for a filler. Keep thinking about those angles. And would you be up for a game or quiz show perhaps?

4) **Give some talks** Call up your local library and offer to give a talk – with a book-signing afterwards, of course. Organisations like the Rotary Club and the WI book lots of speakers too. (Many of which are mind-numbingly dull so a cheery address on the finer points of the perfectly-fitted teapot lid would probably go down a storm.) They may not pay much, if at all, but if you've enthralled them, they may well buy a book afterwards. And then tell their friends about it.

5) **Write some short stories or articles**. There are thousands of magazines and newspapers out there – all needing copy. Most of whom will put a book plug at the bottom of your piece, if you play your cards right.

6) **Use the Internet** You've got a website haven't you? (Time to get one if not). Link to Amazon and other places to buy. Ask friends with websites to put a link to yours on theirs (and return the compliment of

course) and search the web looking for sites dedicated to something relevant – say teapot worship or the history of the teabag – that you might be able to write a short piece for or get a link on. Join forums. Embrace Twitter and Facebook.

7) **Leave a paper trail** Carry your postcards and bookmarks, get some flyers made with the details of your book and where it's stocked and leave them wherever you go.

8) **Talk to people** about your book in the bank queue, or at bus-stops (the beauty of being a writer is that people expect you to be eccentric), give a copy as a present to your most out-going friend and ask him or her to spread the word. All the hype and marketing budget in the world cannot compare with the power of word-of-mouth.

9) **Get round the bookshops**. Make friends with the staff, offer to stock-sign, see if they're up for a signing proper. (I usually take the opportunity to engage in a little judicious re-arranging of the shelves too – but do this when they're not looking.)

10)) **Think Big**. Every best-seller had to start somewhere. Be positive try everything, and when you get a phone call saying, Would you like to....? say YES!

The lure of bookshops

The first thing you might notice about having a book out is that it ruins going shopping. Or going anywhere at all.

For unless you stick to visiting Ye Olde Worlde Village with the one Post Office (recently closed), one pub (about to be closed or made part of the Happy Folks Diners Chain and newly-refurbished in red and green vinylette) and one Olde Worlde Craft shop (full of Olde Worlde Fridge Magnets made, naturally, in Taiwan) sooner or later, you're faced with a dilemma.

Do you dare go in the book shop?

Of course! I hear you cry. And in the beginning, I rushed in too. It was the moment I'd dreamt of for years. Seeing my book for sale. My name on the cover. A real live novel, there sitting on a shelf waiting for people to buy it.

Checking stock became compulsive. Husbands and offspring would glower and groan on the pavement, rolling their eyes at my excited witterings if there were heaps of books on prominent display or the sight of my gritted teeth if there'd only ever been one sad volume, spine out, in the A-Z section and nobody had bought it.

For if you're really masochistic, you can ask. In the early days I used to sidle up to the counter and plead for the computer's statistics. Thus were days made or broken.

I remember wandering into what was then *Books Etc.* on Piccadilly, when my first novel was just out, and loitering hopefully by the till. The sales assistant sighed. How many did they have in stock? Twenty-six, she told me without enthusiasm.

Twenty-six?? My God but that was masses – best-seller quantities – surely the number they ordered when they were expecting BIG THINGS…

"You've sold two," she added flatly.

Oh.

Some years later, now I know about the paid-for promotions and have read all the damning statistics and sad tales that say if you're not in the two-for-ones or three-for-twos you're dead in the water, I try to be realistic.

In my more neurotic moments I ask myself why would anyone buy a book by me? On my doorstep, no problem. My mum will buy everyone she's ever met a copy for Christmas. And locals from various bars I've fallen out of over the years, will buy one to see if they're in it. Some people – Vanessa Webb, who used to manage my local independent bookshop until its sad demise – told me, will buy ANYTHING if it's by a native of the town. (Even if – in the case of one elderly lady – they return it the same afternoon because it's "disgusting".)

But a total stranger in a far-flung city? Why would they pick up my novel among thousands of others? The first time I met someone who had, I did deep breathing exercises to stop myself kissing her. "Oh I just thought it looked interesting," she said airily when I'd pressed her into a corner for interrogation. "I liked the cover…"

I was equally excited the time my aunt told me she'd seen someone reading my latest *on the tube*! Firmly closing my mind to the thought that it might have been one of my third cousins, twice removed, who got it from my mother at Christmas, I saw it as proof that people who didn't know me did really wander into bookshops and for one reason or another, pick up a book by me and buy it.

But why?

These are the reasons I can think of:
1) It's on the table at the front on special offer
2) They've read a review of it, or an article about it
3) They've heard me talking about it on the radio and thought, that book sounds interesting
4) They've seen me on the TV and thought, she looks bonkers I wonder if she can actually write
5) They leant down to investigate something stuck to their shoe and found themselves at eye-level with the Ws

OR – they've bought it because it's got a signed-by-the-author sticker on it, OR they were swayed by the 'this store recommends' card on the shelf in front of it, that had been written out by one of the staff.

The first item on the list is the only one you can't really influence (except by proving to your publisher you're a good bet and worth that sort of sales effort and investment), the next three are down to you getting your second career as media tart off the ground, the fifth depends on happy chance (I shall indulge myself by telling you the heart-warming tale of Annie Ireson at the end of this section) but the last two can be helped along if you've got the neck.

I cannot produce any statistics on the matter but I am convinced that signed-by-the-author stickers make a difference. I think buyers like a little extra something and that signed books are more likely to get snapped up.

This may be by those who collect them (to either fuel their great love of literature or to squirrel away in case the author gets famous and they can be flogged on ebay) or those who think that a signed book will appear to be an added-value present for the friend/relative/colleague they need to keep in with, without spending more than £6.99. It doesn't really matter.

I have checked this theory with three different booksellers and they all agreed – signed-by stickers help shift copies and the bookstore is less likely to send them back (in theory they can't, although I happen to know some bookshops do!) or leave them languishing in the storeroom.

Similarly, if you're in the A-Z section, the 'this store recommends' cards draw the eye towards your book out of the thousands lining the shelves. They may lead the reader to pick up your tome, now that they've seen someone else likes it, and if the blurb on the back sounds appealing.

One Waterstone's manager told me that books sporting such cards had accounted for 7% of sales in the previous week.

So how do you get stickered up and ensure cards are written about you?

Make friends with your book-store

I always fondly imagine that booksellers will be thrilled to see an author hoving onto the horizon ready to lend their assistance to boost sales but I suspect that the reality could well be different. Depending on how you go about it, there is probably a fine line between being helpful and a right royal pain in the butt.

At the risk of alienating every book shop manager in the country who actually, thank you very much, would rather see fewer writers appearing at the doors demanding to see how many copies of their works are face out, rather than more, I will still tell you what I do.

I've always made a point of being a familiar face in the book stores around me. I introduce myself to the manager and staff and ask them if they'd like any postcards or bookmarks to leave on the counter or inside the books.

I also offer to sign any stock (and put the stickers on myself!) and, without actually getting anyone in a half-nelson, mention that I give talks, and am happy to do signings and events.

As a result, I have done many of all three. The trick is to make sure you sell plenty of books at the first one to prove your worth (even if you have to browbeat all your friends into rolling up and getting their hands in their pockets). More of this later.

In the meantime, pop in regularly. Don't make a nuisance of yourself or expect the staff to talk to you when they're busy but make sure you catch their eye and smile and say thank you for what they are doing, when you get the chance. (It also goes down well if you buy the odd book!!)

If the staff think you are a jolly nice chap, they are more likely to decide to have a read of your book and more likely to write out one of those cards or put a review up on their website. "We choose, it's still genuinely bookseller enthusiasm," says Waterstone's manager Martin Latham, of whom I shall say more later, although he offers the additional tip that if an author offers to write a card themselves, few booksellers will refuse.

"As long as," he adds in his inimitable style, "its not a crap or self-published-looking-thing."

At the time of writing, Waterstone's have brought out some new cards that makes the whole thing even easier, as they are designed to be filled out by the customers. So what are you waiting for? Get down there or send your mum!

Your favourites!
Chosen by our lovely customers.

feel every word   WP0505STA9336

If you're in there regularly, you can keep a subtle eye on whether the book is being restocked, whether the 'store recommends' cards have fallen off the shelf, they've run out of bookmarks or some bright spark has picked up your book, decided against it and left it in the cookery section.

Not that that is necessarily a bad thing!

There is a lovely writer called Anne Ireson who I now count among my good friends. But we had never met or heard of each other until, in August 2007, Annie went into the children's section of the Kettering branch of Waterstone's to look for a copy of *Harold the Helicopter* for her grandson.

"There, sitting on the shelf, right by the book I was looking for, was *Wannabe a Writer?* Someone had obviously put it in the wrong section. Of course I just had to buy it. It was an omen for sure. It was as if it being in the wrong place chopped through the chains that made me keep my writing a secret."

Up until then, the only person who knew that Annie wrote, was her 92-year-old Great Auntie Rita.

> She was my godmother and my biggest fan as a secret writer. We had just spent the last five years writing her life story and she desperately wanted me to try to get it published as a novel, but I was unbelievably reticent and self-conscious about my writing. I just didn't see how I was ever going to be able to let anyone else, other than her, read my work. She had always said she wanted to appear on the cover, draped across her sofa like Barbara Cartland, glass of wine in hand, as the real-life heroine of the story.

Sadly, Rita had died just days before Annie picked up my book. She says, "When I saw 'Wannabe' on the shelf four days later, I felt the proverbial shiver down my spine, I can tell you!"

As a result, Annie got in touch with me, met other writers through the Wannabe website, got some confidence up to show her writing around and now has an agent! (Her grandson Tyler – bless him – has given her back his copy of *Harold the Helicopter* because, as Annie says, "he knows how special it is to me.")

I gained a new friend and Auntie Rita's stories about her life have become the first book in a trilogy, which, I am convinced, will be published one day soon. Remember you heard it here first!

And remember too – that if you find your book in the wrong place in the bookshop, don't throw a strop. Perhaps it's meant to be!

For anyone not as touched by this story as I am, who is instead making a time and motion graph and thinking, Huh! All that going in and out sounds like a lot of effort for one bookshop – how many will a single store sell? The answer is: you'd be surprised.

Before the Thanet branch of Waterstone's opened, my local bookshop was the Albion Bookshop, managed by Vanessa who I've already mentioned.

She was in charge of the ordering, the displays and any events the shop got involved with. I barely knew her when my first book came out – but I made sure I went into the shop early on and put that right (how many bottles of wine we've had together since is anyone's guess!)

Vanessa sold the books at my launch parties, brought them to signings, displayed them in the window, and would often pile them on the counter. I went in regularly to say thank you and she knows how much I will always appreciate her support. (Strangely, another local author, who sounded off about stock levels, did not get the same treatment.)

Never underestimate the power of a good bookseller. The floorspace was tiny, the town is small. But Vanessa sold well over a thousand copies of my various books before that shop closed.

What if I'm not in stock at all?

You need to go in with an even bigger smile.

Sadly, with so many books coming out every month, not every title is going to be in every bookshop. But if yours isn't in the shops nearest you, I should make it a priority to get that situation addressed

If it's an independent bookshop, you need to chat up the owner or manager and see if they'll order in a couple of copies to give it a whirl (it goes without saying that you then make sure these are sold pdq).

Take a copy of your AI sheet and any media coverage you've had together with any rave reviews and a list of what is coming up next e.g. if you've got a radio interview planned or an article coming out. Leave a few bookmarks and/or postcards.

Most bookshop owners I've met are pretty amenable to this approach and since they can always send the books back if they don't sell (although you of course, will make sure they do!) then they've little to lose.

It gets a little more complicated with the chains, but while a lot of the ordering is done centrally, most managers have some autonomy and can get additional books in if they so choose – especially if it can be deemed to be local interest. This works best if you've written a history of the town but can apply equally to the fact that you live in the vicinity (I have stretched this to "in the same county" on occasion).

NB If you can play the local card then ask your publishers for a show card to back it up. This is typically a large cardboard sign with your name, LOCAL AUTHOR, book cover, titles and details on it, that your friendly bookseller may agree to put in a prominent position on the shop floor or in the window.

(Yes, even now all these things are paid for, you'd be surprised what they'll do if they like you.)

My first novel wasn't initially taken on by WH Smith. I went to see the manager of my nearest branch and persuaded him to order in some copies as I lived locally. Once he'd said yes (and put my showcard on display), I drove straight to the next town and told that manager what the first one was doing. Once they'd both sold a few copies, I moved further afield. Soon it was on sale in eight different branches and was on the computer system for reordering. When my second novel was published, WH Smith ordered it nationwide.

Love your book-buyer too

And speaking of ordering, if ever you get the chance to meet/schmooze with/throw rose petals at the feet of a book-buyer, take that opportunity as a gift from God and with open arms.

I first met Matt Bates – fiction buyer for WH Smith Travel (the holy grail if you're looking for station and airport sales) – at a Romantic Novelists' bash. I listened to his informative talk and lost no time in elbowing the other hopefuls out of the way when it was time for tea and biscuits and shoving a copy of whatever tome I was currently peddling, into his hands as soon as I decently could.

As it happened, that was *Wannabe a Writer*? and he does fiction, but he kindly passed it on to his non-fiction colleague and put my newly re-jacketed *Perfect Alibis* on promotion. I have thought him a jolly fine chap ever since.

He has kindly offered this insight into the book-buyer author relationship:

> Meeting authors for lunches or dinners can sometimes be a bit intimidating for both the buyer and the author. Over the years of meeting many authors – from celebrity ones to first time writers – I have found that having a much more personal and one-to-one conversation cultivates a real bond between author/buyer and very often the conversation isn't about books at all! You can really connect with people and I am very blessed to have a few authors who are real friends now, following a business lunch! So be yourself and find out what makes a retail book buyer click!

If you'd like to find out, sooner rather than later, enter the competition at the end of this book. Matt is a lovely guy – it will be a good lunch!☺

And if I'm self-published?

There's no point pretending about this. As a general rule, bookshops are wary of self-published books.

Mainly because so many of these books are awful. And they're already short of room for all the thousands of titles published each month by bona fide companies. So if you've published your book yourself, getting it into retail outlets at all, let alone piled high in a prominent position, is going to be hard.

But once again let us not confuse the word 'hard' with 'impossible'. If your book is worth its salt (and I'm sure YOURS is ☺) then the trick is to prove the cynical wrong and take it step by step.

If you are fortunate enough to have an independent bookshop nearby follow the steps above. You can try your luck too by playing the local card at your nearest chain. But don't hold your breath.

What will work, if done properly and the book is worth reading, is selling your book online. This a fine moment to introduce you to the fabulous Catherine Ryan Howard.

Catherine, from Cork in Ireland, self-published her first book, *MOUSETRAPPED: A Year and A Bit in Orlando, Florida* and has been enormously creative in the way she's gone about making sales.

Catherine produced her book using CreateSpace (you can visit her blog **Catherine, Caffeinated**, at www.catherineryanhoward.com for the whole glorious story) and through them was able to get her book on both amazon.co.uk and amazon.com as well as the amazon sites from France, Germany, Canada and Japan, in addition to Barnes and Noble and Books a Million, in the US.

She also sells the book through her own website.

"All you need," she says cheerily, is "a free Paypal account, a box of your books, access to a post office and at least mediocre organisational skills."

She sums up her approach to promotion as "cheap is good, free is better," adding, "Luckily in this new age of social media and the magical interweb infiltrating every facet of modern life, this isn't hard to do."

Catherine has blogged and twittered about *Mousetrapped*, made a Facebook page, joined forums, offered copies as prizes in competitions and even made a trailer for the book and uploaded it to YouTube.

She also did approach a bookstore and did have some success. "I was really nervous about approaching my local independent bookstore and asking them first, to stock my book and then second, to kindly lend me their store for an hour so I could a have a launch there," she says. "But they couldn't have been nicer."

Once the bookshop had agreed a date, Catherine swung into gear.

> I sent out invites, had postcards made, bought a cute outfit, stocked up on books and Signed by the Author stickers, called all the local papers, packed a box of DVDs of the trailer, told everyone I knew that this was more important than my wedding (for one thing, there IS a book launch, there might never be a wedding...!) and hoped for the best.

Her efforts paid off. A good crowd turned up, the bookshop people were happy and there was interest from the local press, including the 'social diarist' from Cork's *Evening Echo* (daily readership of about 250k) who showed up with a photographer and interviewed Catherine for the paper as well as inviting her on to a radio show.

Catherine was able to post the pictures online and blog about the event but says that best of all, "It helped me make friends with my local independent bookseller who then displayed *Mousetrapped* in that coveted position just inside the door and I got to play the part of a real, live writer. Woo-hoo!"

So Catherine is a shining example to us all of just how far you can spread the word if you try. I first heard about *Mousetrapped* on Twitter and have since bought a copy and so have hundreds of others.

By the time you're reading this, I am confident there will be another nought on the end of that. Catherine has generously shared a lot of her know-how and we will return to the fascinating tale of her promotional efforts when we get to the section on using the internet.

In the meantime, your book, published by whatever means, is on sale. Which means that if you've struck gold with any of those book editors you carefully targeted earlier, it's time to keep your eyes open for –

Rave reviews – or not

It is, I'm afraid, more likely to be 'not'. This isn't because your book's bad or deserves a roasting but because the statistics means that it probably won't get any attention at all. It is as Sam Leith, one-time Literary Editor of the *Daily Telegraph*, says, "a question of maths."

Sam wrote an excellent article for *The Author*, the Society of Author's regular journal, in which he explained that the average newspaper books desk gets more than 300 books a week for possible review – what he called "a slow-motion avalanche of Jiffy bags" – and so, very clearly, cannot review them all.

Decisions have to be made on which books to choose and Sam was candid about replying to the question of how he judged them, with the – perhaps unexpected – reply of "by their covers".

"When I stand there judging a book by its cover," he wrote, "what am I asking myself? I am asking whether the author (and indeed the publisher) has a reputation that suggests it will be good. I am asking whether, if it is non-fiction, it deals with an intriguing subject or looks like it will tell us something new. I shuffle the pages to see whether it seems well written or originally treated."

As someone who has successfully bludgeoned the odd editor into pushing my book to the top of the review pile, and who will almost certainly try it again, I asked Sam what else would have swayed him. Lavish gifts? Bribes? Authors chaining themselves naked to the steps of Telegraph Towers…. None of these, as it turns out. He replied:

> Politeness is always a winner for me, in authors, and a book that's well-published and looks like it's interesting to read sells itself. But the maths of the books cupboard makes it rather hard to do much more than follow one's nose. Gifts, pestering and gimmicks don't really work – though I'd be more than happy to see people chained naked at Telegraph Towers now I no longer work there! Basically, being a shit-hot writer is the way to success. That or being on the telly.

I don't think this should necessarily put us off. As it happens, I first came across Sam when we exchanged a few emails back in 2007 when *Wannabe a Writer?* had just been published. I decided to target a few Literary editors myself and sent the following email, which, those with sales training will note, emphasises the book's USP, pre-empts the objections and also engages in some shameless name-dropping. It went like this:

Hello Sam

You don't know me but the kind and ever-helpful Michael Bywater suggested I might contact you. Michael is one of over 100 contributors to my new book, *Wannabe a Writer?* (Accent Press). (Michael shares with Michael Buerk the honour of supplying the most un-repeatable bits :-)) along with other journalists, authors, agents and publishers.

I know there are more writing books than you can shake a stick at but 46,000 people entered the Richard & Judy 'How to Get Published' competition, there are thousands of writing groups out there and as the publisher Alan Samson says on page 201, "It seems as though in every street in Britain someone is writing a book" (adding, "and I do wish they'd stop" :-)) so there is a big demand for such tomes and this is completely different from everything else on the market.

It deals (in a totally hilarious way, natch) with the grim realities of being a writer as well as giving practical advice on how to get noticed in the endless sea of slushpiles and wannabes. Chapters on stress and jealousy and Writers' Bottom (a big chapter that one) as well as how to nab an agent and what to wear to your launch party (the book is nothing if not positive) and hot tips from everyone from Jilly Cooper and Mavis Cheek to Frederick Forsyth and Ian Rankin.

Being an optimist of the bottle being half-full variety (see chapter on The Benefits of Alcohol) I have asked my publisher to send you a copy today. I hope you don't mind and that you might have time to have a flick through. A review would be absolutely fabulous of course. But I hope it makes you smile anyway.

all best and many thanks for reading this far if you're still with me.
jane x

Strangely, Sam did not say, "God, don't you go on?" or even jettison me straight into the delete folder. He sent me a nice reply back saying it sounded great and he was looking forward to reading it (he'd also, as luck would have it, lost Michael Bywater's email address so had a good reason to answer).

To cut a long story – and several more emails – short, Sam was complimentary about the book but didn't ultimately review it. By the time

I'd had the bright idea of chatting up Michael for his contacts and the book had been sent, temporarily lost in the Telegraph offices and then turned up again, we were quite a long way past publication date, which, despite my best attempts to fudge, Sam had checked on the internet.

"If it was May, as the website seems to suggest," he wrote after I'd tried to persuade him, "I'm afraid we're rather too late to do anything on it..."

But not all was lost. Sam, has after all, contributed to this book – thank you Sam[1] – and if he hadn't, rather selfishly in my view, since left the *Telegraph* then the ice would have been broken for me to bombard him with future works.

Wannabe wasn't reviewed by *The Times* either, but after emailing Literary Editor Erica Wagner twice, accosting the editor of the weekend section of *The Times* at a gathering, emailing him when I got home and then emailing Erica again, the following appeared in her editorial.

> But at the moment the river of literary self-help is in spate; there's The Handbook of Creative Writing from Edinburgh University Press; there's Wannabe a Writer? by Jane Wenham-Jones; there's Louise Doughty's A Novel in a Year (based, as it so rightly says on the front flap, on her highly successful newspaper column).
>
> Ms Wenham-Jones quotes the crime writer Bernard Knight as saying, "Writing is cold-blooded hard labour – like digging holes in the road." I admit that I have never dug holes in the road, but I can't say that I agree. Yes, writing is hard work. It's confusing. You wonder why on earth you bother. The list (like the list of stationery) goes on and on. And yet, because somehow you simply cannot help yourself, you persevere.
>
> **Erica Wagner The Times June 9, 2007**

This thrilled and delighted me as you might imagine, and proves once again that sometimes it's worth having a go, even if the odds are stacked against you.

However, there is obviously a mere hair's breadth between managing to get your book a second glance and being a bloody nuisance so please do not start emailing every literary editor in the land and blaming me.

Footnote 1: So the least I can do to plug his book which is *Sod's Law* published by Atlantic Books. It's very good – hilarious in places – I do recommend the tale of George Brown on page 32 which made me laugh out loud.

Particularly do not do this to Erica Wagner as 1) She always strikes me as a woman not to be trifled with and 2) it is one of my small ambitions to one day persuade her to send me more than an auto-reply and she's not very likely to if you lot start flooding her inbox with begging missives.[2]

You may of course, already be very well-reviewed indeed and just reading this book because you can't sleep and someone left it in the drawer in your hotel room when they pinched the Gideon's.

If so, and you take it for granted the fact that most of the editors will fall gladly on your latest work and send it out for review, all you need to concern yourself with is – suppose you get a bad one?

If you do get a bad write-up, I suggest you are philosophical – these things are subjective – and certainly do not allow yourself to descend into paranoia.

As Sam Leith says, Book Editors do not commission 'hatchet jobs' or set out to attack someone's work but he understands how authors can come to react badly to a negative verdict. As he put it in his article, "it must be mortifying to conclude that an intelligent person has carefully, patiently and open-mindedly read your work and found it bad. But that, nine times out of ten, is what has happened."

I have not (yet) had what I would call a 'bad' review in the press –although naturally some critics have not been as enthusiastic as others – but if and when it happens, I hope I will still be grateful to be there at all.

I'd rather my books were in the public eye than ignored altogether and if the review is in the national press, then for the most part at least, it *will* as Sam says, be intelligent and considered.

Which cannot always be said of the reviews that end up on the internet – which by its very nature is bound to be a free-for-all.

Prolific novelist Judy Astley found a review on Amazon that said her book *Other People's Husbands* (Bantam Press) was "a load of pants".

"I cried a bit," she says cheerfully, "because we take such comments personally. But then I noticed the critic's grammar was pretty poor so I felt better."

JoJo Moyes vowed never to Google herself again after coming across a book blog review which suggested one of her novels should go "straight to

---

Footnote 2: And speaking of Sod's Law, sometime it can work in one's favour. I knew if I wrote that line, Erica Wagner would reply to my very next email which she just has. See page 272. Thank you Erica.

a dusty shelf in a charity shop" – but says she takes "thoughtful, intelligently written" reviews seriously and is prepared to learn from them.

Sometimes, however, there is no chance of redemption. I winced when I spotted an on-line review of *Perfect Alibis*, describing it as "very dissapointing, (sic) with a weak shallow and unbelievable plot and characters that you couldn't feel any empathy with" but there is little point in exercising oneself unduly.

When on the receiving end of criticism, I remind myself that at least my books are published and being read and that I can't be the only one who has bought a book purely on the strength of a good slating, just to see if it can really be that awful.

If you write features, articles or have any sort of regular slot in any publication at all, you may well come under occasional attack and become equally hardened.

Having written a column for my local newspaper for many years I am entirely used to readers becoming apoplectic and emails such as the one which began, "Ms Wenham-Jones – I cannot bring myself to call you Dear because YOU CERTAINLY ARE NOT..." no longer faze me.

I smile when a regular correspondent tells me I "talk rubbish at the best of times" or I am accused of everything from having dangerous communist tendencies to being unpleasantly right wing. It goes, as they say, with the territory. And this is very small fry compared to what those on the nationals can expect.

Journalist Robert Crampton was very amusing about this in his column in *The Times*, telling how one Mr Dean had described his writings as "vapid, meandering and utterly uninspiring chunderings" which is pretty impressive, and another reader had accused him of producing "whining effeminate drivel" which I like even better.

Robert, whom, personally, I enjoy hugely as a writer, ended the column on a very wise note by saying "take your work seriously, but never yourself or your enemies".

This, I think, is just about the best advice any of us can hope for, especially in today's internet-driven world where, via comment boards, reader reviews, and feedback forms, every last oddball with an axe to grind can have his or her say.

Which leads us neatly on to:

Amazon – a double-edged sword

There is no doubt that Amazon can be a wonderful tool for the modern writer. Readers can see all your books at the click of a mouse, order them instantly while the iron is hot – when they've just heard you on the radio for example, or seen you on TV – and have access to feedback from others who've already made a purchase..

You can collect glowing reviews, post your own comments and author info and build yourself a profile. You can also become obsessive about your ratings if so inclined. (I am.)

If you have a website, you can link to Amazon and potential customers can click through to the store from there. Many authors have a 'shop' page – I do myself – with thumbnail images of their covers that go directly to the corresponding page at the bookstore.

If you join the Amazon Associates Programme (details on the Amazon site), traffic originating from your site will be tracked and you will earn a commission on any resulting sales – of anything, not just your books.

These small payments can accrue quite nicely and while you're unlikely to be able to retire on them, they may well keep you in chocolate from time to time.

For any author who is self-published or whose books have not been widely distributed in the High Street, Amazon can be a godsend.

You can have a fair idea of whether stock is moving – each book's ranking is updated hourly; there's a lot of cross referencing – "customers who bought this item also bought", etc., which can increase awareness and sales; and customers are positively encouraged to write reviews and comment on the reviews of others – both of which are simple to do. So far so good.

The only fly in the ointment is that as far as the reviews go, there are millions of books on the site, millions of readers posting their thoughts and you may find some of them unwelcome.

Readers are invited to award one to five stars to a book they've read and if you find you've been given only one and your book, that you spent a long year of your life sweating blood and tears over has been pronounced "Unintelligible Bilge that's a waste of the rain forest" you may, understandably, feel upset.

But every one is entitled to their opinion. Sometimes readers will just hate a book and that I'm afraid is something we have to take on the chin. You can't please 'em all and nor should you expect to.

However, it can be galling if the reviewer is clearly just trying to plug a rival book or something of their own, and puts up negative reviews purely in order to bring your average star rating down. What can you do about it? If they're clever about it, not a lot. But they often aren't…

Fiona Mackenzie is the author of *How to Start and Run a Petsitting Business* (How-to Books). She received what she describes as a "heart-stopping" review on Amazon.

My one star review advised that I was "no writer" and that anyone wanting to be a petsitter should join a certain fee-paying association. The review ended with 'sorry sweetheart'."

Since this appeared to have been written entirely to further the reviewer's own ends, Fiona decided to investigate.

> I had no idea who this person was but I did a search on the internet with her username and found her on ebay. It felt good being able to see who she was and that she had links within the pet care world so perhaps had an agenda. I then contacted Amazon and said as I'd had a book published by a highly respected publisher, clearly I was a writer and if they let the review stand it would reflect on other 'How To' books. I tried to avoid making it all about me. Amazon took the review down within twenty-four hours.

Amazon take all complaints seriously but obviously you cannot complain just because someone doesn't like your book and says so.

Everyone has the right to free speech and is entitled to their view – which is entirely as it should be. However, if you feel that any reviews or comments made are actually defamatory then you can say so. Amazon have a procedure for reporting such things.

After two years of largely positive reviews of my first Wannabe book, I had a sudden spate of one star reviews myself.

They came from different names but were all very similar in content – each one seemed to be getting het up over the fact that others had described my book as "brilliant" when it very clearly wasn't, and opining that one would do far better to read Stephen King.

The former was reasonable, if a little obsessive, and I can hardly disagree with the latter since I recommend *On Writing* by the awe-inspiring Mr King myself, in *Wannabe a Writer*?

However, the reviewer, not content with popping up several times saying this, then descended into what amounted to libel by accusing me on several occasions of either writing the five-star reviews myself or asking my friends to.

Several of the reviewer's own 'friends' materialised to agree.

This was utterly untrue. My publishers reported it as defamatory and the offending comments were removed. I can't stop this person reappearing any time he wants to – and from time to time, he does. I'm not always sure what is said because Amazon themselves have often deleted the comments before I've got there – and a note has been left to this effect – but as this has happened, one can assume they fell into the abusive or libellous category.

Such behaviour is not worth getting steamed up about – one could indeed feel sorry for the kind of person who finds this a fulfilling way to spend their time – but it *is* worth keeping an eye out for.

Just to be clear: if reviewers are merely stating their opinion – honestly held – you haven't got a leg to stand on. If they are making any claims that are untrue, and therefore they will be unable to substantiate them, then you have a case to report them to Amazon as defamatory and Amazon will take action. (Details of how to make such a report are clearly laid out on the site.)

For example.

"I hate this book"

"This book made me throw up my breakfast"

"This book is inane, facile, full of useless information and the author is a dork"

(Which, I think, is what my admirer was trying to get at) are all fine but:

"The author has plagiarised A.N. Dork in the writing of this dreadful book", or

"This author is a convicted criminal who roasts hamsters and eats them", or

"This book is the most expensive of its type on the market"

when these statements are false and unproven, are not acceptable and you have every right to ask for them to be removed.

In less extreme cases, inaccuracies can be just as simply dealt with yourself. Novelist Sarah Duncan was surprised to read a review of her first novel *Adultery for Beginners* (Hodder) which referred to the wife in the story having had a Deepo-provera injection – something which definitely doesn't happen in Sarah's story. The reviewer was clearly confused but it left Sarah with a dilemma.

> I quickly realised that whatever book the reviewer was talking about, it wasn't mine. And worse, he gave away the plot of this other book – that the guilt or innocence of the wife was shown by her Deepo-provera injection – so I reckoned people would be deterred from reading *Adultery for Beginners* for the wrong reasons. I didn't know what to do. It seemed petty and somehow wrong for me, as author, to make a fuss. In the end I asked a couple of friends if they would point out the error, which they did, then I felt OK to comment that it wasn't the plot of my book. But it still niggles, and I wonder how many people were put off buying because of that review.

It is extremely annoying if a reviewer gives away the plot – whether it's your book or not. (As Sarah Duncan puts it, "it takes me weeks to plan those big surprise moments!") Or exaggerates in a misleading way.

"Having 'orgasms' mentioned every other page isn't very sensual" wrote one reviewer crossly about my novel *Perfect Alibis*.

I'm afraid I was anal enough to get the original manuscript up on screen and use the search facility. In fact, the word 'orgasms' appears twice in 315 pages, together with 3 uses of 'orgasm' and one 'orgasmic flush'. But hey ho – one man's every other page is another woman's once every five chapters. Who am I to quibble?

In any case, sometimes the odd inaccuracy can work in one's favour.

Wannabe a Writer? has a foreword by Katie Fforde. But because her name is listed first, before mine, searches can throw her up having written the entire book. I can't tell you how many people have kindly emailed to point this out, expecting me to be indignant.

As I always explain, maybe I was for a nano-second when I first saw what had happened. Hang on a minute, I might have thought, *Katie Fforde* as the author?? But I pretty rapidly thought again. *Mmmn! Katie Fforde as the author…*

For let us remember that Katie is a Best-Selling Author with legions of fans and I am quite sure that many more people are going to be searching for her name on Amazon than for mine. I imagine therefore that quite a few people have pitched up on the *Wannabe a Writer?* page that wouldn't have found it otherwise.

Once there, it becomes very clear that Katie wrote the foreword only, so nobody buys under false pretences, but perhaps I get some extra traffic that I can only be thankful for and a few extra readers get to hear about me!

Which is, after all, what we are here to talk about even if we got slightly side-tracked there.

So, back to:

On-line stores in general

Do use them to their full capacity. Get your picture up there if there's a facility to do so, or add your biography. Amazon allows you to create an author page on which you can do both.

No doubt as time goes on, more and more online stores will offer this extra content – see it as free advertising and make the most of it. The aim is to be as widely known, seen and heard of, as possible, but this can be a double-edged sword too.

If not for you – or me – then for others around us.

More than one publisher has suggested I might include the next section! I've called it –

Get over yourself

If you've experienced the sort of rubbish reviews we've been talking about, you are probably suitably chastened anyway, so this section is not for you.

But for anyone still in the first heady stages of being feted and adored, who is looking forward to a future of fame, fortune and minions on hand to offer the peeled grapes after the ardours of tripping up yet another red carpet, let us just take a minute out for a small reality check.

As in: you won't do yourself any favours if you get too carried away. Obviously it's your book, you did the hard work – you wrote it – and of that you should be justifiably proud. But remember that once it is Out There, on sale, being promoted, on its way, hopefully, to making you an author 'we've heard of' then all sorts of other people are involved in making efforts on your behalf and they may not be quite so keen on doing that if you are being a prima donna.

"Don't argue with or criticise your publisher," says best-selling novelist, Jill Mansell, very sensibly. "They would prefer to work with nice authors. If they can only renew the contract of one author and they have two to choose from, they're unlikely to choose the stroppy, difficult one!"

Hazel Cushion, MD of Accent Press, who publishes this book, bears this out. "We have regretfully dropped several writers who developed APD (Author Personality Disorder) on publication," she says dryly.

It can be disappointing if you don't feel you're getting the marketing support you need, aren't in all the promotions you'd wish for, and finding publicity opportunities seems to be left entirely up to you, but let us look at the facts.

The publishers loved your book enough to spend money on it so it is in their best interests to do as well as they can by it. And that is probably what they are doing. What we have to remember is that they have a whole heap of books to do their best by, and – particularly if they are small and/or times are hard – they have finite resources in terms of budget and staffing.

Throwing your toys out of the pram won't change the latter, it will just make everyone at the publishing house fed up with you. Acting like minor royalty in bookshops will alienate the very staff you need on your side and behaving as if you are the only author your agent has on his or her books will pretty soon make them pissed off too.

"Successful authors are usually canny authors," says Hazel Cushion. "They are people who have looked at the whole publishing process, made an effort to understand it and worked out where and how they can help influence things. They realise where they fit into the publishing machine – their book is an important cog but their attitude and professionalism will oil the way to its success. Unsuccessful authors think they are the machine, that publishers are mere maintenance men, poking and prodding at perfection – a necessary evil in the production of their books."

"In these parlous times, publishers need all the help they can get," says Patrick Janson-Smith from Harper Collins. "Authors generally have to be prepared to muck in."

"But," he warns, "authors shouldn't be **too** pushy when it comes to promoting themselves; it's just a question of knowing where the boundaries are between help and hindrance. An OTT author, without the personality to match, may annoy rather than amuse."

Hazel agrees. "Understand that everyone is overworked – your publishers will welcome you flagging up genuine PR opportunities, errors, etc., but do so briefly. One author was livid that I didn't answer all his emails but he sent at least seven a week!"

Far from haranguing them by email, best-selling crime writer, Peter James, suggests entertaining your publishers instead. "Invest some money in taking them out to decent lunches – all who work in publishing love a good lunch – and get them enthused about your book."

Certainly, you should find a way to let them know how much you appreciate all they do. And Hazel also has the following recommendations:

1) Have realistic expectations – most companies have tiny marketing budgets but you can help supplement these with proactive PR on Facebook, etc. You may also decide to print your own bookmarks, postcards, etc.

2) Keep a copy of your contract and read it. You'd be amazed how many authors email me asking things that are clearly covered in their contracts.

3) Don't invest in a big, floppy hat and 'swan' up to signings. See APD above

4) Remember that it's sometimes nice to say thank you. If you're entered for an award, featured in a promotion, invited to a Book Festival or event then someone at the publishing company made that happen for you. Find out who and send a quick note or email to thank them.

The last one, in my humble opinion (fortunately I came out of my 'hat' phase long before I was published), is the most important of all. The words 'thank you' always go down well and should now be hovering on your lips at all times. They will make the next stage of proceedings a whole lot more successful...

ON THE CAMPAIGN TRAIL

Book signings

The first thing to say about these is why restrict yourself to shops? When crime writer Peter James's first Roy Grace novel *Dead Simple* came out in Germany, one of his events took place in a coffin warehouse. "I had to lie in a coffin and sign books," he recalls.

I cannot possibly compete with this but in my time, I have engaged in book signings on cross-channel ferries, at airports, in hotels, and a fine selection of bars and restaurants.

These have been arranged via on-board book suppliers, small independent book shops, large book-selling chains, or me simply getting a cardboard box out of my boot.

However humble or grand the set-up, and however many I do, they all have one thing in common. They begin with that small niggling feeling of 'suppose nobody buys' that lasts from the time I first sit down at the table till someone gets her purse out.

It's a feeling I hate so I always try to get the first sale as soon as I can. There are two ways of doing this. Prime a friend/colleague/your mum to arrive the moment after you do, waving a tenner OR – if you are miles from home/ everyone you know has done that for the last three Saturdays and has, frankly, lost interest – pin on your biggest smile and go straight into chatting up the punters.

This requires a little effort and nerve initially as the first thing you will notice if you've never done a signing before, is that nobody wants to make eye contact. They will walk purposefully past, gaze fixed on the far corner of the shop, scuttle up a different aisle or skirt round your table head turned as if they haven't noticed you.

The best way to deal with this is to tell yourself that they are simply embarrassed and dying to talk to you really but too shy to make the first move.

Once you've cracked one, it will give you the confidence to carry on. So take a deep breath and call out something cheery as they attempt to sidle past. "Good afternoon!" or "Hello!" is a fine opener.

Don't be put off when they look either startled or repulsed – this is usual. Instead, indicate your pile of books, smile widely, and say "Hello I'm J. Arthur Author and I'm signing copies of my new book *The Thinking Man's Guide to Teapots* today. Would you like to have a look?" and then thrust a copy into their unsuspecting hands before they can make a run for it.

Once they're holding the book, go straight into your sales pitch, making a quick appraisal of your potential customer and taking a stab at what might float their boat – e.g. it's set locally / I live locally / this is an ideal Christmas present / recent research has shown that men who like tea pots are better in bed – and the minute you sense any weakness, grab your pen.

Remember the alternative close beloved of double glazing salesman[3], and ask "Would you like me to sign it to you or to someone else?" If it's a bloke, you can then add in something about it being an excellent, personalised gift for his girlfriend / boyfriend / wife / mother-in-law as men are invariably stuck for imaginative gifts for birthdays, anniversaries or to make up for not coming home till 5 a.m., (if it's a female customer she'll a) have more imagination and b) would think up a plausible excuse), and beam again.

Once he's capitulated, thank him loudly and fulsomely so that other customers can hear too, catch the eye of the nearest sales assistant and call, "Gosh, that's 176 I've sold now" and look round to see who else is within shouting distance.

Sometimes shoppers *will* come straight up to you. This will mean one of two things. Either they think you're staff and will want to know where they can find the book that was being talked about on the radio by someone they now forget but her name might have begun with an M, or they are not the sort to worry about the niceties of conversation.

Charles Collingwood (Brian in *The Archers*) tells a lovely tale about when he was promoting copies of his autobiography *Brian and Me* (Michael O'Mara Books).

Footnote 3: Obviously they don't use these words, they say, "Would you like your frames in white or brushed aluminium?" but the principle of offering limited options that both result in a sale, remain the same.

Sitting at a signing desk in a bookshop with a pile of your tomes at your side, be prepared for the crusty old couple, not a smile in sight who stand motionless by your table. Their eyes move from looking at you to the pile of books alongside. Back and forth their eyes shift from one to another until with a shake of their heads, one says "no dear, never heard of him". And they walk away without the slightest acknowledgement that you existed at all.

It was, as he says "hilarious later when told to friends with a glass of wine in hand, but quite hard to take at the precise moment".

Anita Burgh, who has dozens of novels under her belt, is an old hand at this game too. She likens a book signing to being an animal in a zoo. She tells how two customers standing a mere five feet from her discussed her as follows:

'She's fatter than in her picture,' said the first one.

'She looks older,' said her friend.

'And she's not deaf,' said Anita, who was rewarded with "a look to freeze hell".

At another signing, Anita sat beneath a huge poster bearing her picture and name. "Excuse me," said a shopper, "are you Rosamunde Pilcher?" When told that Anita wasn't, the woman looked askance. "I AM disappointed. I so hoped you were!"

She then picked up a book, leafed through it and asked Anita if she'd read any Pilcher. When the answer came that she hadn't, the woman looked shocked. "Then I think you should," she said.

And, as Anita adds wryly, at the end of this tale, "She didn't buy either."

You can often tell fairly quickly who will and who won't and it's worth expending your energy accordingly. We can all be taken by surprise at times, but, as a general rule, if you're flogging a chick-lit book you're better off targeting young women than old men and if you're offering *The Gorgeous Gay's Guide to Happy Clubbing* there's not going to be a lot of mileage in pinning down the harassed-looking mother with the three kids who's hanging onto her husband's arm.

I gave author Sally Zigmond the benefit of my considerable advice before she embarked on a book tour around the north with her novel *Hope Against Hope* (Myrmidon Books). She soon identified that her typical reader was "called Joan or Beryl, aged about 75 with a tight grey perm and a mobility scooter".

However, this wasn't foolproof when it came to predicting sales. Sally reports smiling brightly, pen poised, at a woman gliding towards her.

Sally: "Good Morning! Lovely day!"

Woman: "I came in here to buy a specific book and it's not yours."

If you can possibly get yourself somewhere where your book is going to be of interest to pretty much everyone, then grab that chance with both hands.

Elaine Everest is the author of *Showing Your Dog, A Beginner's Guide* (How To Books). After having the bright idea of contacting *Our Dogs* magazine, she did a signing on their stand at the Earls Court Exhibition Centre when an event called Discover Dogs was being held. She was delighted to find herself facing a queue of people with books in hand and some canine customers too. "There are some really clever dogs out there as I signed many a book to Fido and Trixie and wished them good luck with their showing careers!"

Later she did it all again at Crufts which she describes as "hectic" but again she sold lots of books.

"Signing at dog events is really different to a bookshop signing where we can sit at a table and look elegant," she says. "By the end of my sessions I was hot, almost deaf from the noise and covered in dog hairs and a fair amount of slobber!"

Elaine also visits pet events, fun dog shows and dog training courses to sign and sell books. And is currently doing the rounds with her latest tome *Canine Cuisine* (How To Books) a cookery book for dog owners!

Illustration by Shirley Webb

The first time I did a signing in Wales, I looked a bit like a dog's dinner myself. It was in the Cardiff branch of WH Smith with my friend, novelist Lynne Barrett-Lee, to promote *Sexy Shorts for Christmas* (Accent Press) – an anthology of short stories to which we'd both contributed, to support Breast Cancer Campaign.

I wasn't in the best possible mood, having got up at five to drive through freezing fog for four hours to get there and having, in the days before Sat Nav, taken a wrong turn which meant I arrived with minutes to spare. Just enough time, it transpired, to change into my 'costume'.

The mere word brought me out in a rash as I still hadn't recovered from the hours spent at Gatwick airport for a 'Tolkien Day' which we had assumed would involve a huge array of colourful characters dressed as Gandalf or Gollum but which turned out to be just us in Now You're Tolkien T-shirts trying to flog our own chick-lit offerings to bemused long-haul passengers who really wanted the latest John Grisham.

This time, Lynne had had the brilliant idea of dressing us up in festive gear and was proffering a Santa suit – a short-skirted, red, fluffy white-edged affair with matching cape, belted in at the middle. It would probably have looked very sweet on someone of seven years old. But was not the sort of thing middle-aged women want to be seen sporting in Cardiff City Centre.

"I promised the manager," she said calmly while I spluttered. She was referring to the WH Smith events manager for South Wales, Phil Trenfield, who seemed amused to see us tripping about among the decorations and wrapping paper, looking ridiculous, trying to sell a raunchy book to stony-faced Welshmen.

Amused enough, anyway, to get involved in the next *Sexy Shorts* anthology himself and to invite us back for several more signings over the next couple of years (mercifully in our own clothes!).

Phil, who arranged over 150 events and signings during his time at WHS has worked with first-time novelists as well as some of the biggest names in the business. He admits that choosing who to book was often driven by how much revenue they might generate but this was not necessarily dependent on how famous they were.

He explains, for example, how he would try to tie in book signings with local events or other books being launched.

When *Harry Potter and the Half Blood Prince* was released I organised for a brand new author, Shelley E Parker, to have an event signing copies of her children's book *Return to Allapatria* which had similar appeal. As the store was already teeming with customers in to buy the Harry Potter, this gave the author and publisher a perfect opportunity to attract a new audience by publicising Shelley's book. We ended up selling over 150 copies of her book in two hours.

On another occasion, Phil took advantage of the fact that there was rugby on in Cardiff.

I arranged for two of the players to attend the store to sign copies of *Breathing Fire* which was a book all about the Grand Slam. The book was quite expensive at nearly £30 a copy and wouldn't normally have flown off the shelves as it was more of a considered purchase but with the rugby stars there, we ended up selling nearly 100 copies in under an hour.

So it's worth being tuned into any opportunities for tie-ins and/or associated events and we should find the above encouraging.

If your book on cooking comes out at the same time as Nigella's it might not be all bad – there could be lots of foodies filling the shopping malls.

And if you've written a book about the Olympics and it's 2012 – obviously you're laughing (except for the fact that I imagine there will be about 5000 books on the Olympics so make sure yours involves how you lost a leg in the 100 metres/shagged a gold medallist/were the first person to drop the flame on his foot).

However brilliant your concept for self-promotion, however, keep smiling and accept it if the bookseller does not share your enthusiasm. They know their customers better than we do and Phil says he would know instinctively when something wouldn't work.

A lady phoned me who had released a new book of knitting patterns and wanted to arrange a signing. I politely refused as I knew most customers would not attend that kind of book signing so it would have been a waste of time and resource. I advised the author that maybe she should contact her local library and at the same time she could arrange a practical session to give knitting demonstrations at the event.

Similarly, if he suspected the author him- or herself wouldn't attract a crowd but signed copies of the book would probably sell well, he'd go for a stock-signing instead, encouraging the author to come into the store to sign a quantity of their title and then putting up a display of the stickered books. As Phil says, "This would guarantee good sales without an author's ego being dented by lack of a queue."

Phil offers these top tips to make your signing or event go well:

1) Always come prepared with your own pen as some book stores won't even think of things like that.
2) Dress well, as you want to make a good impression.
3) Don't be afraid to approach shoppers in a bookstore. Most book sales are through word of mouth, so tell them about the book and that you are there doing a signing. If you approach five people and only one says yes, you've still sold one more than you would have normally.
4) Be prepared for questions,
5) Contact the local press and let them know you are doing a book signing. They normally love a local girl/guy done good story and it's all free publicity. It normally also means you get a bit more attention from the shoppers in the book store if a photographer is clicking away.
6) Use social networking sites to attract friends, family and contacts to the event. Target other authors on these sites and ask them to advertise it to their friends. If only ten percent of 100 people turn up that's still ten books sold.
7) Always ensure you are polite and courteous to the book store staff. I was always put off by any rude authors and it usually meant I never asked them to come again.
8) Advertise the event well. Ensure that the book store has posters, show cards and even leaflets to pop in customers' bags advertising the event. Let your local tourist information office know and also the surrounding libraries as they will usually advertise for free. Contact local radio stations and try to blag an interview. If you have a good story you can normally get some good exposure.
9) When you are at the book store ask them if they would like you to sign some copies to sell after the event. Customers do love a signed copy and they make great gifts.

10) Send the book store that you have been signing in a thank-you card or note. It's always a nice touch.

Phil Trenfield knew how to throw a signing together – always a fun day out.

And just to add a few of my own fine tips too –

1) Take several pens. a) there's nothing worse than one running out on you mid-signature and b) in my experience, there's always someone who'll nick anything.

2) If you've got anything you can give away – bookmarks, postcards,

pens – then this will always endear you to the canny shopper who likes an added extra. When I was doing signings for *Wannabe a Writer?* I would often take along some complimentary copies of *Writing Magazine*, a pile of entry forms for short story competitions or some advertising material for writing courses. A bowl of chocolates on the table can work well too…

3) Ask the bookshop to put a large sign outside, indicating that you are within – you may get some extra visitors who come in out of curiosity, just to see what you look like. **NB** This works particularly well when it's raining or the bus is late.

4) Always check how to spell a name, before you gaily start writing. Is it Nicky, Nicki, Nikki or Nykki, for example? I have come across all these variations.4

5) Remember to say a big thank you to your customer as well as the book store. While you're doing this, it's worth telling your new reader where you will be signing next in case she has a cousin/sister/aunt in the town who might also enjoy your book.

6) Smile! People are more likely to gravitate towards you if you appear happy. So look as though you are enjoying yourself even if you feel a prune.

Bookshop events

If you are lucky – and go about it the right way – you may be able to cajole your local bookstore into holding something a bit more meaty than a mere signing.

Giving a talk is the obvious thing to offer but hold fire before you rush for the High Street to break the good news to your local manager. If you live in Canterbury, he may be underwhelmed.

Footnote 4: This reminds me of a pleasing joke about dogs' names.

Two posh dog-walkers in Kensington Gardens:

"What's yours called?"

"Fido."

"Fido?" (disdainful look) "That's rather common isn't it?"

"Not, (equally disdainful) when one spells it P h y d e a u x…"

Martin Latham is the longest-serving Waterstone's Manager, having been appointed by Tim Waterstone himself. He now runs the Margaret Street branch in Canterbury where well over 100,000 people have attended events in the store, coming to see everyone from AS Byatt to Norman Wisdom, including such diverse personalities as Stephen Fry, Nigella Lawson, Jilly Cooper, Tony Benn and Melvyn Bragg. Martin has organised upwards of 3000 events so is well placed to hold forth on what works and what doesn't. He also blogs for *The Bookseller* where he wrote:

"Authors are often rotten at holding an audience. Novelists are the worst and should avoid reading from their books unless they are performers. Put them in twos or in conversation."

While I wouldn't be quite so categorical about this – I know plenty of novelists who are excellent speakers – I think the idea of combining authors is a good one.

If you don't feel confident you can be spell-binding on your own, give the audience two for the price of one and ask a published friend to interview you or hold an 'in conversation with'. He or she will probably be delighted as long as there's a pile of his or her own books on display too.

I know I was, when I was asked to do just that by Judy Astley and Victoria Connelly at the Notting Hill branch of Waterstone's.

Victoria was publicising her novel *Molly's Millions* (Allison & Busby) while Judy was there with her *Other People's Husbands* (Black Swan). I asked them both questions about the individual books, as well as the whole writing process and their lives as writers.

I think it worked well and the audience seemed to enjoy it. From the authors' points of view, they didn't have to worry about running out of things to say or keeping their eye on the clock. I timed it, kept the conversation moving along and chaired questions from the audience. (This can be an art in itself. They were a very well-behaved bunch on that particular night, I remember, but there is generally always one who wants to explain the plot of his own unfinished manuscript and needs to be deflected.)

Victoria was so taken with the concept that she's since set up a group "Let's talk about Love" with three other authors, and they regularly give talks in bookshops and libraries. She says:

An author event can be a scary prospect especially when you have to face an audience on your own so I found doing my event with Judy and Jane at Notting

Hill's Waterstone's really helped to calm my nerves. It wasn't just me on my own that night – I had two good writer friends with me. Plus, it was enormous fun because we were all sharing and learning from each other along the way. Doing an event with fellow authors helps take the pressure off and it becomes a really enjoyable experience.

When three's not a crowd.
Victoria Connelly e
Judy Astley in Notting Hill.

Photo by Roy Connelly

On the other hand, if you'd rather go it alone – and I've always been perfectly happy to – Martin Latham, for all his grumbling, says he'd book an event if an author had "some charisma" and some "guaranteed press". This means real local coverage that comes off, not just the promise of some, and not you simply relying on your friends and family to come. "Don't tell me: 'I can promise a full house just from all the people I know'," Martin says. "Those feckers will not come out on a rainy night."

How close the event is to the publication date doesn't matter to him at all but a long lead time does. "What's the rush?" he asks. "Why give three weeks notice when you can arrange an event three months in advance and get a lot more people? Give me six months," he offers, "and I can fill an event with a tramp reading out the Berkshire telephone directory."

(Speaking as one who, at the time of writing, has just arranged an event with Martin in five month's time, I am suitably reassured.)

He is keen that authors don't "just drone on" and emphasises the success of events where the author is "doing something".

He has booked authors who've carried out painting demonstrations, past-life regression therapy and guided meditations, as well as reiki healing and head massage. These are the kind of events that make a profit for the shop – which after all, is what it's about.

"Get authors to do what they are best at," he says. You could be forgiven for thinking this is writing books but Martin is looking beyond that. "Ray Davies brought his guitar," he recalls, "Dankworth his sax, Hom his wok and Brian Blessed his climbing kit."

So, you may think of yourself primarily as a writer, but if you know how to play the combs or the spoons, can eat fire or lick your own elbow – this could be the time to give those skills an airing. Particularly if they relate in some way to your book.

If it's a manual on dog training bring along a pooch to jump through a hoop or two, if your novel is set in 19th century India, produce a sari and show how it was worn or produce some slides of the prominent sites in the story.

I had the pleasure of doing an 'in conversation' with Susie Boyt, author of *My Judy Garland Life* (Virago Press) in the Guildford branch of Waterstone's some years ago and the audience were enthralled when she handed round shoes and items of make-up that Judy Garland had actually owned and played old records of the star singing.

As Martin puts it, "If you are not local, or famous yet, you have to be engaging: remember the store does not need to do any events at all. The event may seem like a banker to you, but booksellers get paid peanuts; why should they stay late and put chairs away or have to bother returning the post-event surplus because stock budgets are tighter than ever?"

You can't be told much straighter than that! Remember what we've already said about being thankful and appreciative of your bookseller? Do it with bells on if you're anywhere near Martin. His enjoyable tips for, and rants about, authors also include:

1) You must be able to perform, hold an audience, so tell the bookseller if you were a teacher, or that you have experience of public speaking and so on.

2) Keep your friends and family away from you on event night. Talk to the strangers, who've come to see you. So many authors want to turn a talk into their private party, with us booksellers as waiters.

3) Find your own way to the shop! Satnav, Googlemaps, ask a policeman – I don't care. I am amazed how even travel authors demand directions in advance, or to be met at the station. Sheeesh! Middle classes still wrestling with 'the servant problem' I say.

4) Don't push it. One author MADE me wear his disgusting body belt with illegal drugs in during the talk. Another made me check his teeth. Another DEMANDED a snickers bar at the last minute.

And if you're wondering after all this, why Martin does it – it's because he loves it really. He describes a good book shop event as "magical" and finishes, "I sound gloomy but really, a good event is the most exhilarating, inspiring part of bookselling: I go home after a big event so high I can't sleep."

Newspapers & magazines

I get like this too, over pretty much any publicity opportunity that goes well. Despite all the competition, I still believe those opportunities are there in shedloads, if you only know where to look. And, more importantly, you know how to go about it.

When it comes to getting into the press, we must remember that with over 100,000 books being published each year, jaded editors are going to be largely unimpressed by all but the most ground-breaking, and are already up to their eyes in authors clamouring for a plug. So you need to be looking at turning yourself from someone who's written a book into **a story**.

We've already talked about having an angle but it's worth re-visiting, especially as since I wrote that bit I have had an entertaining chat with Kelvin Mackenzie, ex-editor of *The Sun* and something of a media tart himself.

All these years on, he still pops up on everything from *Question Time* to *Celebrity Bird Watch* – where, he tells me, he singularly failed to spot any birds at all (we are talking the feathered variety not the sort he favoured for page three) – and has characteristically colourful views on the best way for authors to get themselves into the limelight.

Leaving aside his more encouraging words (sorry, new scribes reading this with hope in your hearts), "Everyone thinks their book's going to be a literary sensation but it's not – it's probably shite and is going to be used to prop up beds," – let us look instead at what he suggests.

"Ask yourself why your book is interesting. Answer: on its own it's not! If you got up one day, decided to write a book, you wrote 100,000 words and it took you three years – nobody gives a damn about that! There has to be something about YOU that joins with that book: a broken heart, a disease in the family, the fact that there you were, a mother with two kids, walking down the road when lightening struck a tree and broke it in two and you stopped and thought, this is a sign...."

Long-time journalist Melanie Whitehouse agrees. "I write about authors all the time," she says. "And they have to have a very strong personal story that tallies with their latest novel if it's to make an article a newspaper will commission." For this reason, she considers it much easier to promote non-fiction. "With non-fiction at least they are writing about real lives."

But Kelvin takes a more creative approach. "I'm not suggesting it has to be 101% true," he explained. "What you can do is extrapolate – surely an author of all people, should be able to do that. Take a germ of a story and make it up. Who's to know and who cares? If your kids don't like it, you just say, 'Look son, this is paying the bills.' And it will. Everyone likes a human interest story."

There is no doubt that the media certainly do. As novelist Christina Jones, found out when she married a man 20 years her junior.

The fact that we met at work and I was his boss simply added to the frisson. Oh, the daytime telly programmes LOVED it. The Toyboy Trucker and I were invited on every show possible – *This Morning, Esther, Kilroy-Silk, Breakfast*, all the morning/evening news programmes (local and national), every 'relationship' slot in every chat-show and even, yes, honestly, *Newsnight*. Then the women's magazines and the newspapers also jumped on the bandwagon. It was crazy. And fun. And huge, huge publicity because of course I got to mention the novels at the same time.

You might now be thinking, wow, lucky Christina! as she's sold plenty of books as a result, or you might be cringing in your seat at the thought of your relationship being spread across the TV screen.

But remember, you don't have to answer nosy questions! Christina always made sure she stayed in control:

The Toyboy Trucker and I became very adept at fielding the bordering-on-sleaze questions (Is he hankering after a dominatrix/mother figure? Are you unable to cope with a same-age relationship? What's the sex like? What happens when you get too old? Does he mind being called a toyboy? Why are you a cradle-snatcher? and many others too intrusive to mention) and turning each one into something linked to my latest book. I even deliberately wrote age-gap relationships into *Tickled Pink* and *Hubble Bubble* so that the interviews would be relevant.

But she is delightfully unrepentant about spilling a few beans in order to plug her books and in fact, thoroughly recommends it.

If you don't mind telling the world about ANYTHING remotely personal that they will find fascinating, odd or outrageous, then go for it! Everyone has something tucked away – make it your USP. Link it to your novel. And don't be afraid or ashamed of it. Be proud to tell the world that you've eaten nothing but baked beans for the last 15 years or that because of your OCD you polish your lipsticks on a daily basis or that your belief in reincarnation means your cat is called Elvis for a Really Good Reason.

This all applies whether you are being interviewed or writing the article yourself. And now that you've sent out your press release to the papers and magazines, done a little judicious chasing as necessary, and, I hope, arranged some features, interviews and reviews, it is time to offer to do just that.

AND: if you can write short stories – some can and some can't – try to knockout a couple of those too. (By knockout, I mean – naturally – sweat blood over them, hone and edit them to within an inch of their lives and make them the very best you can. I don't want the womag brigade, of which I was/am one, foaming at the mouth.)

Getting a short story published is a very good way of publicising a new novel. Magazines like *Woman's Weekly* and *My Weekly* are usually more than happy to mention your title at the foot of the story – they've both done it for me – but cast your net wider too. I've also had several short stories published in *Your Cat* where they included a jpeg of my latest cover and full details of how to buy the book at the end of each.

I'm not sure if there's a *Your Tea Cosy* or *Your Stick Insect* but if you think you could write a story on a particular subject – I can always bring a cat into things – then it's worth doing some research to see if a suitable publication exists that carries fiction.

And if it doesn't, then you could maybe write an article for them instead.

If you have written a non-fiction book then you have your subject matter right there in front of you – distil the basic message of your book, pick out a few hot tips, etc. – but if you've written a novel? What should your article be about then?

Anything, is the basic answer. If you ask nicely, you can usually negotiate a book plug at the bottom of the piece, whatever its subject.

It doesn't even have to be on the same theme as that in your book but where there is overlap, then clearly you can exploit this.

"As a former journalist I am quite used to anticipating what features desks do and don't want" says novelist Jojo Moyes, who makes a practice of offering pieces for any books she has coming out.

When her novel *Night Music* (Hodder) was published, she wrote an article for *The Times* about her experience of renovating her 400-year-old Grade II listed farmhouse in Essex (the heroine in her book moves into an old house that needs an enormous amount of work) and appeared on those pages again with an enchanting account of how her childhood was spent riding her horse around the streets and canal paths of London to coincide with her next book *The Horse Dancer* (also Hodder). Details of the books appeared at the foot of both.

By the time it came to *The Last Letter From Your Lover* (Hodder as above) Jojo was thinking features long before it hit the shelves.

I was conscious even as I wrote it that there were lots of opportunities to write accompanying features. I can't say it made me more likely to write THAT book – you can only write the book that's in you – but I did know that the publishers would find it an easier book to promote as a result."

So it's never too soon to start thinking up ideas of your own. To make sure you leave no stone unturned, it's a good idea to have another brain-storming session with yourself and rake up all the things you've experienced/know a bit about/could hold forth on as an 'expert' or otherwise.

Include anything you know anything about, however vague or common. Even if it has nothing to do with your book, you can still probably get the title and details included if you smile a lot.

My list of topics, for example, might look something like this:

- Why Women have affairs
- How to get away with them (second novel – *Perfect Alibis*)
- The damage they cause (read the whole book)
- The realities behind the middle-class dream of owning a wine-bar (third novel – *One Glass is Never Enough*)
- Being a landlady/ The perils of the buy-to-let market (first novel *Raising the Roof* based on same)
- Being married to an older man
- Second Marriages
- Having adult step-children
- Being the mother of a teenager
- Being a columnist
- Being in one's forties
- Suffering from PMT/ Having a hysterectomy
- Depression – from point of view of relative/carer (third novel)
- Daytime television – experiences of being on
- Becoming a writer/ How to get published (*Writing Magazine*'s agony aunt and author of *Wannabe a Writer?*)
- Being self-employed

I have written about most of these at some point or other and remain poised for any chance to do so in the future.

Stop now and write your own list. Think past and present – anything you've done that either a) the vast majority of people haven't e.g. you've: climbed Everest; won *X Factor*; given birth to quads; had a sex change; won the lottery; found John Prescott attractive OR b) the ordinary things in life that only you can bring a unique slant to e.g. Having teenagers but making them live in a cave in the garden; being married but she's 7 ft 3 and you only come up to her armpit; having parents but one of them is a troll and the other used to make you tap-dance naked in front of Asda and then pass round the hat; loving cats but you own 147 of them; being exceptionally thin without trying (Cow!) or hugely fat when you live on carrot sticks (a likely story).

Start your list here: (you can always add to it later)

What you have included will depend on how much you are prepared to reveal about yourself – you may not want to share with the nation the fact that you've been divorced fourteen times, even if it would undoubtedly be seized on by any editor looking to cover your manual on the secrets of a happy marriage – and the lengths to which you will go in the name of publicity.

Amassing a list of these topics now is good for two reasons: so you can put them forward yourself, and so you can be poised for any opportunity to contribute further to items already in the news. Let's go back to your novel about the lap-dancer.

If an MP is caught in a lap-dancing club, a mother of six is criticised for not using a registered childminder, someone in the media starts ranting on about the portrayal of women as sex objects or a move is made to outlaw sex clubs, then you want to be in there like a tramp on a kipper.

Immediately offer yourself to the editors/journalists (or radio shows) who ran or wrote the original piece.

Kelvin MacKenzie emphasises that when pitching to write a piece, you should keep your initial email short. "A paragraph is sufficient," he says. "Nobody's got time to read more."

Kelvin put it like this, "I've written a book about being a lap-dancer. I used to be a lap-dancer myself. Would you like 800 words?"

You might feel you want to make your pitch just a little longer than this but the advice is solid.

In your first contact, just get the salient details across – the editor/TV researcher/radio producer will soon come back to you if they want to know more. So if our MP is caught with a couple of dancers on his lap, your email might read:

Dear Blah

I am the author of Lap it Up, a novel about a single mother who becomes a lap dancer. Following the recent coverage of The Right Hon Grabbit being caught with his trousers down, I can offer insights into why men in power frequent such establishments and can provide real-life anecdotes from my time spent working in The Happy Lapper Club as a dancer myself.

If you are interested, please call me on 07654 1234444

For more information see www.lapitupnovelist.com

Regards

Iona Story

NB to save you constantly typing the same thing (and at the risk of teaching most of you to suck eggs) it is sensible, and time-saving, when on the publicity trail, to have a default signature on the bottom of your emails with all your contact details, title of book, etc.

Something like this covers most bases:

Wannabe a Writer We've Heard Of? by Jane Wenham-Jones is published in paperback by Accent Press at £9.99

www.janewenham-jones.com

http://twitter.com/JaneWenhamJones

http://twitter.com/UWannabeawriter

NB: If you're contacting a lot of journalists/radio producers, etc. include your mobile phone number too. If you are replying to 'fan' mail, best delete that bit before you press send (most people who take the trouble to email you will say nice things and mean them but we will discuss the joys of attracting the occasional oddball when we get to our chapter on weirdos).

Even if you're only emailing to complain that you've had another estimated gas bill despite having had to stop work and let the meter reader in three times in the last month or that the scented candle you ordered online did not smell like Lily of the Valley, but next door's cat's bottom, it's always worth casually leaving your book title there.

Someone, somewhere, may think, gosh she's a stroppy cow but hey she's also an author. And spend the next five minutes finding out more.

However, even if the curiosity factor occasionally works with bored admin assistants who'd rather look you up on Google than process another invoice, it's not going to cut the same ice in Fleet Street (or Wapping), over the airwaves or on the TV screen. In those arenas writers are two a penny, and readers and viewers can easily turn the page or flick over to another channel if you're even a tiny bit dull or samey.

If you're lucky enough for anyone in the media to want to investigate you further you have, as the cliché goes, only the one chance to make a good impression. You need to be fascinating, gripping, entertaining and to ooze allure. So start thinking now about 'the interview'.

"If you're sitting there waiting for someone to say that your one book, out of 100,000 published, is tremendous, then you're wasting your time. You've got to get out there and sell it. You are now a publicity machine. That's your job."

Kelvin Mackenzie, newspaper columnist,
broadcaster and ex-editor of *The Sun*

The interview

An early piece of advice I received on the interview front was, "Think of Ann Widdecombe!" (This was before I decided she should be PM – or possibly Queen). What my advisor meant was that when interviewed, Ms Widdecombe was very adept – as are most politicians – at saying what she wanted to say rather than bothering with the minor detail of what the question was.

While we are not politicians and your average magazine journalist or chat show host is not Jeremy Paxman (more's the pity!) it is still useful to have a very clear idea of what you want to get across and how you can say it, whatever you are asked.

If you are on television or on stage at a book festival you're going to have to rely on your memory for this, but if you're on the radio or being interviewed down the telephone line for a magazine, then you can have a crib sheet in front of you and I strongly recommend you do so.

This may be in the form of your press release or AI sheet and your own notes, including your definitive answer to 'what's it about?' and your favourite version of how you became a writer. You should also keep a copy of the book close to hand in case you need to consult the blurb on the back or remind yourself how much it is.

You may think all this information is indelibly engraved on your brain but you'd be surprised how that organ can fail you when under pressure.

The first time novelist Sue Moorcroft went on air from a radio studio, having only ever done interviews by phone before, she was left waiting in the reception at BBC Radio Northampton until the last moment and describes becoming "twitchy" as time went on and she heard herself being announced as "on soon" but nobody came to fetch her. By the time the interview began, she recalls, "my adrenaline was working against me."

Asked for the name of the heroine of her novel, *Uphill All the Way*, her mind went blank until the interviewer, Anna Murby, filled the silence, by saying kindly 'I think it's Judith.'

Some interviewers, you will find, will have read your book and know more about it than you do, some will only have read the press release, and occasionally you'll end up with one who seems bemused to find you there at all (I will tell you about my inglorious time on the Russell Grant show later!)

It is best to be prepared for all three. And to remember that whatever the scenario, it won't be all bad. "You need to know very quickly what the interviewer knows about the book," says PR Simone Klass, "because if he doesn't know much, it's a golden opportunity for you to tell the listeners yourself!"

Simone carries out question and answer sessions with her clients so they are ready for any scenario. So they know, as she puts it, whether they are working from crib sheet A, B, or C. "I tell them they've got to be prepared in advance for every possible situation – so they can handle it."

If you can't afford to hire Simone, you could do this with a friend or by just asking yourself every question you can possibly think of that might come up. Popular topics are going to include: Why you wrote it/where your inspiration comes from/your life as a writer/discipline required when working on your own/difficulty of getting published, as well as the specific themes/subjects covered in your book. The more you think about all these things beforehand, the more confident you'll sound when the time comes.

Simone Klass, too, likens the process to that of the media training given to a politician and urges us to make the most of any opportunity on air as it will only be short. "It's the only bit of time you're going to have and you cannot let a presenter kill it for you. You've got to have control," she says, adamant that any interviewee needs to be ready with his or her own agenda, whatever is thrown at them.

"There's no such thing as ad lib," she finishes, firmly.

I know what Simone means but I would say there sometimes has to be. I once went on BBC Radio Wales thinking I was going to be talking about the joys of being a novelist, only to find myself plunged into a discussion about whether the British tell lies.

If you do get asked something you've never thought about before – and it's live – you just have to do the best you can. Say the first thing that comes into your head and try not to um and ah too much. If it's a pre-record or a magazine interview then obviously there's some room for thinking time but it helps to get used to thinking on one's feet.

This will come more easily the more you do it, and the greater the fund of material you have at your disposal, the simpler it is to smoothly change the subject to something you DO know about.

Tom Maddocks is a former radio and TV reporter who's worked for the BBC, IRN and Channel Four. He's now Course Director at Media Training Associates, which runs media and presentation coaching and training courses.

Tom also believes that preparation is key. "Polish up your sharpest anecdotes and self-deprecating one-liners. You need a good stock of pithy 'soundbites', preferably sharing some of the choicest pearls from the book. Rehearse them to yourself, then run them by your loved ones for constructive feedback."

You might want to have a stop watch to hand for this bit too, as Tom also has some useful technical advice. "Around 30 seconds or so is usually a good length of answer in a broadcast interview – too short and you can sound defensive, too long-winded and you will be interrupted just as you're getting to the good bit."

But however well-rehearsed you are in reality, the trick is to still sound fresh and spontaneous.

"Don't be boring – don't be repetitive," says Simone Klass. "You don't want to be like one of those American actors plugging their autobiographies who've just learnt their lines." (Imagine this said with a truly magnificent and disparaging snort.) "They're not being interviewed – they're just giving their party piece, and because they're famous, they get away with it. But your average author is not going to be in that lucky position so he or she's got to prove herself on the couch. She's got to be so much more interesting and flamboyant. Always engage with a presenter – don't let him just ask you questions – have a conversation with him!"

At least if you are being interviewed on radio or TV you will have some idea of how this conversation is going to sound. Unlike a magazine or newspaper interview where the final column inches may bear little resemblance to anything you remember saying.

I squirmed recently to discover a so-called interview with me, advertising a forthcoming talk I was giving, where I was quoted as saying

"… you'll never hear me preach. I always speak with a pinch of salt and a good laugh attached. My advice is to turn off Jeremy Kyle, shut down the computer, have a glass of bubbly and listen to me drivel on for a bit. You never know it may just hit the spot. And if you never do make it into print, at least you'll fail smiling."

The only bit of that I recognise is the word 'drivel' which is one I probably overuse. I would never, ever claim in an interview that I am funny (even if I'm hilarious!) or 'a good laugh' as such things are in the eye of the beholder and I don't want to sound any more of a tosser than necessary. As for Jeremy Kyle – he's on in the mornings. My talk was at 8.30 p.m.!

Little one can do about it, though, except to shrug and put it down to experience. As I did over an early magazine 'interview' the thought of which still makes my toes curl.

But it at least means I can share with you another important lesson I've learned, namely: Beware the closed question! By this I mean one to which the question is either yes or no, or, more to the point – where the interviewer has already decided what they want you to say. For example –

"So when you first met your lover, you instantly felt he was the man for you?", or

"So that must have been the happiest day of your life…"

These questions (statements) are often put by very experienced journalists, in the sort of friendly, easy going, we're-all-girls/boys-together-here, type tones that cause you to forget you are being interviewed at all.

I first realised this had happened to me when a women's magazine did a double page spread on my relationship with my husband (the hook was that it was a second marriage for him and I am much younger) which involved chatting for about an hour to a feature writer on the phone.

It was only later that it struck me that she had done most of the talking with me mumbling "sort of" and "I suppose so" from time to time. And that was when I discovered she was clearly a frustrated Mills & Boon writer who'd had a field day.

Seeing the resulting "our eyes met across a crowded room" fairy tale when it got into print – along with some nauseating photos of us supposedly tripping romantically along the beach (I couldn't stop squinting because they wouldn't let me wear sunglasses and my husband had a face on because he was the missing the cricket) – still goes down as one of the most utterly cringe-inducing moments of my life.

It is why I now prefer to write such articles myself and if I am interviewed for a magazine or newspaper, make a point of talking non-stop so nobody else can get a word in!

But do not let me make you paranoid. Better to listen to the sensible words of novelist Emma Darwin (yes, since you probably wondered when I mentioned her last time, she IS a descendent of Charles) who says "Journalists aren't trying to catch you out – they're chiefly interested in a good story. So if you offer them a good story, you're happy to tell, everyone's satisfied."

Things to do when you're going to be interviewed

1) Have a mental or physical check list of things you want to say – and try your best to get them in whether you're asked about them or not.

2) Carry a copy of your book. You can refer to it if you're on the radio and ask to wave it if on TV

3) Be polite and smiley to the interviewer or presenter – if they think you're OK they'll be on your side and won't ask you anything too tricky. **NB** I'm not sure this works with Jeremy Paxman but he doesn't usually do authors. (Unfortunately [5])

4) Remember you're there to plug your work. I was once interviewed by a paper in Worcester. Called upon to comment on the area and keen to substantiate my claim to have spend my formative years visiting a maiden aunt who lived there, I spoke about the cricket ground. I had never been there in my life and know nothing about cricket but it was all I could think of. I made the cricket-ground sound stunning – they probably needed to take on extra staff to cope with the unprecedented influx of visitors – and made my book sound as boring as bat-shit.

5) Also remember you're not on oath. I routinely lie about my age, my exotic lovers and my solitary childhood in the book-lined castle of my adoptive hermit and nobody raises an eyebrow. If you want to say the plot came to you in a dream, that you were born on a remote island in

---

Footnote 5: I have had a penchant for JP ever since he leant across me in the Conrad shop on Marylebone High Street to reach for one of those see-through staplers. He did say "excuse me" first. I wouldn't have minded if he hadn't.

the Caribbean or have posed naked with a rose in your teeth, go for it. Just don't libel anyone.

6) Practise lowering your voice.

Radio

You may not need to concern yourself with that last point but I did. The first time I appeared on the radio, I sounded like Pollyanna on speed.

I knew this because I asked someone to record it for me and was then duly horrified to hear the high-pitched, breathy, gushy voice that held forth relentlessly until even I longed to slap its owner.

I am a lot more relaxed on air these days and my voice has duly gone down a few octaves, though I lapse into 'Fannit'[6] vowels occasionally, according to whether I've got out much, and still have a tendency to squeak when I'm over-excited.

Tom Maddocks recommends you, "Project your voice a bit and give it plenty of energy – what may feel a little OTT in the studio usually sounds about right when coming out of your loudspeakers at home."

While the well-known TV and radio presenter Sue Cook advises, "Don't gush. Above all, keep natural."

Both emphasise the benefits of a smile. "You can smile with your voice, and should do so – if you sound warm, people will warm to you." says Tom Maddocks, adding the warning, "If they decide they don't like you they certainly won't go out to buy anything written by you."

"Keep a smile in your head as you speak," agrees Sue. While the only way I can do it is to keep one plastered on my face. Now I automatically grin down the phone whenever I'm doing an interview and if I'm in the studio, make a habit of beaming at the presenter throughout.

Do try to speak fluently too. The other day, I heard a debut novelist on Radio Four who said "Umm" so many times it made my nerves jangle. I soon found I'd stopped listening to the content of what she was saying and was just bracing myself for the next hesitation.

Footnote 6: I refer to the Thanet accent – a blend, I am reliably informed on wikipedia, http://en.wikipedia.org/wiki/Estuary_English#cite_note-9 of working-class London and Estuary English with occasional notes of cockney.

We've all done it, but it made me think how important it is to practise covering your thinking time with something else – even a tinkling laugh or annoying giggle before each answer (and that soon becomes VERY annoying) – is better than ers and ums.

Slowing your delivery a little and using fillers like "That's an interesting question," or "ooh – I've never been asked that before…" and "Now, let me think…" gives you time to formulate some sort of answer.

And don't overly stress about what that answer is – just try to be bright, cheery and engaging. Very much like being a writer in general, you're basically there to interest and entertain.

"The key is to remember that you have to sing for your supper," says Tom Maddocks, "it is a performance. Earnest though well-meaning answers to the questions, except on the most serious of subjects, will probably send the audience nodding off or fleeing to another channel."

"For my show," says Sue Cook, who presents *Write Lines* for BBC Radio Oxford, "it's the author's personality that attracts me more than the merits of the book he or she has written."

So how do you get on to these shows and make sure that your personality shines through?

"Don't delay," says Sue Cook. "As soon as you know your publication date, identify the shows you think might be interested in the kind of book you have written and get in touch with them. Find out the producer's name. A phone call is usually the easiest way to do this rather than trying to use the net. Jobbing producers are often on short contracts and move from show to show like sheep to clover patches."

Lead times for radio programmes vary enormously. At the time of writing I have a booking four months ahead but I've also been called, lots of times, to hold forth on some hot topic, the night before or even the same day.

As Sue says, "It depends whether the programme is 'live' or recorded. Features for a 'live' show will be planned rather less in advance than a recorded one. Regular topical programmes such as breakfast shows and daytime feature shows will plan their running orders more 'on the hoof' while series such as *A Good Read* and *James Naughtie's Bookclub* will be planned more carefully ahead. A two-hour live show will work much closer to the transmission date. There will be 'holes' in their running orders right up to the day before."

When approaching the producer of your targeted show, you or your publisher will need to send them a copy of the book and the press release, but I personally wouldn't despatch this until you've made contact and had some sort of response. They get hundreds of books sent in and, in my experience, individual ones soon get lost in the general melée unless your name/title is fresh in a producer's memory.

Send a short email in the first instance, setting out the details – what you've written, any connection you have with the area the radio station is in (use your imagination!) and what might make you and your book interesting subject matter for an interview.

Sue Cook recommends, "A friendly letter and a couple of sentences (and I mean just a couple of sentences; producers are always desperately busy) about yourself. Suggest any angles or lines of questioning the interviewer might like to take. Add a line about what you particularly enjoy about the programme or its presenter. It demonstrates that you know what the show is about and that you think you are just the right kind of guest for it."

"Make the letters or emails a little bit different," says Laura Earl, producer of the Pat Marsh show on Radio Kent, "point out any Kent connection and include any interesting stories about how you came to write it or get it published."

Laura gets about 10 emails about books a day and can only arrange for 3-4 authors to be interviewed by Pat per week. A couple of these will be 'famous' and unknown authors will probably only make up one slot a week.

When deciding which ones to choose, she says these are the factors that will sway her:

- if they are local authors or their story is set in Kent
- if they are well known and the book is the next one in line, "like Patricia Cornwell or Robert Goddard"
- if they're writing about an interesting subject that the audience would like. "We know from audience research what people like to hear about so if the subjects fall into that category then we may book them."

Be prepared to wait. "Producers almost certainly won't book you straight away," says Sue Cook. "They'll want a balanced running order and will probably wait until they know what other elements are going to be included in their shows, so don't feel bad about a friendly follow-up call to check they received the book and ask whether they need any more details from you. Your reminder nudge might come through to the production office at exactly the right moment!"

Once you start pitching to national radio stations the whole thing gets even more competitive – obviously every author in the land is clamouring to get on *Open Book* or *Midweek*. Andrea Zemmel, who has worked as a freelance producer for both radio and TV describes *Woman's Hour* as 'the pinnacle' and you certainly see books shooting up the Amazon charts once they've had an airing on any of these.

(Although personally, my lifelong and enduring ambition is to go on *Just a Minute* – never mind the book-plugging. Thought I'd mention that, just in case....) [7]

"I have to say that, sadly, I don't think there's an easy way to get booked for a radio or TV appearance," says Andrea, who's been a producer for LBC, as well as the Beeb for both TV and radio and LWT (London Weekend Television that was). "The market's extremely competitive, producers are inundated with press releases for new books and can afford to be very selective."

But at least you don't have to have the perfect face for radio?

"Radio is more forgiving on the appearance of course," Andrea concedes. "But your voice is paramount. You must be clear, eloquent and above all engaging and interesting."

No pressure there then.

"Of course, the best way," continues Andrea – who I have to say, is all of those things, damn her – "is to have a genuinely compelling or topical subject that will just capture someone's eye. But being topical is the luck of the draw quite frankly – i.e. maybe you've written about lying to get kids into school and then that very subject explodes in the news and you're hot property. Also, a biography about someone who's just become newsworthy could be good."

In this respect, Andrea thinks it's often easier to plug non-fiction.

"You can promote yourself as an 'expert' on your topic and then would be filling a different slot. For example, in radio phone-ins, they often have

---

Footnote 7: I remain a hopeless optimist and am nurturing a small fantasy that the relevant producer or Paul Merton will happen to pick this book up and the page will fall open here. (Hi Paul ☺ love you xx)

experts taking calls. 'How to' books can be good in this respect because authors can take calls from people who want to do the same!"

Andrea has a very important rider to add here, however. "But don't give away all your secrets – tell them to buy the book!"

Andrea Zemmel's advice for approaching radio stations includes:

1) Go a stage further and phone producers, introducing the book and topic to see if they may be interested. Don't be pushy – remember they're inundated! Just sound confident, like you do this all the time.
2) Be creative. For example, if you've written a novel about a serial cheater on a poor wronged woman, you could 'hook' it on to a recent celebrity scandal and offer yourself up as an authority on the subject. After all, you ARE an authority – you've written a book!
3) If they like you and invite you on – be brilliant! A good producer will always remember good guests and perhaps use them on other occasions.
4) When you leave, tell them you'd be delighted to come back if they ever need this topic covered again. You've always got something to say haven't you?
5) Ask them to recommend you to others and perhaps add you to their list of 'approved pundits'. You never know!

But if you don't manage to get yourself on to national radio – yet – don't be too disappointed. Sue Cook admits, "National publicity is of course more precious than pearls," but still maintains that "local radio stations have a more intimate relationship with their listeners and I reckon the buyer to listener ratio is much higher."

When going on local and regional radio you can always double the impact by tying in with a signing or talk.

Bookshops will be more interested in booking you if you tell them the event is going to be announced on the radio and if you tell the radio station that you're doing an event that day, that makes you topical. And as Sue Cook says, "Radio shows love topical."

"Once you've got an event booked, contact the radio station and ask which show might be interested in an interview with you." she suggests, adding a final tip that I think is worth putting in bold:

Don't come over too desperate. Producers want winners not whiners.

I would endorse all of the above advice and have a few random tips of my own:

Illustration by Shirley Webb

Keep a smile in your voice...

1) **Water** Always take some with you or visit the station's water dispenser before you go into the studio. Your mouth may feel dry if you're nervous and I have never forgotten nearly choking to death on BBC Radio Leicester.

2) **Freebies** I would normally suggest offering a couple of books as give-aways or prizes. But this only works on commercial stations now. Unfortunately there has been a BBC wide ban on this practice since the famous phone-in scandals. "Which is why," says producer Laura Earl wryly, "our cupboard is bulging with unread books".

3) **Imagination**. Use it. Radio shows get loads of authors on. Try to stand out. If you're talking about your lap-dancing book, for example, demonstrate on the presenter or take in your own pole and do a bit of

a dance on air. (The latter was Kelvin Mackenzie's idea – no surprise there! "Someone will pick that up and it could lead to something else," he said.) (I should think the possibilities are endless!)

4) **Other avenues**. Mention that you are something of an expert on other topics too (what was your previous book about? What are you working on next?) They may keep you on file and come back to you another time. I have been re-booked more than once on this basis.

5) **Time-keeping**. Don't be late. Allow masses of time to get there. Especially if you're on during rush hour. More than once en route to Radio Kent, I have heard myself being introduced while still crawling down the A26 into Tunbridge Wells.

6) **Listen and learn**. For the first few times you go on the radio, line up someone to record it for you. If you're lucky enough to be on Radio Two or Four or selected regional BBC programmes you can 'listen again' online, of course, but if it's Local-station-run-from-Room-Over-Chippy FM then have a friend or relative poised with some sort of recording equipment so you can hear yourself afterwards. Once you've got over the shock of discovering you sound nothing like you thought you did, this is incredibly useful to help you improve your performance for next time.

7) **Notes** – carry them but don't read from them verbatim because it always shows. As well as your book and AI sheet and any other prompts you might need, take a small list of things you definitely want to say: your website details perhaps and the publisher and price of your book. The presenter will usually include these at the end but there's no harm in it being said twice. **NB** twice is max. Don't annoy everyone by plugging titles and sites every few seconds or it could be the end of a beautiful relationship before it's begun. The novelist Sophie King suggests agreeing how the book will be publicised before you start the interview – i.e asking the presenter if he or she will mention all the details at the end. This is a good idea if you get to speak to them first – you don't always.

8) **Speaking up**. Don't feel you have to wait to be asked about something. Most interviewers will be quite happy for you to prattle away – saves them having to ask too many questions.

9) **Keeping still**. This is a time when it doesn't matter if you wave your hands around – I always do – but don't bob about so much that you

127

move your mouth away from the mike. Smile at the presenter and don't panic if you fluff your words or forget what you're talking about – he or she will rescue you.

10) **Language**. Don't swear. Or tell any filthy jokes or – if you're on the BBC – use lots of brand names. You won't be asked back. However, a little controversy can make the programme go with a swing. I had a most entertaining time with John Warnett on BBC Radio Kent after I'd made a small jest about the Germans and referred to them as "Krauts". The EFL teacher who phoned in to berate me was very cross. (So was 'Helga' who phoned next!)

11) **A great face for radio**. Remember the audience can't see you. It's no good pointing to things, miming or doing the actions. Sue Moorcroft also tells the tale of being on the Bernie Keith Show on BBC Radio Northampton. "I plucked a magazine out of my bab and tried to *show* him a picture! He must have thought I was very dim."

12) **Small mercies**. Be thankful the audience can't see you. You don't have to get too neurotic about clothes and slap8

"Just relax and talk to the presenter. Don't try to think about the listening audience or you'll freeze."

Jill Mansell, best-selling novelist

Photos part two

It will be time soon enough to worry about your appearance when you're writing for, or being featured in, the press. Once you start getting yourself interviewed, or you pen some articles, you will find the larger magazines and newspapers often want to take their own photographs rather than using yours. This can be a rather hit and miss affair.

Footnote 8: That was for my female readers and this is for them too. Personally I would still stick it on with a trowel and wear something slimming – I always think if the producer/presenter (of whatever gender) thinks you're a bit-of-all-right it can only help for the future. Seeing them recoil as you wander in with your hair unwashed and your worst leggings on, will put you off your stride.

The picture editor often has a very clear vision of how they want you to look and this may not fit in at all with how you see yourself.

One particular newspaper, who shall be nameless in case they suddenly want to give me a double page spread, always wanted me to put on a nice bright frock whenever they came to photograph me, while another used to straighten my hair to within an inch of its life and use so much face powder I was one big crevice.

The portrait of the latter delight was used to accompany the (jokey) piece I'd written on longing to get away from the family. And by the time they'd finished, I looked just like the sort of hatchet-faced harridan who'd abandon her children at the drop of a hat.

Yet when the same newspaper ran an article I'd written about being a step-mother, they had me sat on the lawn, floral skirt spread out around me, holding a child in my arms, looking like something out of the Waltons.

In the early days I went along with it all fairly meekly but these days I will (politely) speak up, if I think I'm going to look too ghastly.

And there's plenty of time to speak your mind. The whole process takes hours!

Jeremy Clarkson wrote a hilarious column in the *Sunday Times* about spending time in a photographic studio, which he described as "the most miserable day of my working life".

"The camera does bloody well lie," he continued. "I know what I look like; I see myself in the mirror every morning. And yet in a picture, I look like me, but with special needs."

I sympathise. I have had way too many photos taken where I look like me but weighing twenty stone and with several chins. And I entirely felt for Jeremy when he complained about how long the entire process took.

By 11 o'clock this morning, I would have happily swapped with someone who collects semen from racing pigeons for a living. At two in the afternoon I sat down for a tea break and gave serious thought to killing myself. At four I gave it a bash.

The longest day I ever spent was in a studio off the Kings Road, for a photo shoot for *Family Circle*. It was August but as the feature was for the October issue of the magazine, I had to be dressed in autumnal clothes. As the day wore on and the heat increased, my long-sleeved two-piece jersey number stuck to my back. There was another poor girl there in cashmere who was almost expiring. No wonder real models always look so miserable.

I smiled throughout, because I couldn't believe my face! "We're going for a demure look," the stylist had told me, looking a shade doubtful. I'm not sure that's exactly what they achieved, but I know I wanted Julie, the make-up girl, to come and live with me and made me look like that every morning.

Which isn't always the way. Sometimes I have actually jumped when I've caught sight of myself in the mirror after a 'make-up artist' has been at work.

Whether the photographer and make-up person come to your house, or you go to a studio, they will pretty much decide how you're going to appear.

I have learned that "what colours do you normally wear?" and "we'll make it quite natural" is just small talk. It will still go on in layers and may be purple.

Novelist Judy Astley recommends taking along your own tube of Clarins Beauty Flash balm & making sure it's the first thing that gets put on your face. "It's magic stuff that tightens up skin just that crucial bit for several hours," she says. "Most make-up artists will have it," continues Judy. "But it's possible the younger ones will look at you blankly because they can't imagine the need for help with looking youthful."

Oh those happy days! Perhaps Clarins would like to send Judy and I a couple of kilos of the stuff in grateful recognition for bringing it to your attention. (I wonder if it can be smothered over one's entire body.)

Sometimes the package involves a stylist who wants to dress you as well. I have done photo sessions where clothes have been provided, others where I've been asked to offer several alternatives from my own wardrobe.

NB if the shoot is taking place in your own home and they ask if you have anything "brighter" it is best to say no. On no account let them look in your closets themselves. I have no idea what the male equivalent might be, but if you're female, I guarantee they will immediately home in on the Laura Ashley dress circa 1988 you've been meaning to give to the charity shop for twenty years. Or the ill-advised blouse you bought when you were feeling hormonal, that your mother likes.

Judy Astley has things to say about this too.

If you won't see 35 again the 12-year-old stylist is going to look at you and see Mother of The Bride/pastel floatie. If you're really brave you can protest that you've got more rock-chick credentials than Jo Wood and Anita Pallenberg combined and insist they let you have some say in the clothes. Truth is, though, that you're likely to end up opening the relevant pages months later and see yourself dressed as the Queen on Ascot Ladies' Day.

This has not happened to me yet although I remember one stylist who was intent on putting me in frills. "Do I have to?" I pleaded as yet another high-necked, pearly-buttoned number was held up. "I'll look like a Sunday School teacher".

The girl raised her brows as she studied my green and pink beaded hair extensions. "Hardly", she said.

Once these small battles are over and you are suitably tarted up in all respects – they will do some strange things to your hair too, involving straighteners and possibly those corkscrew ringlets – the photographer will set up the shot and tell you how to stand or sit.

But as long as you're not too bossy, he or she won't mind you making suggestions too. Show the photographer which side you look best from and ask if you can have a look at what they've got so far when they've taken the first few shots. Photos are often displayed on a laptop as they go along. Otherwise a friendly photographer will show you them in the back of the camera.

If you don't feel comfortable in a certain position, say so – nicely. In fact it's worth being as lovely as possible throughout the entire session, so the photographer and any assistants, like you and make sure you're shown in the best possible light and don't look too much of a dork.

There will be times, however, when despite your best efforts, you'll still think you look awful and there's not very much you can do about that, except grin, bear it and hide all the papers.

Alison Penton Harper tells the tale of a photographer from one of the tabloids who was "quite evidently some kind of deviant" who, she concluded, probably took rather different sorts of pictures in his spare time.

Fat, ugly and sweaty (him, not me), he kept suggesting I 'open my mouth a bit' and that kind of thing. When the article finally broke I nearly died. After being tipped-off by my cleaner, I had no choice other than to go trudging up to the village shop and buy every copy to sling on the bonfire. Whoever it was that said there's no such thing as bad publicity had probably never run the gauntlet of a pervert with a wide-angle lens.

I have cursed the wide-angled lens myself on many an occasion when I have appeared to have gained five stone and this has been the explanation offered by kindly friends.

At other times I've had to accept I was just not presenting myself to the best advantage. Once when taking a workshop, I had made the mistake of wearing a slightly cropped T-shirt and was leaning across the table when a photographer from one of our local papers turned up to record this auspicious event (another slow week for happenings in Thanet) and began snapping away.

The photograph that appeared a few days later was truly horrific, showing me sporting a vast expanse of flaccid white stomach and a couple of extra chins to match. As soon as I saw it, I phoned Mike Pearce, the then editor. "How could you use that photo?" I wailed. "I thought you were my friend."

"I am your friend, he replied, "you should have seen the others."

I should have known I'd not get much sympathy. This was the man who, when faced with an irate woman who complained that he'd published a photograph in which she looked 'awful', replied, "I think your quarrel is with God, madam, not this newspaper."

One thing to remember about newspapers is that they have a habit of digging out the same photo again and again. The one of me with the hatchet face and powder problem came back to illustrate further articles and there is a photograph on file at the *Isle of Thanet Gazette* that I have so far failed to get deleted.

It features me with my friend Janice at a local beer festival. Janice looks fine – I appear to have no eyes. "My God," I said to one of my more supportive friends, "I look as though I've got three weeks to live."

"No," he replied, "you look as though you died three weeks ago and they've just dug you back up."

The sub-editors at the paper now use it as revenge. If I've complained that they've been heavy-handed with my column (it is one of the laws of journalism that whenever a sub has to cut a line it always contains one's best joke) that picture reappears and readers stop me in the street to ask if I've suffered a terrible trauma (yes – I've just seen that photo again!)

Beware the sartorial cringe-makers too. The picture that comes back to haunt *Times* columnist, Carol Midgley, is the one taken when she went undercover as a cleaner at the Royal London Hospital in Whitechapel, and was sporting a nylon cleaner's outfit, no make-up, thick, black tights and trainers. "It's about the most unattractive photo of me ever taken," she says. "and that's up against some stiff competition! My friends on *The Times* distributed hundreds of copies of it to guests on my wedding day as part of a mocked-up front page. Bless them...."

Dressing up as someone other than your usual self is OK, of course, if it's at the glamorous end of things. Motoring author Maria McCarthy was thrilled when she got to pose in a Lexus sports car in shades and a hair scarf, Grace Kelly-style and loved the "fabulous" photo that resulted so much that she begged to be able to use it on her website (unfortunately the fee requested for a mere year's usage put this out of the question).

But as a general rule, anything involving unusual garb or an outfit that's "themed" is going to be dodgy.

I carefully avoided being photographed when I was doing my bit to promote the *Sexy Shorts* anthologies and although I agreed to pose in a Father Christmas hat one year for the local paper, I flatly refused an offer of an elf costume (unlike Lynne Barrett-Lee, who announces happily that she's "been an elf on several occasions").

And 'comedy' costume is best treated with caution unless you're ready for the joke to run and run.

Kelvin Mackenzie tells the story of how, when he was Chairman and Chief Executive of talkSPORT, he was interviewed by the *Financial Times*. For reasons best known to himself he thought it would be amusing to dress up in a Gladiator costume (it was around the time of Russell Crowe's hit film). This made the front page of the *Financial Times* but from then on, whenever he wanted to talk about anything, this picture would reappear.

"So if you are going to pull a stunt – be prepared to live with it for evermore," he says, admitting the shareholders "got a bit po-faced about it."

As he puts it, "the trouble is once it becomes a library picture, then no matter how seriously you want to be taken in the future, out comes this bloody photo..."

At least Kelvin had nobody to blame but himself. A friend of mine, Lisa Payne is an actress. She's gorgeous but often ends up playing roles that rely on her looking as unattractive as she possibly can! One such character is Denise, a single girl who has decided she will seduce the pizza delivery boy – by performing a strip tease. During the routine, she not only pulls a number of peculiar faces but wears a costume that is "a two sizes too small pink girdle and huge knickers."

Lisa bravely shares the story with us:

Being a curvy girl – I have a little bit of a tum, and this rolls over the girdle, in a very unflattering way. But that's fine – it is part of the act. What I hadn't counted on was that at one particular event, there would be a photographer…

This photographer took loads of pictures which he then promptly put up on his website, much to Lisa's horror.

In the context of my act it is fine – funny even – I have control over that, but taken out of context I just look like a mad woman who has squeezed herself into a too-tight pair of pants. I cringe every time I see it.

I am of course, hugely empathetic. There are photos of me floating about like that where I haven't even got the excuse of being a comedy actress. I think the only solace we can take is that, if they ever reach a really wide audience, it will mean we have become of much greater interest than we are now.

It is best to resist 'themed' attire…

Photo by Bill Harris

As Lisa says, "I fantasise that when I become famous, *The Sun* will manage to get a copy and alongside the fabulous airbrushed image of me at some Hollywood party – there will be that one!!!"

In the meantime, for anyone worried about this sort of thing happening to them, there is another crumb of comfort I can offer. However bad you think you look in a photograph, that's nothing to how you can come across on TV.

TV

C'mon baby, light my crow's feet

"LIGHTS. CAMERA. ACTION. That was the old Hollywood call that went out in the LA studios and for anyone who has agreed to do a television interview, it still rings true today."

So says Glenn Campbell, a TV journalist who came to film me at home recently for the BBC's *Inside Out*. I became an instant fan of Glenn when he rooted around the house for a small lamp which he placed strategically at my feet. "You look 30, darling," he emailed later, when the edit was in progress.

I was pleasantly surprised myself. There was one slightly saggy-jawed shot at the beginning where they'd panned in too close but even my son (who was cringing and keeping a weather eye on Facebook in case his friends had seen me) admitted, when it hit the screen, that I looked "OK".

Praise – as other mothers of teenage boys will know – indeed.

Glenn, I decided, would therefore be a good person to quiz on the finer points of looking half-decent on TV. His words of wisdom are as follows:

Think about the **LIGHTING** and how it makes you look. Natural outside light, especially if it's strong and in your face, will show up all your natural faults. It will also make you wince as your eyes try to deal with the increased light levels. You can't wear sunglasses, they'll make you look 'suspicious'. Also, beware prescription spectacles that darken in strong light conditions. They'll make you look shifty too!

If you are lucky enough to be interviewed on camera indoors, then make sure the camera operator has plenty of time to set up a couple of lights. If you are in a rush or pushed for time, the crew will set up quickly and that's when the lighting gets either forgotten or bodged. Good lighting makes you look good. It can add years to you, or it can flatter you beyond all recognition. It can make you look like a movie star. Why do you think they insist on seeing how they look when lit? After all, you may have a baggy chin, but a good lighting cameraman can make it vanish!

(I hope he wasn't thinking of my own chin when he said that)

And that brings us to the next point. The **CAMERA**. The crew have most probably travelled a fair old distance to interview you. They've carted in all their kit, including hopefully a couple of lights, so while they set up and spend time sorting out those lights, why not make them a cuppa? And then when you bring it in, ask politely if you can have a quick look at 'the shot'. How you look on camera. Is your hair ok? Did that bit of make-up properly cover the childhood scar? Are YOU happy with the lighting they've done? Are there any personal family photos in view that you'd rather weren't?? You get to see the shot in exchange for a cup of tea. You'd be surprised the number of people who treat a camera crew like they were strangers who'd barged in just to read the electricity meter!

(I am pleased to report that I certainly made Glenn and assistant producer Jon Greaves, a cup of tea. My usual habit is to open a bottle of wine but it was a bit early.)

Finally we come to the **ACTION**, or in your case THE INTERVIEW. If you are doing a 'live interview', ask how long the segment is and what the 'shot' will be. A single framed shot on you (this will be close up) OR a 2 shot that includes the reporter and / or another interviewee? (This will be wider and therefore you won't be shown in so much detail, but a word of warning, the camera can always zoom in.)

They certainly can, as I know to my cost. News-type programmes do not generally have a make-up artist in tow. So if you have any spots, stray hairs or warts waiting to be removed, get to work with the concealer before they switch the camera on.

If your interview is LIVE, it may appear to be a precarious situation. Will you fluff your words? Will a police car go screaming past just as you were making that all-important point? But just think, live interviews can't be edited. What you say will go out to the public. That's good if you want to push a specific point or perhaps plug your business or product. They can't cut it out. Also, think about timings. Live interviews are usually pretty short, so think about writing down 4 main points you want to cover and memorise them in 10-20 second 'bites'. As far as reporters are concerned, it's their interview. The way you need to think it that its yours too!

This is really good advice. In my experience, live interviews flash past so quickly that it feels as it they're over almost before one's drawn breath. So be very clear in your own head about what you want to say, and get it in there a.s.a.p.

The last time I was interviewed live, it was outside a café for BBC News 24 and I had a list of points to make about the decline of Margate as a tourist destination and my views on what should be done to redress the matter (e.g. hold some council elections).

I'd thought about these quite carefully and consulted some key people in the town. I had my ideas summarised on a postcard and had experimented with expressing them in ways that would sound both enterprising and revolutionary, conducive to engaging viewers drawn to the common touch of the woman-in-the-street while being erudite enough to invoke empathy among the Intelligentsia

We ended up with less than a minute on air. I got as far as, "Look how many people are on the beach..." before they thrust the mike at the Chief Executive of the council. I wished afterwards I'd just shouted KICK THIS LOT OUT and had done with it.

If the interview is pre-recorded or 'as live', then this means you are going onto tape (or a digital chip inside the camera). In a nutshell, what you say can and will be edited to suit the length and editorial slant of the item. So, first of all, find out what the interview's about and what the 'slant' is. What's the exact agenda here? Do I want to take part..and if so, what can I contribute? Once you've worked out the answers to these two questions, then the way to deal with this experience is to try and treat it as a normal conversation. Odds on you can normally chat away about say, your job or hobby without making any mistakes, so try to do that here. If you are nervous about being interviewed on a street with people passing by and looking on, then say so and ask if it would be ok to pop into a local park.

I take the view one can always contribute something. If it's a direct interview about your book, then brilliant. But even if it isn't, you will be spreading the word obliquely.

When I did the *Kilroy* programme (God Help Me) it was 'as live' which basically meant we carried on regardless unless somebody died. The discussion topic was extra-marital affairs. My book got mentioned under my name "Author of..." but I didn't speak about it directly. However, it got coverage in a follow-up newspaper article about the fact that I'd inadvertently said "shagging" on daytime television after being warned not to.

And being seen by another producer, led to a further TV booking. So nothing wasted really. (Except me in the filming that came next. But more of that later!)

Because right now, you may be asking yourself, how on earth you get on television in the first place. There's no point beating about the bush here. The answer most people in the know will give you is "with difficulty".

"If you've written a novel," says our one-time producer Andrea Zemmel apologetically, "then you need to realise that how you sound and how you look will go a long way in getting you used. When I was producing TV, no matter how compelling a book topic, if the author sounded dull, couldn't express themselves properly and quite honestly looked a mess – they wouldn't be used."

This may sound harsh, she adds, but only fair. "No producer wants to be responsible for putting on a 'dud guest'."

"You need to be bright, engaged, entertaining and presentable. If you can't interest the producer, you won't interest the audience. Common sense really."

Do not get too disheartened at this point. I have been on TV a dozen or so times without trying too hard and I'm sure you can too. But we'll listen to Andrea first:

All I said about radio applies except it's even more competitive to get on TV! Moreover, there aren't so many feature magazine shows any more. You may succeed better locally, i.e. the local news programmes rather than national shows. If you've done a radio appearance, that will always help. It shows the producer that someone else took a chance on you and you've got some experience.

List the shows you'd love to appear in, contact the producers and ask, genuinely, how you can get on, explaining about your masterpiece that needs a good shot of publicity. Don't make the mistake of selecting the wrong shows – you need to make sure their programme does cover whatever fascinating tales are in your book!

Show you have something to say, and quote any previous media appearances.

Good advice – I'd go with all of it. And I'd also add that if you know anyone who even vaguely works in TV – or has a second cousin twice removed who did back in 1987 – then chat them up, pick their brains, and get some names to conjure with.

Most of my TV appearances – and pretty much everything else – have led on from someone speaking to someone who'd interviewed me after I'd emailed them and mentioned a person I'd been on radio with previously. Say what you like – I think that's how an awful lot of it is done.

And I suspect Andrea would agree. Her final tip after all that, is this:

Failing that – just befriend someone, buy 'em a drink and hope for the best!

I would also say: get yourself in the tabloids. I was invited on to *Kilroy* after writing a piece for the *Sun*. I was asked to be a guest on *Loose Lips*, having been seen on *Kilroy*. And so on.

And I've been on both *The Politics Show* and *Inside Out* for the BBC because they picked up on my local newspaper column which appears online.

I think the important thing is to get yourself on, by whatever means, at least once. You could be surprised at what may follow.

And when you are there – sitting in a studio, trying not to put the nation off their TV dinners, do attempt to enjoy it. It's best to treat this like any other interview and if you can, put out of your mind the fact that you're spread across a thousand screens, and just concentrate on the person talking to you.

As novelist Sarah Duncan says, interviewers (for daytime television at least!) are generally chosen because they have a warm and friendly persona, and will do their best to put you at your ease. Sarah was an actress before she turned her hand to fiction (spot her as Rodney's girlfriend in *A Royal Flush*, The *Only Fools and Horses* Christmas special of 1986) before she turned her hand to fiction.

I asked her what tips she could share:
1) Always relax as much as possible. I find that waiting to go on is the worst part as when it's live, I concentrate on what's going on and completely forget the cameras, lights, audience, etc.
2) Think of questions they might ask you and be ready to answer them.

3) Or have answers prepared and use them regardless of the question – well, it works for politicians. Think of sound bites. You might only get 30 seconds of air time, so use it well.

4) Think about how you'd like to come across – personally I think it's charming when people being interviewed are honest and say if they don't know an answer rather than waffling with a look of desperation.

5) Listen to what the other interviewees have to say and don't butt in all the time, you'll get your moment.

6) If desperate, look at the bridge of the other person's nose, it'll appear as if you're looking directly at them but avoids eye contact.

7) If you find your mouth goes dry, lick your teeth – it works like magic.

8) Watch out for waving your hands around all the time, you'll look like a mad professor. Press your thumb and middle finger together, it'll give your hands something to do so you won't feel they're hanging down by your sides like great useless lumps of meat.

Thank you Sarah. I also have some advice of my own:

Don't sit on the set
In fact don't sit anywhere until you're told to. When I went on the (live) *Heaven and Earth Show*, I absent-mindedly perched on the end of a shelf-thing while waiting to go on. It turned out this structure was strictly for display purposes only and was delicately balanced to house a huge lump of crystal. I watched the lump crash to the floor and shatter into a thousand pieces moments before presenters Alice Beer and Ross Kelly walked forward to pose in front of it as the opening credits rolled.

Keep smiling.
I could blame it on the trauma of the above but the footage that ensued did not cover me with glory and taught me an important lesson. Keep smiling or at least look interested. It doesn't come across well if you appear to have a face on.

You may already be thinking I was an odd choice for a programme that explored what I believe the BBC described as "ethical, spiritual and cultural issues" (and strangely I was never invited back!) but I should explain that it was around the time David Beckham had (allegedly) been caught up to no good with that Spanish bird. And the theme of the discussion was: Is

Monogamy Overrated?

I was on with a German writer called Ulli Springett who had written a Buddhist-inspired book called *Soulmate* in which she argued that utter fidelity is the key to perfect happiness and feeds the soul. I'd been booked to give the opposite view.

Obviously I was on slightly shaky ground, because the general consensus of opinion tends to be that if you find out your husband's been spending every Thursday night, not at his car maintenance class as you thought, but locked in passion with the woman up the road, you have every right to feel thoroughly betrayed and to weep, wail and very probably beat him to a pulp with his jump leads, but I did my best.

I ventured that there were worse things you could do to your partner than have a quick bunk-up with someone else – engaging in physical violence/being tight about shelling out on decent holidays/saying: yes, actually love, your arse does look massive in that – and that these things happened when you'd been married too long or had too much to drink and it wasn't worth getting too hysterical over one testosterone-fuelled footballer who probably loved his wife really and had already forgotten his transgression by the time the tabloids obligingly got hold of it.

Understandably, this rather flabby argument did not wash with Ulli whose speeches in return became ever longer and more earnest and her accent heavier. I didn't think about what I was doing while she held forth or consider that my expressions might be broadcast to the nation (or the God-fearing segment of it, anyway).

But every time the camera panned to me I was sitting there looking as though I'd just been told my flight had been delayed for 15 hours and there were no drinks vouchers.

"Grumpy," said one friend. "Bored" said another.

Now whenever I am filmed with others, I keep my mouth fixed into a permanent beam and my eyes trained firmly on my co-guests, to show how utterly enthralled I am by every word they are saying.

When I was on with our local MP, I looked as though I longed to marry him.

Keep quiet

Once you've been miked up – usually with a power pack attached to your waist somewhere (for this reason it's useful to wear a skirt/trousers and/or a belt rather than a slinky dress, although all is not lost if do you opt for the latter – it just has to sit on the chair behind you) and a small lapel microphone, make sure it is switched off before you a) say anything rude about the producer/your fellow guests and b) you go to the loo.

Stories abound of entire production crews listening to the sound of the uninitiated having a pee, dealing with their nervous flatulence or discussing their sex lives with whoever's in the next cubicle.

Check someone's doing your make-up
There usually will be someone if it's a magazine/celebrity type programme, and usually won't be if it's current-affairs/news job. But this is not set in stone.

I went on something called *The Good Day Show* on Legal TV, a Sky channel, a few years ago and made an assumption. So I sat around, flicking

Don't pull silly faces...

through magazines, waiting to be called into make-up, only to find time had marched on, and the call was to go straight into the studio.

I knew I was in trouble when I glanced at the monitor to see the young and beautiful American presenter, Tracy Falke appearing to be at least a decade older.

With that lighting, I'd have been struggling if they'd employed their entire cache of concealer but with no time to even get on any slap myself, I realised I'd look about ninety.

"No, you didn't look great, love," confirmed my friend Lyn-Marie Fabes. "Rather tired."

"You looked fine," Hazel, my publisher, declared loyally, adding doubtfully, "though I noticed you weren't wearing any lippy," which I realised translated as: you were so ancient your mouth had disappeared.

If you're doing your own make-up, have a steady hand

And take your time. I still have a small eye injury from hastily stabbing myself with a mascara brush before presenting a short film on Margate for *The Politics Show* back in 2007. By the time filming had finished – it took all day – I could barely keep that eye open and by the next morning it was swollen shut. I had to drive to Brighton to do the voice-over wearing a patch and whining. There is a still from the programme on the internet, showing me scowling, with eyes like slits. Aside from that it was a great experience – even when the locals came out and started yelling at me.

Keep your nerve

And talking of yelling … If you ever get invited on to one of those 'discussion' programmes where the participants start getting over-excited and there are bouncers at the back of the studio, may I recommend deep breathing and repeating to yourself over and over, "it's only television".

Although, when I went on *Kilroy*, I must say, it was that very thought – of this spectacle being broadcast across the land and particularly into the living rooms of anyone who knew me – that sent the sweat running down my back.

As I attempted to defend myself – some of the audience had been bussed in specially to do booing and hissing – against the accusations that it was women like me, tempting hapless men to break their marriage vows, who were the root cause of 98% of all known crime, death, destruction and the inexorable slide towards the demise of the planet my resolution to talk about my book in a calm and dignified manner, no matter what, went out of the window and I was soon squawking and waving my arms around with the best of them.

I watched the video through my fingers. I hadn't had my make-up done on that show either.

Thrilled to be with Kilroy....

Never work with animals or children...
On *The Wright Stuff* they did do my make-up but I wished I'd done it myself.

Comments from friends ranged from "Did you have a hangover?" to "Did you need a doctor?" to "How come they made you look like Esther

Rantzen?" (I wish! Frankly I would much rather have resembled the fragrant Esther than the hatchet-faced crone I appeared to be.)

Heavy purple eyeliner never helps and once again it was the sort of lighting that left one appearing rather raddled. Or as Lyn-Marie put it this time, "Yes love, you looked like the sort of woman who'd leave her kids on their own while you went off to Turkey for three weeks."

I was on the programme as a result of the newspaper article I'd written about longing to escape from the family, and, against my better judgement, had taken my son with me. He was going to be in London with me anyway, and the researcher thought it would add something to the proceedings if he were sitting in the audience to witness my diatribe about the current media trend to make one feel guilty if skipping round making fairy cakes and having baby princess manicures wasn't one's idea of total fulfilment.

To my surprise, he was quite keen. So, despite my misgivings – I did not want my little soldier traumatised if my opinion that playing shops was mind-numbingly dull and infinitely inferior to going out with one's girlfriends and getting slaughtered[9], proved so controversial with the stay-at-home-I-simply-love-wearing-a-pinny brigade that I was subjected to a whole lot more Kilroy-style berating from the back rows – off we went.

And as it turned out, I sounded a veritable earth mother compared to the phone-ins.

Sharon from Essex called to say she had seven kids and didn't like any of them (why go on breeding like a rabbit then, dear?) and the lines got jammed with an assortment of parents attesting to the crushing tedium of child-rearing in general.

Beginning to worry about the effect this might be having on these unfortunate children – nobody really wants to hear one's mother telling the whole country how boring one is – I felt moved to mount an impassioned declaration of my adoration for my son, who went white. "Did you have to say you loved me?" he demanded afterwards, when he'd been given sweet

---

Footnote 9: I should like to make it clear that I have loved being a mother even if I was never the gluing and sticking sort and still feel an immense gratitude towards the inventor of PlayStation. The Yummy Mummy however, is an important role-model and has a vital part to play for those of us who are writers. May I suggest that you pal up with one who spends school holidays so overcome with joy that she's got her little darlings 24/7 that she won't notice if yours go round there too.

tea and had a blanket put round him. "My friends might have been watching that."

He claims to be scarred by the experience still and has refused to get involved with any sort of publicity I have ever done since.

...Or hairdressers

Remember *The Salon*? The 'reality' show where members of the public could go and get their hair done in a TV studio converted into a hairdresser's where a lot of juveniles spent all day prodding each other and sniggering?

I'd never seen the programme when I had the brilliant idea of appearing on it. Others told me it was dreadful bilge but I had my eye on the viewing figures – which were huge.

For the last eighteen months I'd sported fetching purple and turquoise hair extensions to match the cover of my first novel. So wot a laugh, I thought, to have my whole head a mass of pink, cappuccino, orange and black in the shades of the second one. *The Salon* would have a wacky hairstyle to create and I'd get to witter on about my new book to an eager nation.

I spent some considerable time tracking down direct email addresses/phone numbers for the producers who weren't as immediately thrilled by the prospect as I'd hoped. We had protracted discussions over whether I could show the book (I couldn't) and whether it was OK to say what it was about (it was), what constituted 'plugging' and if I could be trusted not to do it every two minutes.

I wasn't to be allowed to show the actual book cover so had to spend hours making a colour card instead, by – rather artistically I thought – chopping a cover into tiny pieces and creating a mosaic on the back of a postcard so that the colours were displayed but nothing remained that could vaguely identify it as having come from a book by anyone, least of all me.

Despite all the negotiations, the card was still confiscated the moment I arrived at the studio in Balham High Street (somewhat hot and flustered having run up it the wrong way), by a tall skinny bloke of about sixteen who sighed, scratched his head and disappeared to "check with legals"

Someone else aged fourteen arrived. "You can say you've written a book, but you won't mention the title, will you?" she asked anxiously. What should I do if Mel (she who was supposed to be doing my hair) asked what it was, I enquired. The fourteen-year-old looked stricken. She didn't know.

After I'd made a lot of promises I didn't mean a word of, I was eventually allowed into the studio, where 'Mel' examined the colours on the card that had been grudgingly returned, and went into a huddle with John-have-I-told-you-I'm-gay-for-the-fourteenth-time who made a show of mincing over to inspect my head.

"Nah," he said, "we can't do 'em. Not wiv 'enna on it."

I tried arguing the toss until he got petulant. Having bleach on top of henna, he insisted, would make my hair go green and fall out. This would make gripping television, I suggested. "NO!" he squealed.

With no colours there was no story and although I made a point of droning on about the book while Mel did things to my hair that basically left it the same as it had been before, and gave her a lot of hot tips on how to find someone more interesting once she'd been married to her fiancé – another adolescent – for ten years and he'd started grunting, I knew very well they wouldn't show it.

So I amused myself by watching Frankie Dettori being peroxided in the next chair along, and the 'staff' alternately sulking and giggling over the weirder of my fellow clients (on the other side of me was a 72-year-old bloke in a skirt having his nails done and boasting about where he had piercings, trust me– you don't want to know) and made mental notes in case there was an article in the whole experience.

Which, as I later wrote, was like a cross between being in a group of thirteen year-olds in the school toilets and finding yourself unexpectedly in a transvestite club.

But all in all, I walked out of *The Salon* looking much the same as when I went in. I was on air for about three nano-seconds having my hair dried. Friends who were loyally watching blinked and missed it.

All was not entirely lost. I did get an article out of it – with a book plug at the end – and the girl who washed my hair emailed me later to tell me she'd bought a copy of *Perfect Alibis*. A lot of trouble to go to for one sale maybe but hey – it's filled a page or two now!

Don't buy the wrong potatoes

Presenter Ross Kelly should not have been surprised when I was a walking disaster on *The Heaven and Earth Show* because he'd worked with me before.

Then I was cooking (a loose term as the running gag in this house is that I don't know where the kitchen is) for a programme called *Just for Starters*.

Remember what Andrea Zemmel said about buying 'em a drink and hoping? Well I didn't have to do that for Trevor McCallum, director of Red Door TV, who made this series for the Good Food Channel (then UKTV Food) – he bought one for me. Trevor was a regular in the wine bar I co-owned for a couple of years and soon picked up on my media tart tendencies. (Perhaps it was the way I kept serving up my publicity shots along with his wine and shouting "Make Me A Star!")

Trevor suggested that I, along with my friend and co-owner of the bar, Jacqui and one of our staff, Will, might like to take part in one of the programmes. We had to prepare a course each and then come together at the end as if to have a dinner party.

I chose to do the main course.

This was mainly so I could demonstrate one of the few things I know I can do well, which is to make perfect mashed potato[10].

I usually do my supermarket shopping in Waitrose (product placement, Mr John Lewis?) but on this particular occasion, for reasons I now forget, I was forced into a rival supermarket to get my ingredients.

This one did not have the helpful little signs I was used to: *suitable for mashing,* etc. so I bought 'general purpose' spuds.

Which, despite being endlessly boiled, remained like bullets and responded to my enthusiastic wielding of the masher by shooting from the saucepan and hitting the cameraman.

We had to stop filming while everyone became hysterical and then pulverise the things with a hand-held blender. The resultant mass was like over-thick wallpaper paste. Later we had to eat it.

It tasted fine. The potato was the topping to my own recipe, a Mediterranean twist to a British classic – Spicy Turkish Goatherd's Pie. I have just done a Google search and found that amusingly, the recipe is still up on the internet – now more boringly named Turkish Shepherd's Pie and not attributed to me. (Although I suppose the latter is fair enough since all I did was look up how Delia made the standard version and then add half my spice cupboard.)

Footnote 10: The secret of which, since you ask, is to use hot milk. Cold milk does something funny to the starch in potatoes. Hot milk makes them all smooth and creamy. Try it – you'll be amazed.

Two web-surfers/viewers of the Good Food Channel have even tried it.

"very very yummy!!!!!!!" says StellaN65738 while 'Pammi Wammi' thought it so delicious she made double and froze it for her husband who "adores" it.

I am popping it in here in case you're short of an idea for dinner yourself.

Spicy Turkish Goatherd's Pie

What you need
- 2 tbsp olive oil
- 1 onion, chopped
- 2 cloves garlic, crushed
- 450g minced lamb (or beef if you don't like lamb)
- black pepper
- 1 tsp ground cumin
- 1 tsp paprika
- 1 tsp curry powder
- 1/2 tsp ground cinnamon
- 1/2 tsp turmeric
- 4 tbsp chopped coriander
- 3 tbsp natural yogurt
- 1 tbsp tomato purée
- Large glass red wine
- a small bunch of basil, torn
- 450g canned chopped tomatoes
- 1kg potatoes, peeled and chopped (NB suitable for MASHING ?)
- 150ml milk – or more if needs be
- 25g butter
- 4 spring onions, finely chopped
- 115g cheddar cheese, grated

What to do with it
1. Heat the olive oil in a large frying pan. Fry the onion and garlic gently until soft. Add the lamb and fry, stirring as you go, until the mince has cooked and browned. Season with salt and freshly ground pepper.
2. Mix together the cumin, paprika, curry powder, cinnamon and turmeric with the chopped coriander, yoghurt and tomato puree.

3. Add the spice paste to the browned mince, mixing well. Cook for 5 minutes. Throw in as much red wine as it looks as if it needs and drink the rest. Cook for 2-3 minutes. Add the basil and chopped tomatoes, mixing well. Bring to the boil, reduce the heat and simmer for 15 minutes (or until you remember to turn it off).
4. Meanwhile, cook the potatoes in a large pan of boiling salted water until tender; drain and return to the pan. Preheat the oven to 200°C/gas 6. NB do not go on twitter/check emails at this stage. It will all boil over and make a mess.
5. Heat the milk either in a small pan (if you want to look professional) or just in the bottom of the potato saucepan (if want to save on the washing up). Add the butter and mash until smooth. Mix in the spring onions and 55g of grated Cheddar. Season with freshly ground pepper.
6. Transfer the spiced lamb to an ovenproof dish. Top with the mashed potato, spreading it evenly. Rough up the surface with a fork. Sprinkle over the remaining Cheddar.
7. Bake the pie for 45 minutes until golden-brown. Serve with a green salad (or a Greek one if you really want to have a cheese fest). Plus rest of bottle of red wine (if there's any left).

Voila! Or Afiyet Olsun as they'd say in Turkey. Just call me a Goddess…

NB in case you are wondering what the hell all this has to do with promoting oneself as a writer, I popped a postcard featuring the cover of one of my novels up on the dresser in my kitchen before beginning my culinary performance and the cameraman obligingly panned in on it.

I was working on the basis that viewers might think, She can't cook – let's see if she can write instead….

Check what your caption's going to be BEFORE the camera rolls

I should know by now you can't trust the media as far as you can throw 'em. And I wouldn't be able to throw Russell Grant far. In fact, I couldn't lift him. Neither, probably, could your average winch…

So began the column I wrote when I returned from appearing on the Russell Grant Show in January 2004. And looking back at it now, I think I was rather kind.

Someone from the Sky One show had written to me offering "free publicity for you and your novel". You'll have gathered by now this is guaranteed to get my nose twitching. OK says I, what do I have to do?

It sounded harmless enough. Russell was going to read my chart – he does the Royal Family you know, said the researcher – and I would talk about my book.

I mentioned that I had once got a letter about *Perfect Alibis* saying I would burn in hell for promoting adultery (I knew at once they hadn't read it), containing various biblical tracts. Marvellous, she said, you can say that.

Later it emerged they had also booked 'Tanya,' a 'serial mistress'. She was going to talk about how she'd rather sleep with other people's husbands than find one of her own and I was to 'banter' with her.

Hmm, I thought. But, yes, OK, I said. But I am not coming on, I added, just to make absolutely sure, unless I am introduced as a novelist and the book is mentioned.

No problem, the producer assured me.

She said it again when I arrived, reminding me to tell the anecdote about the hellfire (which had clearly captured her imagination) and introducing me to Tanya, who took my breath away. Not only because she claimed to have slept with 100 men and I don't wish to be unsisterly but my goodness they must have been short on options, but also because she had a body odour problem of a magnitude I have never shared such a small space with before.

While we were hanging around waiting for a rehearsal that didn't materialise, someone asked me if I was "the other mistress", I said no, I was an expert on infidelity. My suspicions aroused I again checked out my biog with the producer. "Oh yes," she said. "Russell's got all the notes." Yeah right.

It went out live. We were sat on a squishy sofa while Russell pranced his way to his chair where he read his notes, wobbled a bit, looked totally bewildered by Tanya's account of her torrid sex life, referred to my 'double-barrelled name' without actually managing to say it and then asked me what I did when I went 'on the prowl'.

Wot? No, I smiled through gritted teeth, I didn't do that. I had written A BOOK.

A book? Mr Grant looked even more bewildered, I managed about three words extolling its finer points and they moved on.

Well, I thought somewhat irritably, that was a lot of writing time wasted for not very much (there wasn't even any wine!). But I'd shrugged it off and put it down to experience until I got home to see the video.

We had captions under our names. *Tanya – loves to sleep with married men* and Jane... Novelist? Author of best-selling book and all-round good-egg? Nope. *Self-confessed husband-snatcher.*

Whose husband? I enquired when I was giving the producer three barrels by email. From where exactly did I grab this unfortunate individual?

A speedy apology was forthcoming. The caption was "meant to be taken in a light-hearted way" (I was overcome with hilarity as you might imagine) and "Russell was obviously overpowered by Tanya." (Actually we all were – they were lighting scented candles and spraying Impulse about every time she left the room) so that "things slightly lost their thread".

To cut a long story short, I made a big fuss, my solicitor made a big fuss, an apology was broadcast and a small sum handed over in lieu of any further action being taken. After it was all over and the cheque had been sent, someone from their legal team thought to request an undertaking from me that I wouldn't speak or write about the matter.

I have made a point of including it in every after-dinner speech I've ever made since.

Set your recorder or get someone else to.
Not only so you can check on your captions, but in case you want to make a show reel, see how much you were waving your hands around/look out for unfortunate facial tics, revisit the experience in order to write about it later. Someone from the TV company might promise they will send you a DVD but they generally don't. Hence back in the days when I didn't have Sky and couldn't track down a friend who did, I never did see myself on The Property Channel or on Legal TV (the latter can probably be considered a blessing – see the case of no lips, earlier).

Be prepared for anything
On *Loose Lips* on Living TV, I was called upon to give off-the-cuff relationship advice as part of a live phone-in.

I'm not sure what sort of counsel I cobbled together – the woman in question was having an affair I seem to remember, so I probably said, For

God's sake don't get caught – but it was the first in long line of situations where I've had to think on my feet.

In fact, over the years a variety of magazine editors, radio producers and fellow hacks doing the Ten Top Tips trick when there's nothing else to say, have called upon me to dispense guidance on everything from handling a first date to spicing up one's marriage to how to cope when he lives a continent away (sounds ideal to me). It's OK if it's by email and you've time to have a stab at wording it intelligently, but not so easy if you didn't know it was coming.

I once nearly spluttered on air having just heard myself introduced by one regional radio station (clearly desperate to fill five minutes before the travel news) as a "relationships expert" and finding I was being called upon to offer guidance to Helen who felt Kevin no longer loved her, when I'd thought I was just there to plug a novel.

"A special night out," I suggested vaguely, trawling my memory for every cliché from every agony aunt page I'd ever read, "a quiet night in when you can really talk… Communication is so important," I simpered, getting into my stride, and talking candlelit dinners, even though I knew that Kevin, if he was like most blokes, would probably much rather watch the football than have any sort of discussion about his feelings and would be totally aghast when Helen switched off the TV and served up chicken a la mode in the dark instead.

(In fact I obviously showed a bit too much enthusiasm for her plight because they then rather misguidedly kept me on the line and offered me Veronica and her problems with her mother over which I was utterly lost – "put the old dragon in a home" evidently being not quite what they were looking for.)

So even if you are convinced you really are on to talk about the book and nothing but the book – it's best to get into the habit of having a ready opinion on anything – which is easy if you remember that, if you're up against the wall, it makes very little difference what it is. (**NB** it might, though, if you want to be invited back – see later sections on 'a media presence' and 'expanding your repertoire'.)

Don't drink too much
Often you won't get the chance. Usually TV companies are careful not to let you get at too much booze in the green room beforehand, but if it IS around –

or there's a pub nearby – then it's best not to let the quick snifter, to steady your nerves, end up being enough to make you slurry. (You know how embarrassing it looks when celebrities have done it, let alone us mere scribes.)

Alison Penton Harper, who was one of the prize-winners in the *Richard & Judy* How To Get Published competition, run in conjunction with Macmillan, concurs, though she puts it a little more bluntly:

> Try not to get horribly pissed before facing the cameras. While doing the R & J Show, they foolishly left 5 writers together with no supervision from the production team, so we snuck off to the pub and accidentally got a***holed, which didn't go down too well at all. The film was unusable and I got my worst telling off since leaving school.

I can think of two occasions when I've slightly overdone it myself.

Once was when I got involved in a "documentary". Again I was supposed to be talking about affairs, and how to get away with them. When I got there – this time "on location" to a frighteningly expensive house in North London – they wanted me to shave my legs on camera. The director – who looked about twelve – was the creative type.

They were also filming a Betrayed Wife, the suitably scary Lady Sarah Moon – she who cut her husband's bespoke Savile Row suits to ribbons and distributed his vintage claret collection around the village.

We met in the hall. "What are you angry about?" she asked me. I opened my mouth to explain only to find it covered by one of the crew's hands.

"For God's sake don't tell her you're promoting affairs" he said as she was taken down to the kitchen to hack off chickens' legs with alarming savagery, and I went upstairs where it was considered jolly arty to have me sitting in the bathroom half-dressed (the cameraman squashed uncomfortably in the bath with the lighting man on top of him) pretending to get ready for a night out.

I haven't shaved my legs for years (this is not an admission of German ancestry – I have them waxed by Gina) and was apparently not much cop at pretending.

As I sat there under a weight of shaving foam doing Take Fifty-three, repeating the same sentences over and over again, I not only drank all the rest of the Lady Chicken-chopper's cooking wine to get me through the ordeal but persuaded the runner to go out and get me another bottle.

This was, on balance, a mistake. I will spare you the rest of the story but it involved slurring, agreeing to greater states of undress and nobody telling me my make-up had run.

Most of the footage ended up on the cutting room floor – thank the Lord – but in the bit I saw, I looked utterly deranged and in need of a good social worker.

At least when I went on *Ready, Steady, Cook,* I didn't get smashed till afterwards. Although it was touch and go. It was because I had such a thoroughly lovely time on this show that I was bitten by the TV bug and was tempted by other, lesser programmes, that probably did me little good except for giving me something to write about here. So another tip should probably be:

Don't have too much fun first time out

But I'm glad we did because it was *enormous* fun – and I still have my pinny.

Once again I was with my lovely friend, the author Lynne Barrett-Lee, whose idea it was that we should offer ourselves as a brace of novelists and apply for an audition.

This took place in a classroom in a university building somewhere behind the British Museum and involved us acting out the presentation of our ingredients using rolls of Sellotape, with a roomful of other hopefuls.

I think there is an argument for not trying too hard in these situations. We both giggled and dropped things and generally wittered on aimlessly, but Lynne was supremely confident we'd be chosen and we were – to the evident fury of the couple before us who, in a well-rehearsed and orchestrated double act were poised to launch into the full Hamlet to Ophelia Get-thee-to-a-nunnery scene when they were thanked and sent off.

When the actual filming came, in a studio in Wandsworth, we were there pretty much all day, having our hair and make-up done – beautifully – watching the earlier recordings, eating a lovely lunch, etc.

The actual recording went really fast and since the question everyone always asks me is, do they really cook it all in that short space of time, I can tell you, yes they do. My only contribution was to chop a few broccoli stalks, grate some cheese and stare lovingly at Ainsley Harriott who is very gorgeous and as nice off camera as he appears on it.

My chef, Tony Tobin, did everything else and we won against Lynne and Phil Vickery, although I can't claim any credit – see above. I had simply followed instructions to the letter: don't stand there doing nothing – wine or wipe. In other words, when in doubt, mop at the surfaces or pour a drink. No contest. We were given more wine afterwards and allowed to eat the wonderful food. By the time the car took me to the station, I could barely stand.

Other things to think about
Clothes
Remember what we said about having your photograph taken? For TV, similar rules apply, only more so. You will usually be told all this when you're booked but just in case:

- Avoid small checks, stripes, dots and patterns.
- Avoid outfits that are entirely white or entirely black (though I will always do my best to get away with the latter because it's slimming and TV puts ten pounds on you!)
- Don't wear anything with a prominent logo on it – you generally won't be allowed to
- Aim for bold and bright – they like that! (**NB** I was persuaded into a bright orange T-shirt for *Ready, Steady, Cook* and looked like fat wasp)
- If you are travelling far, make the journey in something else and change when you get there OR wear something that won't crush. If you take three trains and a bus in a linen suit you'll end up looking like a bag person
- Take a change of clothing anyway – just in case nerves make you throw coffee down your front
- Don't wear jangly bangles or chunky necklaces that will clatter as soon as you move – it will come across on the mic
- Belts are good – for attaching the mic to
- Don't wear perilous heels unless you're sure you can walk in them – you don't want to break an ankle on the way to the sofa
- Wear something you feel good in. If you feel good, you'll look fine too.

Networking opportunities
Make sure you come away with the producer/researcher's business card – or at least an email address/phone number. If you're on with any interesting guests, chat them up for theirs too – you never know in this game.

Why you're there

Remember, if you're allowed to, to actually plug your book!

Remember, if you're not allowed to, to do it obliquely.

It's easy to get so carried away with the conversation and the fact that it often seems to be over before it's begun to come off air and realise that the audience didn't even know you were a writer.

Practise saying things like "As a novelist…."

Or "because I work from home – I am an author, you know –…."

Or "It's funny you should say that – the same thing happened to me when I'd just finished writing my first book – *A world full of teapots…*"

Your friends will find you the most terrible bore but at least you'll be prepared when *Newsnight* calls….

> TV can be tricky, but I think it's just a case of trying to speak a little more slowly than usual and letting your enthusiasm and interest come across. Interviewers might be hard on politicians, but they are usually gentler on writers.
>
> **Kate Williams, author, historian and broadcaster**

Public speaking

If the notion of standing up in front of a roomful of people and holding forth fills you with unspeakable horror there are two things to keep in mind.

1) you are not alone
2) that's no reason to dismiss the idea

"I always thought that speaking in public would be terrifying," says novelist and journalist, Emma Lee-Potter, "but it really isn't."

The first time Emma undertook a speaking engagement it was at a literary festival in Oxfordshire.

"I worried about it for weeks beforehand. I felt so nervous on the morning of the event that I felt too sick to eat and couldn't settle to do anything. I also had visions of arriving at the hall and finding rows and rows of empty seats! But the moment I was up on the stage all my nervousness vanished into thin air. The hall was almost full and the audience asked loads of questions."

I find this reaction is fairly typical. As with so many things it is the thought of speaking to an audience that's the problem not the reality – many writers find they get to quite relish the whole experience once they've tried it a few times.

"After my first event I felt fantastic," says Emma. "I realised that public speaking is almost enjoyable. After all, you're speaking about a subject close to your heart – your book – and you know your characters backwards, so there aren't going to be questions you can't answer."

Questions are certainly good – this is the easy part of public speaking – because you don't have to worry about what to talk about, someone else has done that for you. The problem is, you will often be required to fill anything from twenty to forty minutes off your own bat before you get to that happy juncture. Or perhaps even longer…

"How long should I talk for?" I asked, the first time I was ever booked for an after-dinner speech.

"We generally recommend," replied my host, the president of a Dining Club for Gentlemen of Mature Years, "that you keep going until half the audience is asleep…"

The average age in the room was 86 and one chap had already been snoring for ten minutes before I stood up. I punctuated each anecdote with any large noise I could muster. "And then there was a knock at the door," I'd cry, slapping the flat of my hand hard down on the table and waiting while the front row jerked awake.

"And the woman next to me shrieked…" I'd add, illustrating this with an ear-piercing scream to make sure they didn't drop off again.

It was apparently the most excitement most of them had had for years – previous speakers had held forth on "The Workings of the Local Authority" and the "History of the Rubber Stamp" (with slides) – and word soon spread about my ability to bring on a coronary and my speaking career was forged.

I've done Ladies' Diners and the WI, Past Rotarians and the Round Table, The Over 41 Club, The Under 65 Society, Young Wives (they were 70 if they were a day), Old Mothers, Small Businesses and more Writing Circles than you can shake a stick at, and now consider myself an old hand.

Why would you want to be, I hear you enquire with a shudder. I'll tell you.

If you can master the art of speaking to a crowd in a reasonably relaxed and entertaining way:

1)   You can earn money from it

2) You can offer yourself to writing conferences, literary festivals, clubs and groups without fear
3) You can sell extra books
4) You can spread your name surprisingly far and wide and become a 'writer we've heard of' more quickly than you would otherwise
5) You may come to like it.

It might not happen straight away, but give it time. I was pretty nervous the first few times I stood up and spoke, and I still get butterflies if the audience is very large or the gig is particularly important to me, but I'm fine once I get started, and so will you be. The more one does it, I promise you, the easier it gets.

After years of largely avoiding having to speak in public, *Times* columnist Robert Crampton decided to advertise his services as a speaker in his column. "I did this, not because I was any good," he says, "but because I wasn't and wanted to be."

He received more than 400 requests and over the next year travelled the country fulfilling as many as he could manage from a Rotary Club in Gillingham, Kent, to a church in Cheshire and a prison in Leeds.

When Robert subsequently wrote an article about his experiences, he described feeling "the first stirrings of what might just be enjoyment," and said he felt he had rediscovered his 'showing-off gene' which had been dormant for 30-odd years.

Writer Elaine Everest, who describes herself as "quite a shy person" has also found she can now happily talk to groups and has benefited from increased book sales as a result:

"I've visited writing groups where I explain about writing non-fiction books and I also visit dog training classes where I talk about showing – both sets of groups buy copies of the book for differing reasons; one group to study how to write a book, the other to learn how to show a dog," Elaine says, finishing with a smile, "Occasionally I meet someone who wants to write *and* show – I see them off with teeth bared in case they are better than me!"

Saga writer Jean Fullerton has a diary full of speaking engagements since she auditioned to be an official WI speaker, with her talk entitled "Inside the Writer's Mind".

She is full of enthusiasm for speaking as a way of boosting her readership.

"I have managed to not only identify my natural audience but have put myself in a position where I can reach a great number of them – often 50+ women at one go – and do three things: sell books, get my name known, and spend time with some lovely people."

There are lots of groups out there, looking for speakers. Not all of them pay but they'll give you the opportunity to sell your books afterwards and get some valuable experience for when the paying gigs do come along. Often you'll get dinner, sometimes wine or flowers, and as Jean says, you'll meet some great characters too.

Even if you still find the prospect alarming it is worth trying it at least once. When you do, it's useful to remember the wise words of Emma Darwin, "Remember that audiences aren't trying to catch you out. They want it to go well, they want to like you."

Or most of them do. Try not to be intimidated by the one person who is glaring at you – there is always one. Don't take it personally.

Do your best not to look at that particular individual but at someone else in another part of the room who is looking smiley and interested. Sometimes the one with the face like an arse isn't really glaring anyway, I can't tell you how many times the member of the audience who's been looking the most bored/annoyed/unimpressed throughout my entire performance has been the first one to come up afterwards and tell me how much they enjoyed it.

I remind myself that I too have a tendency to appear rather straight-faced when concentrating and have been told off by my son at school events for looking miserable or bad-tempered when in fact I was enthralled and proud.

Also keep your eyes away from anyone who falls asleep – or employ the tactics I described earlier. Maybe they were up till 4 a.m. And when the bloke in the front shouts, "Can I heckle? Ha ha ha" (there is always one of them too), smile sweetly and say you'll be delighted.

On the basis that a) he won't have the balls to do it really, b) I find a little light heckling can actually add to the proceedings and c) frankly, they can do what they like as long as they stay awake.

Other suggestions to make your talk go smoothly include:

Use a microphone if you can
Some speakers don't like using amplification but I do. I think it lends authority to one's voice – makes humour that relies on changes to one's

pitch – e.g. using asides – easier to execute and saves you worrying about the 90-year-old at the back who keeps cupping her ear and bellowing, "What's she on about?"

If you're offered the choice of a 'walk-about mic' as I call them – a radio affair that can be pinned on your lapel – even better! This leaves you free to use gestures, tell stories with actions and move about freely without tripping over yards of cable.

Just make sure it's adjusted properly so your voice doesn't disappear as soon as you turn your head – you should always do a sound check with any microphone – and wear clothes that allow the rest of it to be easily attached to you (there will be a power pack with on/off switch).

As per dressing for TV, belts are good or at least a garment with a waistband. But if you forget, do not panic.

Despite my own advice, I turned up to do a talk recently in a sheer dress but was able to fashion a belt from a cardigan tied round my waist. If you don't have a cardigan with you, demand to borrow a belt from a member of the audience. It will be an ice-breaker. (Especially if his trousers fall down)

Material

Have plenty of subject matter up your sleeve (or written as headings on a postcard). If you have to talk for twenty minutes, take material for forty. There's nothing worse than looking at the clock and realising you've only been going for fifteen minutes, are booked for thirty and have already run out of things to say.

Take a clock

Correction. There is one thing worse – not knowing how long you've been going at all. If there's not a clock in the room, and you don't wear a watch (as I don't) then borrow one to lay in front of you, take a small clock you can put somewhere discreet or put your mobile phone (on silent) in view.

I have occasionally forgotten to do any of this and it can be quite disconcerting to have no idea if you're five or twenty-five minutes from when you're supposed to stop.

Include some humour

Even if it's feeble. You'll be surprised what people will laugh at, so do lighten the proceedings with some amusing anecdotes about how you had a book signing and nobody came (yes, I know, bloody hysterical, but others will be amused) or tell your favourite 'knock knock' joke.

"If you can make people laugh early on," says Robert Crampton, "they'll pay attention, hoping to laugh again."

I would totally endorse that but would add the rider: but **gauge your audience.** I'm not saying *you* should, (it may not work at the WI) but what I do, just by way of an example, is slide in the word "bollocks" early on. If there are nods or grins, I'm home and dry. If I look round at a sea of mouths like cats' bottoms I move swiftly into my nice-woman-from-next-door-routine.

Having said that, it's a mistake to make assumptions. Never imagine that the well-bred ladies from the Flower-arranging & Fine Dining Circle won't appreciate a couple of risqué one-liners or that the old boys nudging each other and peering at any passing cleavage, will.

One of my early talks was to an all-female supper club. I kept it pretty light-hearted, and talked about what had inspired me to write a novel about serial infidelity and gave tips on how they could have a go themselves without being caught. The audience – who were mostly in their 40s and 50s seemed to find it amusing and one of them booked me to do the same thing for another group she belonged to, that met on a Wednesday afternoon in a local church hall. I think they were called the Young Wives.

When I arrived, the woman who had booked me was the youngest in the room by thirty years. I looked at her in some alarm, wondering what else I could talk to these old ladies about for the next forty minutes (I did not have the repertoire then I've built up since). "Just do what you did for us," she told me calmly. And because I was due to start three minutes later and my mind was a blank on any alternatives, I did.

They were an even better audience than the one I'd had first time around. They cackled and heckled and nudged each other and completely warmed me with their enthusiasm. When it came to question time, the oldest of them all put her hand up. "Does your book tell you what to do if you're actually caught in bed NAKED with another man? she asked with relish.

Er, no, it doesn't, I admitted.

"That's a pity!" she yelled, as the room erupted into squawks of laughter and cries of "You're a one, Doris!"

Afterwards they all queued up and bought a book and the afternoon remains in my mind as one of the best of the hundreds of speaking engagements I've now carried out.

"One side-effect of my year," says Robert Crampton, after telling an anecdote about speaking to a congregation, "was affirming my belief that Middle England is not nearly as conservative or fuddy-duddy as we in the media often make it out to be." I would certainly second that.

On the other hand, it has sometimes happened that a member of the audience has made it very clear that she (it is usually a she) does not like me AT ALL. The only thing to do in this situation (and it probably won't happen to you because you've been too well brought up to say bollocks or write a "disgusting" book, as one of my more ardent fans once put it) is to look at someone else and carry on regardless. Tip six is therefore:

Don't be put off. Ignore any negative facial expressions (they may just look like that naturally) and don't let it throw you if someone leaves. Tell yourself they've had a crisis by text and need to make an urgent phone call, have a weak bladder or ate some dodgy seafood for lunch.

Or they're putting the kettle on. Novelist Fenella Miller recalls giving her first talk to the WI a few weeks after her first book came out. "To my horror two women got up and walked out. Only later I discovered they were making the tea."

Take questions

Emma Lee Potter is, as you may have guessed, the daughter of legendary *Daily Mail* journalist, the late Lynda Lee-Potter, who was herself a wonderful speaker. (I have fond memories of her delighting us at a Romantic Novelists Association lunch some years ago). Emma has benefited from her wisdom.

My mother started her career as an actress and some of the advice she'd given me was brilliantly helpful. She said it was vital to project your voice to the back of the hall and always to look at the audience (never read from notes). When it came to questions she always said, 'I'll answer any questions, apart from how old I am, how much I earn and what I think about X!' (This was whoever happened to be a rival columnist at the time.) It always got a laugh and got questions off to a great start.

I love question and answer sessions because it's a chance to be more informal and to address the subjects the audience really want to know about. And if you get some wacky queries to deal with, then it all adds to the entertainment. Children are best at asking the unexpected.

A schoolchild once asked Emma how many books she was going to write in her lifetime, and another asked me what I wore while writing (my pyjamas, was the answer). I've also been asked, and not necessarily by children (!) what football team I support, whether I think men should still open doors for women (absolutely!)[11] and where I'd like to see myself in twenty years time (see page xx)

I would just give you two small pieces of advice about question time. 1) Be firm with the person (there is usually one of them too) who wants to tell a long unrelated story about something that happened to them in 1976 and 2) if you've any friends or allies in the audience prime one of them to ask the first question, if nobody else does. Once one brave soul has spoken up, everyone else will. Should you be speaking to a roomful of total strangers and nobody seems willing to break the silence (and I usually find a cheery, "come on, somebody ask one or I'll feel a prune" deals with that) then ask yourself something.

i.e. "the question I'm most often asked is…" and then launch into it. **NB** preferably make it one to which the answer is short and witty to encourage them.

But fret not. You probably won't need to do any of the above – I usually find the problem is too many questions – especially when the hall is booked by the badminton club next and Gladys the Hon Sec is tapping her biro and twitching towards the clock – and never not enough.

Take books
Arrange in advance to have a table at your disposal and make a pretty display of your books (back list as well as your latest tome) before you start, so that they are visible throughout your talk.

Take change
Everyone will proffer a ten or twenty pound note.

Ask for help
If you can, ask someone to assist you by taking the money while you sign

---

Footnote 11: I've also no objection to having my bags carried, my wheels changed, or the plumbing fixed. Champagne, Green & Black's chocolate and flowers don't go amiss either.

the books – the person who booked you, perhaps, or someone you know from the audience. This saves everyone having to wait too long and helps you keep track of who's paid. Particularly if there's a stampede.

It grieves me to share this with you, but on TWO occasions in the last couple of years, some smiley, smartly-dressed woman of a certain age has made pleasantries, got to me sign a book for her and then melted away without opening her purse. Both times it happened so quickly I couldn't even be sure which one it was in the crowd of other smiley, smartly-dressed women. So I said nothing. But was very annoyed.

Offer freebies
If you have anything to give away, it will bring people to the table. I usually say something like: do come and help yourselves to bookmarks and postcards and have a look at the books if you'd like to.

(Unless I've already had a drink, in which case I just yell, "Now come and buy a book, you tight wads!")

And if I've done nothing after all that valuable advice, but deter you even further? You're in good company. Lucy Mangan is happy to answer questions but doesn't enjoy having to give "an actual speech".

> It's too difficult and requires too much confidence. I think it's just too different from what I'm used to doing all day, which is sitting at home and typing and going days without talking to anyone other than the cat.

I first met Lucy when I was chairing "Girls' Night" at the Guildford Book Festival and she was on the panel with Helen Lederer and Mil Millington (who isn't a Girl but we made an exception for him because he's so funny). It was a great success – the audience loved all three of them. And Lucy said afterwards, that she'd had a really good time.

> I love interviews or being part of a panel because you get a chance to talk about writing with and in front of people who you know are not going to be bored by the subject (which I very rarely otherwise do, because none of my friends is in the trade). This gets me out of the house and interacting with other people without giving me a stroke from the stress of speechmaking.

If this speaks to you, then it's time to think:

Literary festivals

"Literary festivals can still be creaky, featuring the same old suspects, orating to an audience of Rotarians, divorcees, solicitors, and what Alan Bennett calls 'Saga louts'"

So wrote Martin Latham in his Bookseller blog of June 2008 on the subject of literary festivals. And I think it is true to say that some of them can be quite traditional and the organisers can have quite fixed ideas about the sort of authors they want. The audience can be a bit like that too.

I will pop in a bit more of Martin's blog both to give you a flavour of what I mean and because it makes me laugh:

The best festival guests are the ones who talk. And talk & talk .....☺

Photo by Bill Beminster

*"The atmosphere is reverent; one longs for the Pink Panther's assistant Cato to come flying through the wall during a discussion with Julian Barnes. It was a festival-style audience member who once berated me for not wearing a suit to introduce an Edward Heath talk. I wanted to say, "I do not possess a suit and I have not spent 15 years organising 1,200 bookshop talks to be insulted by a **Daily Mail** reader." But I didn't."*

It is also true to say I have quite limited experience to speak from as I haven't been involved in very many literary festivals myself (Martin may call for "fewer literary novelists, please" but I still think I may be a tad lowbrow ☺). The only one I can talk about with any real authority is the wonderful Guildford Book Festival where I have chaired events and/or spoken myself for a number of years.

Martin, while conceding there is "so much to admire in the blossoming book festival scene," also added this caveat, "but I wish its directors could reflect wider reading tastes, attract a broader demographic, stream more happenings on the internet (Edinburgh is excellent at this), and move away from the 'talking head' event."

In my opinion Glenis Pycraft, the director of the Guildford Festival, has succeeded in doing just this. She and her assistant director Pamela Thomas do their best to make the programme varied and interesting to all ages and to "encourage a love of books and reading".

I've done bits of presenting and interviewing for them for the last few years and they've booked some fabulous guests.

If possible they like to hear an author as well as read their books before they book them. "The book may be good but it doesn't mean that the author is a natural speaker," says Glenis. "We like to introduce new authors but have to take in to consideration the likelihood of only getting a small audience."

For this reason, Glenis prefers to be approached by publishers rather than the authors themselves, to save embarrassment if she has to decide against using them.

In case she does book you – and the festival is lovely and attracts some big names so it's worth getting your publishers to ask – I managed to pin her down for a few thoughts on how to get the thumbs up.

- Very few authors can read aloud from their books in a way to engage the audience so we prefer not to have this.

- Ordinary festival audiences don't want to hear a lecture read out either.
- Regardless of how many or how few are in the audience, they are there to hear the author so the author should make just the same effort to engage the audience for a few as he or she would do with many.
- Even if they don't want to be there and are only doing so on their publisher's orders, they should at least try to hide it from the book buyers and organisers.
- Many books are sold by word of mouth and a bad attitude can affect future possible sales as the public will tell their friends.
- Most organisers will have their own black list!

I would just like to say from my point of view that the best 'guests' for me are the ones who talk – and talk! Forget here your fifteen second sound bites and hold forth with abandon. The good chair/interviewer will head you off in another direction if you're blathering on about the same thing for too long (and do please heed their signals!!)

The easiest 'in conversation' I ever did was with Richard Madeley when his *Fathers and Sons* (Simon & Schuster) was first out. He was wonderful (and charming and really rather attractive). All I had to do was pop in the odd phrase like "And then what happened?" and he was off for another fifteen minutes. We could have done double the time easily and the audience adored him[12].

The worst was with a panellist who shall be nameless who just would not draw breath or give me any chance to interject and let someone else get a word in edgeways (and I'm pretty good at interrupting).

If you are on a panel, remember the idea is that all of you should get roughly the same amount of air time each so try not to be a shrinking violet but don't dominate either.

Actress and writer Helen Lederer is always a joy in this respect. Helen is very good at not only jumping in when there's any danger of a lull but drawing out her fellow interviewees if they aren't saying much. I love working with her because she's so supportive and generous. Not surprisingly, she's just been asked back to Guildford for the third time.

Footnote 12: I developed a small crush myself

Writing conferences

There seems to be more of these around, every time I look. I wrote in *Wannabe a Writer?* about the pleasures of being a delegate – and many published authors still like to use the conference as an excuse for a weekend to hang out with fellow scribes – so I won't go over that again.

But if you are published now, then you could also offer your services as a tutor or speaker.

I have spoken at most of the big ones and quite a few of the small ones and have usually had a very good time but it is worth bearing in mind that the term 'writing conference' can mean pretty much anything, ranging from the nice hotel, three-course meal, wine flowing end of things to What-am-I doing-here? moment of considerable proportions.

You'll find plenty of information on conferences, courses and holidays (all of which will hire speakers, tutors or facilitators) on the internet but it is best to ask around and find people who've actually been, in order to gather intelligence on the finer details – like which ones have the good food and accommodation, which are well organised and how many writers are likely to turn up, longing to buy your books (I sold over six hundred quid's worth straight after one of my talks to a fantastic audience at Swanwick and ran out of stock.)

Frankly, I could write an entire book on the residential weekend, and the ins and outs of teaching and doing one-to-one consultations at same – and may well do, one day. But there isn't room for that here. So for now, I have boiled my knowledge and experience down into six major survival tactics.

1) Check for the word 'ensuite'. I still shudder to remember my visit to one of our older university buildings where I was shown to student halls. It is no exaggeration to say I've seen more inviting-looking rooms in a documentary about Holloway. I might just have stood the green nylon carpet, graffiti-scrawled walls and strip lighting if I'd had my own bathroom. I don't do padding about the corridors with a sponge bag. Especially without a drink.

2) Familiarise yourself with bar serving times and pack a corkscrew. I arrived at one particularly grim establishment after a four-hour drive to be offered – at what was clearly gin and tonic hour – a cup of tea!

"Where's the bar?" I asked politely. It was closed. What time did it open? 10.30 p.m. After the workshops had finished, as one of the organisers explained helpfully, looking round for assistance as I shrieked, "I don't teach sober!" Fortunately, I pride myself on being resourceful in times of crisis and on this occasion managed to bribe a bottle of white out of the kitchen staff. I was consequently mobbed at dinner, which is another minefield.

3) Check the catering arrangements. Eat-What-You're-Given can work well for those on restricted calories but it might be wise to request a special diet. I have seen waiting staff grow increasingly tetchy as, upon sight of slabs of greyish animal product of indeterminate origin being brought forth, a sea of hands has sprung up with cries of "I'm a vegetarian", even though their lists show only three people had requested Bean Bake. Good food can be hazardous too. At the Help-Yourself outfits, you will need a will of iron when tray upon tray of delicious-looking fare is laid out before you three times a day – plus cake in between – and all you have to do is waddle up and eat it. If you can put on a pound a day on a cruise, it's two when you're sat on your Writers' Bottom. Pack either crispbread or your running shoes.

4) Check the age of the audience. The older they are, the louder they'll cackle at your filthiest jokes. The younger, the more books you'll sell. Note for delegates and speakers alike (especially the youthful or picky): if you're hoping to pull, you're likely to be disappointed. (Although never say never!)

5) Check the turnover of the audience. Some of them have been going for twenty-five years. If this is your second visit, you'll need a different set of filthy jokes from last time.

6) Be prepared for anything. If you're going in blind, take a hip flask, Kendall's mint cake and a couple of pensioners, just in case.

Signings, talks and festivals may not look like much when they're looked at individually, but there's an accumulative effect which should pay dividends in the longer term.

Patrick Janson-Smith, Publisher – Harper Collins

One thing leads to another

The way the 'accumulative effect', works, I find, is that the more you do, the more you get asked to do.

I have seen a direct chain response more than once which has gone: local paper coverage > picked up by press agency > national paper/magazine coverage > invitation to appear on TV or radio.

On other occasions it's been as simple as one person hearing me speak and booking me for another event, or meeting a features editor at someone else's launch party who happens to be interested in something I can hold forth on.

So be open to anything. If someone asks you to supply a few writing tips for their new website – do it. You never know who might visit who'll think you sound just the sort of person to give a workshop, or at least order one of your books.

An online review of someone else's work can lead to some interest in your own; making a competition shortlist may flag your name up to those who'd not heard of you.

I have sent contributions to the American *Bylines Writer's Desk Calendar* a couple of times, both because it's a great idea and in case it might get a few US readers/writers vaguely interested in finding out a bit more.

I had no idea whether that had worked – though the calendar is a really nice thing to have so it didn't matter much – until this week I was alerted to a blog mention in South Dakota giving out my web address (thank you Karin!). So that's one person who noticed ☺ – and now her blog followers have heard of me too.

It is very rare for me to do *anything* that doesn't – eventually – lead to something else – even if it takes three years for it to come to fruition.

And it will be the same for you too.

However, it would be a mistake to spend those years sitting back and waiting for this to happen.

Much better to follow the old adage:

If you don't ask, you don't get

"You get to do so much stuff," said another author to me once.. "Nobody," she added, a tad peevishly, "ever asks me to speak anywhere…"

If I'd been feeling generous and she hadn't been banging on for the previous half hour about how brilliant she was (which explains her bemusement at the above), I could have told her that actually they didn't ask me either.

In the beginning I went out and canvassed for everything I did. I offered to speak or teach or write articles/columns and talked (pleaded/cajoled/bribed) my way into pretty much every publicity opportunity I was given.

Recommendations, word of mouth, a plug here, being spotted by a researcher there, were bonuses and mostly came later.

In the early days it was about banging on doors, sending query letters, putting out pitches and picking up the phone, taking a deep breath and persuading the person at the other end that I'd be a good guest/tutor/contributor/writer to hear more about.

The inspirational Valerie Dwyer, whom I met through *The Speakers Agency* – we are both on their books – describes herself as a Serial Entrepreneur, Coach and Mentor, Business Development Specialist and speaker, as well as a writer.

Valerie is the Founder of My Wonderful Life Coach™ and several other enterprises, including a marketing and PR agency, and is an example to us all when it comes to going to the mountain rather than hoping it might call by and say hello to you.

Valerie has tales of physically turning up at newspaper offices when she thought 'significant events' were happening for various of her enterprises, and asking for the Business Editor and an interview.

On one such occasion she hit it off so well with the editor on a large regional newspaper, that she was featured on the front page of the next Business Edition.

"That started a long relationship of being called upon for expert commentary on my topics as well as them using clippings from my news releases. In most cases, my news or stories have been taken up and used in full or in part, more often than not leading on to requests to write other material."

You may not be brave enough to do this – I'm not sure I would be either – but the principle is certainly a good one.

Remember that the worst anyone can say to you is NO – and while that's not very nice, you won't die of it.

Have courage and take the risk because in the early days of one's career as a media tart, sitting back and waiting for opportunities to come to you, just doesn't work.

I keep a piece of paper attached to my monitor shelf on which I have scrawled a quote which I have spent my whole life believing was from Goethe but have just this minute via Google discovered in fact originates from William Benjamin Basil King (1859–1928) the Canadian-born clergyman who later became a writer. (One of those common misconceptions, apparently, like people thinking it was Emmeline Pankhurst not Emily Davison who threw herself in front of that horse)

Anyway, it says:

Be bold and mighty forces will come to your aid

Which I hang onto when losing heart or feeling a wimp about phoning someone up. And to which, when doing our own PR, we might interpret as follows:

Don't sit on your bottom, waiting to be famous. Go strut your stuff…

PUTTING IT ABOUT – THE ART OF EXPOSING YOURSELF

Keeping up the momentum

If we really want to be someone others have heard of, we need to view it as an on-going process. Yes, you need to make the most of those first few weeks when your book is hot new stuff but publicity opportunities exist long, long after that. And the better you can spread yourself about and get yourself known, the easier it will be to promote your second (third, fourth, twentieth) work because by then all your contacts and media outlets will be in place.

You need, in other words, to establish and then maintain:

A media presence

If you aren't media savvy, your 'airspace' will end up being occupied by someone else. There is no such thing as a vacuum after all ...

Carole Blake, Literary Agent

A week may be a long time in politics but it is bugger all in the PR game. Those who apparently become famous overnight are often reaping the rewards of a long and concerted campaign to get themselves known. Others really do come to attention in a short space of time, but then quickly fade back into obscurity.

It is worth analysing why some figures remain in the public eye long after they first became noticed.

Newspaper editors come and go and there have been plenty heading up national papers whose names we now barely remember.

Compare and contrast them with Piers Morgan – who is now a household name through *Britain's Got Talent* and TV programmes various – and someone like Kelvin MacKenzie who, decades after being editor of the *Sun,* still appears all over the place. How?

I was amused when *Times* writer Janice Turner referred to his inclusion on the panel of *Question Time* as a "comedy irritant". And when I quoted this to Kelvin, he laughed too. But what's the real reason for his longevity? Is it because he's deliberately controversial?

"I'm a journalist," he said. "I'm always going to have an opinion. And I enjoy sharing it."

Sounds simple enough but of course, to be invited back, not just any old opinion will do.

"Make it strong," says Kelvin. "Not just the same as the bloke down the pub. An opinion needs to have either an intellectual or statistical substance to it. Otherwise you sound ridiculous. Have some passion about it! Go with your gut instinct. You have to have heart too. Both are more important than head."

It's always tricky when interviewing Kelvin to keep him on topic and we'd soon moved away from being a writer we've heard of, to the wider world – "If head dominated the world, then every single company in Britain would be run by a maths professor. In business, two plus two doesn't always equal four." – but I include it because I think this is still relevant to us.

Speaking, writing, being interviewed from the heart – with honesty and passion – is far more effective that reciting a well-rehearsed marketing pitch.

After a brief rundown on why David Cameron won the election (speaking without notes[13] at the conference was a plus point I seem to recall), I got him back onto longevity and this is worth repeating too:

"It's down to hard work and perseverance – perseverance first, hard work second and a long way last, talent. If you've got talent that's fantastic. But if you look at the way a lot of races are run, you'd be amazed at how many times it's dogged determination that works."

This is my experience too. The trick is to keep on keeping on and give the media a reason to call you and seek your input. If you have a very specific area of experience or expertise then this obviously happens faster. Be prepared to milk it to death and expand it to its furthest limits.

Maria McCarthy, author of *The Girls' Guide to Losing your L Plate*s and *The Girls' Car Handbook* (both Simon & Schuster) has taken part in over 200 radio

---

Footnote 13: Even if you don't hanker to be Prime Minister (and why would anyone remotely sane?), speaking without notes always looks good. Try it yourself if possible.

interviews – including *Woman's Hour* on Radio Four and Radio Two's *Drivetime* – since the first of those books was published.

"Only about 20 were just on *The Girls' Car Handbook* and why I wrote it, and about 30 were specifically on the L Plates book," she explains. "All the rest were as a result of becoming a 'rent a quote' on local radio. I now get asked about anything from fuel prices to the rising cost of car insurance, potholes, men vs women drivers, older drivers and so on."

At the time of writing, Maria has just been on TV too. She sent through this piece of advice should you be asked to do anything similar. Which I'll include as a useful word of warning:

> If you're involved in an outside broadcast using a 'satellite truck', it's not a truck, it's a little van – with nothing in it apart from sound and camera equipment. Don't expect make-up, tea, or a loo but take along whatever you need (a flask, make-up, an umbrella, something to read) to be totally self-sufficient. This is based on my experience of sitting in the aforementioned van in a driving test centre car park between 6-9am, while rain lashed on the roof, getting out occasionally to do a quick piece about the 75th anniversary of the driving test. Comments afterwards, from friends who'd watched it were mostly along the lines of: 'I felt sorry for you, you looked so bedraggled.'

And there's no doubt that even if you haven't got any particular area of authority – but just the angles and experiences you listed earlier – if you show you're prepared to talk about everything and anything, you'll get the calls.

I've been interviewed on BBC Radio Kent many times. To start with it was always about whatever book I had out at the time. But then one day, the head of the station, Paul Leaper, happened to hear me and suggested to one of the producers that I might make a good guest on the John Warnett show. At that time John used to be joined by some local figure each Friday to discuss the week's news, the burning issues of the day and to join in with a phone-in.

I was really pleased to be asked and thoroughly enjoyed it. And it led to being asked to spout opinions at other times.

When Broadstairs came second on a list published by the *Guardian* for having the best beach or being the prettiest seaside or some such (St Ives won it, I seem to remember) I set the alarm for half six so I could make enthusiastic – if bleary – noises. And they called me again when journalist

Rachel Cooke complained in the *Observer* that she couldn't find any fresh fish to eat here.

Now I go on for all sorts of reasons and get called by other radio stations in other counties too. And if ever I have anything I want to plug, from a new book to a charity event, they are great about giving me some airtime.

Remember that it doesn't matter what you're there for. If you are introduced as novelist Jim Jones or writer Sally Smith on radio or in an article you can usually negotiate to get a book mention at the end.

And even if this doesn't happen someone might feel sufficiently interested or moved by what you had to say to look you up on Google later.

I have had emails from people who heard me on the radio and ended up reading one of my books in this very way.

If you get good enough at being a 'gob on a stick', then there might be a bit of dosh in it too. The local stations rarely pay, unless you do some actual presenting for them, but BBC Wales, Ulster and Scotland will make a small payment, as will GMTV, Radio 5 Live and shows such as Jeremy Vine's.

It always worth pleasantly enquiring – because if you do it a few times, the fees do add up.

Also bear in mind that what you are an 'expert' on, or feel passionate about this week, is not set in stone. Next week you can hook into a new topic and all of these can be developed and expanded on.

Fay Weldon is very good at this. Whenever she has a new book out she always crops up saying something surprising, controversial or provocative. And it's always just the right thing for the media to grab onto.

As I'm writing this she's just been on Desert Island Discs. And already, a day later, the nationals are carrying the story. Her comment on air, "There is a degree of second sight, I think, on occasion,'" has become **Fay Weldon Claims To Have Psychic Powers** in the *Telegraph* and **I was born with psychic powers says Fay Weldon**, in the *Daily Mail*.

And good for her! When you're 78 and have been around as long as Fay has – I fell in love with her writing in my teens and she'd already been going a decade then – it is quite an art form to still be able to hit the news with original snippets about yourself that nobody has heard before.

We can do worse than to follow Fay's example and keep our own profiles fresh.

"Change your mind, change your mood, change your strapline!" says personal advocate, Simone Klass. "Be ready to feed into news stories – you want ultimately to be an authority on your subject – so you're on all the journalists' databases, so they know you'll always have something to say."

I would say cast your net wide and aim to be an authority on as many subjects as you can muster. Or at least to have a view on them. Sometimes simply responding to the opinions of others can lead to a name check – which I discovered by happy chance.

I've always admired Anne Robinson as a writer – particularly when she had a column in *The Times* some years ago. I emailed her one day – long before I'd ever written a book – to comment on something she'd written, for no other reason than it had made me laugh, and was surprised and flattered to find my message quoted in her column the following Saturday. A few months later it happened again. It didn't promote me as a writer – I barely was one back then – but was an interesting lesson that journalists do read their mail and if they like what you say, might use it.

(I certainly do this myself, in my own small columns, and am always delighted if I get a witty/rude/confrontational email I can build something round).

I'm not suggesting you immediately bombard every columnist in the land with your thoughts on their pronouncements but sometimes a well-judged contribution to a debate can pay dividends.

Mick Hume mentioned my first novel in *The Times* after we'd struck up a correspondence and Robert Crampton referred to my second in the Saturday magazine. Jonathan Gornall who was 'Microwave Man' in the same newspaper for a long time, quoted something I'd said to him about infidelity – again mentioning my book – and I later got column material not only from our subsequent lunch but the Sexplained[14] Quiz we did together – along with Mil Millington and Louise Wener – as a direct result of our meeting.

This details of this are a little hazy now but the evening was sponsored by Trojan – a leading American contraceptive brand who were entering (no pun intended) the UK market. My involvement in the event caught the interest of the editor of one of my local papers – a kind of tabloid affair styled on the *Sun* – and I gained further column inches, being described as

---

Footnote 14: This is a charity set up to give information on sexual health matters. There's no room to go into the full ins and outs (still no pun intended!) here but If you are want to know more see www.sexplained.com.

the author of 'sexy' books and photographed clutching a handful of Trojan condoms. (A pose slightly spoiled by the fact that I held them the wrong way up).

Later – which has no relevance at all but which may give my female readers a wry smile – I offered to send readers of my newspaper column free samples from the considerable stock of condoms I came home with. All they had to do was send me an sae and an indication of their size. I had a little bet with myself that every bloke who took up this offer would request them in 'Extra Large' and sure enough…. ☺

When promoting products always hold them the right way up.

You may not aspire to be plastered across your local rag clutching contraceptives – and who can blame you – but there is a lot to be said for developing the sort of relationship with local editors that means if you want to, you can. The more often locals see your name in their paper the more likely they are to think they might as well try one of your books....

So let's take a little look at:

Cultivating your local paper

We've already looked at approaching papers in the first instance to say your book has come out. But when it comes to your local paper, don't leave it at that.

As Mike Pearce explained earlier, the local press are often understaffed and stretched for time and so will be hungry for easy snippets of news with which to fill the pages. It can therefore can be a mutually beneficial relationship that can run and run.

And it's worth re-iterating that 'local' is an elastic term. But certainly you should be on good terms with the editors of whatever paper(s) cover the town where you live. If you're in one of the cities it's harder, I grant you. But then the choice is wider – free newspapers, etc. – and the rewards will be greater too, via a much larger readership. Nothing ventured, etc....

Mike's successor, my current editor at the *Isle of Thanet Gazette,* and now lovely friend (I knew we'd hit it off when she turned up to our first meeting waving a bottle of wine) Rebecca Smith, has kindly offered her own list of dos and don'ts of approaching a local newspaper, to complement his.

This applies to whether it's your first book, your 54th, or you want to get a name check – mentioning that you are an author of course! – for the fact that you've just raised £500 for the Society of Impoverished Scribes Who Need to Get Out More by doing a sponsored Chocolate Gorge.

Rebecca says:

1) Do drop me an email outlining your situation: that you are local and have written a book. This is not in itself worthy of the front page or even anything more than a couple of paragraphs so anything that might tantalise the newsdesk is helpful (if your book is set in the area

covered by the paper or it details your acrimonious divorce from the leader of the council it might merit more coverage).

2) Don't send me your life history in the first instance unless it is VERY interesting. I don't care about your GCSE results. No, really I don't.

3) Do give me a call to check I got your email. A local newspaper newsdesk gets anything up to 300 emails a day people wanting their product or service featured so yours might slip through.

4) Don't assume that I will know exactly who you are and to what you are referring.

5) Do ask if its a good time to call. Ringing five minutes before deadline will mean I am not listening even if I sound like I am.

6) Don't be grumpy if I ask you to call back or I sound vague. It probably IS five minutes to deadline.

7) Do be prepared to do some of the legwork whether it's to write a first person piece or provide a photo of yourself. Both offers will be appreciated by an overstretched newsdesk.

8) Don't assume I will drop everything and rush a reporter and photographer around to see you at once.

9) Do call and say thanks if you like the article. It rarely happens and is much appreciated and will go someway to ensuring further coverage if you have a second book.

10) Don't give up. Something that doesn't make one week might well make the next if it fits with the news agenda or if there's a great big hole to fill.

So what sort of thing might fit in with the news agenda? As Mike Pearce says, if you're looking for a follow-up story on your book, the paper will probably not be overly-concerned about how well it's doing, unless it has rocketed into the best-sellers.

"But news," he adds, "i.e. anything noteworthy or unusual, will always be welcomed." You may recall his example of Miss Clipper and her wretched novel about dog-breeding.

"Miss Clipper signing copies of her book won't send pulses racing. But if she tracks down the chap who gave her that first job at the dog track, a nice feature could result."

(I have to say this wouldn't much send my pulse racing either – surely she'd be better off having riotous sex with him in the Paris Hilton and discovering his fetish involving a prize poodle – but I'm sure we get Mike's drift.)

"Don't be ashamed to come up with a stunt," he says. (This is the man who had me photographed in fur[15] coat and dark glasses, champagne glass in hand, draped across the Welcome to Broadstairs sign, claiming my novel was based on local scandals, for the front page of the *Thanet Times*). "One of Miss Clipper's clients might be the son of a soap star. Lean on him to see if his celebrity dad will say how much he enjoyed your book. Then a short piece with picture of celeb should be pinged off to the paper, revealing the author's delight that a telly star is one her readers."

Mike also suggests getting involved in local issues. E.g. *"Miss Clipper (author of The Great Alsatian Scandal) has joined in the controversy over whether dogs should be banned from Boomtown's beaches. Speaking from her seafront writing retreat, where she is working on a sequel, she told reporters...."*

I can vouch for this as an effective way of getting column inches myself. Having made a noise about lots of local goings-on in Thanet, I am now frequently asked to spout my views on anything from what I think about nude sunbathing (bring it on) to whether the council should sell off the tennis courts (at their peril) or what I think of Tracey Emin's latest visit to Margate (Fabulous. Love Tracey).

And just to show it works, I often find taxi drivers peering at my hair in their rear view mirrors and asking: are you that one who writes books? (Before of course, they proceed on to whether I'd like to ghost their life story. Sorry, mate, can't say I would, really.)

Mike also mentions the newspaper's marketing department. "Offer copies of your book as prizes. The competition might give you a quarter-page of publicity, which would have cost you a jolly sight more than the price of a few books."

He and I did this too. And also ran a promotion with the local bookshop whereby readers could get my novel at a discount on production of a coupon from the paper.

"More books sold, more papers sold, readers got a bargain – everyone won," he says.

The aim, Mike advises, is to be friends with the editor or at least a

---

Footnote 15: Note to mad animal activists: not real fur. You can hold the poo and petrol.

reporter on your main local title. He suggests you take them for lunch or at least meet them for a drink.

"You will know you have 'made it' when *they* start approaching *you* to see if you have any story ideas....."

Expanding your repertoire

OK so let's have a bit of a recap: you've been on the radio, and maybe the TV too, you've written articles, been interviewed, toured the bookshops, taken part in the festivals and conferences, hit the speaking circuit and the editor of your local paper is your new best friend. What next?

1)   you do all that again
2)   You stay alert for any new opportunities.

E.g. **Keep an eye on the press**
Especially the weekend supplements. Are there any **new** columns or slots you could contribute to, since you last looked? My Last Meal? How I Met My Wife? My Oddest Love Affair?

Go through the glossies – spend an hour in the newsagents flicking through all the magazines looking for same (or it you want a seat and your immune system's strong enough, hang out in the waiting room at the doctor's).

Look at everything and anything. I've had a book plug at the bottom of *Confessions of a Tourist* in the *Sunday Times* Travel section, given relationship advice in *Best,* had 'the last word' in *Scarlet Magazine* and even grabbed a mention in the *Independent*'s education section.

Keep in touch with any journalist friends and contacts – they may well want 'readers'' views at short notice or need someone, who's been there or done that, to give them a quote. If they know you'll always come up with the goods, you'll stay on their lists.

Rosie Millard called me several more times when she had her 'Tales of a Landlady' Column in the *Sunday Times;* journalist and broadcaster Sue Hayward used me in an article about blagging for the *Daily Express.* I've also written about doing Sudoku for *The Times* when the newspaper was canvassing opinions on the then-new puzzle.

Newspapers often invite contributions from readers and will include a sentence about your occupation if they use you – it doesn't take long to bash out a paragraph on what you think about keeping guinea pigs or making children eat their greens or whatever the burning issue of the day happens to be.

If you feel like being a little more erudite, pen a missive to the letters page.

When another author wrote to *The Times* about the amounts charged for in-store book promotions and the difficulty of getting his own tomes displayed in his local Waterstone's, I knocked up a quick reply in the chain's defence.

> Sir,
>
> While I share the quiet despair of many authors over the increasing and swingeing pay-to-display policy adopted by booksellers, I feel I must defend Waterstone's over the issue of local writers.
>
> I have not had the same experience as H.R.F. Keating (Pay and Display Letters June 20). The branches of Waterstone's nearest my home have always been most supportive – displaying my novels in their local interest section and often utilising additional POS material or a "recommended" note. No money has ever changed hands.
>
> May I suggest that instead of looking to his or her publisher, H.R.F. Keating approaches the store manager – with a large smile.
>
> Jane Wenham-Jones
>
> Author of Wannabe a Writer?

Of course they dropped the book title (it was worth a try) but the letter appeared. I not only got a mention as a novelist – and my husband got an email from a long-lost school friend as a result, proving that people do read these things – but it pleased my local Waterstone's manager, who then flagged it up to head office, no end. (I am trusting they are recalling my fine PR on their behalf right now as they order this book in shedloads.)

So it's worth doing on several levels.

For the extroverts who do not mind half the country hearing them bang on about the price of beans or what happened when next door wouldn't cut back their leylandii, radio phone-ins can be another splendid opportunity to get your name out there.

Can I suggest however, that if you have aspirations in this direction, you make sure you have the contact details tattooed on your arm. (Or at least written on a card in your car.)

I missed a perfect opportunity to get myself on the Jeremy Vine show once because I didn't know what number to call. I was driving back from Wales, with only a mobile that came out of the ark and my laptop – dongle-less in those days – in the boot.

I heard the good Jeremy introduce the journalist George Monbiot who was proposing that nobody should own a second home, since it was Londoners in their weekend cottages who were ruining the environment, and who, according to George, were entirely responsible for the lack of available housing and levels of homelessness in this country.

I wasn't particularly gripped – it was the usual dreary protests from the "I-pay-my-taxes-and-I'll-do-what-I-want" lot – until one Clive Aslet, billed as Editor at Large of *Country Life*, with a holiday home in Ramsgate (the next town along from me) came on and things began to liven up.

George thought Clive selfish taking a home from the needy while Clive, who also pays his taxes, said there wasn't a shortage of housing in Ramsgate anyway. Oh yes there is, declared George.

I suddenly decided to phone in and knew instinctively they'd put me through. How could they not? Columnist on the local paper, owner of property in Ramsgate (rented out no less), author of hilarious book on same and possessor of the real facts and figures.

I'd just written a piece about a count of the homeless in Thanet (two – and while that's two too many, I knew it was a matter of mental health issues and a need for assistance with benefits rather than Clive having snapped up the last pad in town), I knew exactly how many vacant flats there were to let and how many new ones currently unsold on the market. I had views on the need for the Weekenders (or DFLs – Down from London – as we call them here) to boost our economy.

"What do you say to that, hey George?" I chortled, as I perfected a tone that would sound intelligent while accessible, show wit but not sarcasm and would work when I slid a couple of book plugs in.

Phone us or text us, entreated Mr Vine, without giving out the number as I rooted around for a pen I didn't need.

The traffic came to an obliging halt on the M25 affording me the perfect opportunity to hold forth without losing the signal or driving into the lorry in front. But there was still no number[16].

For the next thirty minutes Mr Vine cheerily invited listeners to phone, text or email without any contact details whatsoever, as I got increasingly fractious, listening to other callers making repetitive points with a lot less verve than I would have done and my fifty seconds of fame slipped through my fingers.

Something came out of it because I wrote my next *Isle of Thanet Gazette* column on the matter and sent a copy of it in to the Beeb, using the opportunity to chat up a researcher by email and get myself put on their list of contacts (Tim – I'm still waiting for your call!) but it was a lesson on being prepared (and having a phone that connects to the internet).

Notable dates

While you're keeping your eyes open for opportunity, keep one of them on the calendar too.

Lots of features and articles are written around certain dates so it's worth contacting editors and radio producers to see if they've got anything planned. If you are a writer of romance, Valentine's Day is ripe for quotes and plugs, if you write horror you should be geared up for Halloween. Lesley Cookman, who as well as writing crime fiction, has written, directed and appeared in numerous stage productions and is the author of *How to Write a Pantomime* (Accent Press) is always in demand in December!

"I get a lot of exposure at Christmas, when local radio stations all over the country are desperately looking for seasonal snippets. I've been on air from Dublin to Manchester, from Cornwall to Norfolk, and I live in Kent!"

Think about any seasonal hooks for your own works. It you've written a book on depression, make sure you know when World Mental Health Day is (10th October), if your novel's a post-feminist tract embracing the enduring quality of sisterhood and female stoicism in the face of adversity, get in touch with the press in plenty of time for International Women's Day (March)

Footnote 16: Should you find yourself in a similar position, it is 0500 288 291.
You can also text 88291.

If you're a diet guru, offer to comment on Eat Your Body Weight in Pies Day and so on. These days there's a day for every bloody thing – and if there isn't, you could always invent one!

Plugs & stunts

And while we're talking inventive, a bit of a stunt will always attract attention.

Before Peter James was the chart-topping crime writer he is today, he was a film producer. When his horror movie *Children Shouldn't Play With Dead Things* came out in 1972 the world premiere was held at the Ziegfield cinema in New York. He recalls the lengths they went to theme the evening:

> I had to dress up along with the director and other key members of the producing team as a ghoul and stand outside the entrance handing out life insurance policies to all ticket holders, guaranteeing a million dollar payout if they died of fright during the screening! We also gave each of them an 'Upchuck Cup' – an empty bucket to vomit into!

Lovely! I've been trying to think of something I could do along these lines next time I do an event. Hand out Nurofen perhaps, with copies of *One Glass Is Never Enough* or dress in a strait jacket when promoting *Wannabe a Writer?*

I don't where one would track down a designer of clothing for the seriously unhinged but I mention Nurofen so often I should probably be negotiating a product placement deal. (If Waitrose, Kettle Chips, Green & Black's chocolate, or any purveyor of champagne is reading this – I'm up for talks with you too).

Such an agreement, of course, can bring its own wave of publicity. Fay Weldon famously negotiated with Bulgari before publishing *The Bulgari Connection*, in which the Italian jewellery maker gets plenty of mention and a few years later, Carole Matthews signed a deal with Ford to mention their cars in several of her works.

I'm afraid I don't have any inside tips on how to go about this. I can only tell you to do it before you start writing and not later.

In my first novel, my heroine Cari mainlines Cadbury's chocolate fingers throughout and creates a whole diet around them. When the book was published I wrote to the boss of Burton's Foods who made these delightful biscuits in those days (they're probably produced in Taiwan now), what, although I say it myself, was a brilliant letter, extolling the virtues of a joint promotion. (Or at the very least, the wisdom of him sending me a couple of free packets.)

I enclosed an article I'd written for the *Daily Express* – clearly mentioning his product, and suggested he might like to advertise my book on the back of each packet, give each of his loyal staff a signed copy, spread the word in his company newsletter and pin my postcards on his notice boards. I even offered to after-dinner speak at his Christmas bash and to personally drive to Blackpool so he could take me out to lunch and discuss the matter.

He – Adrian Sharpe – clearly a man with a humour deficit – did not even have the decency to reply. I have just researched him on Google and see that he left the company a couple of years later. That's what happens when you don't know a good commercial wheeze when you're offered one.

If you can have your own means of splashing your book title about, rather than having to rely on short-sighted biscuit executives, then go for it any way you can.

Peter James is also a keen motor racer, who covers his cars with panels advertising which ever is his latest book. Thus in June 2009 when he had what he describes as "a big smash" at Oulton Park race circuit, he attracted plenty of attention as he stepped from the wreckage of a car emblazoned with the words DEAD TOMORROW. Which, as he says, "had nearly been prophetic!"

If you can't run to a racing habit, you could perhaps put a sticker on the back of your Skoda – as long as your book isn't called *Mr Cool*, *Sex on Wheels* or *Why Don't You Drive into Me?*

Game shows

But if you want to really attract attention to yourself, there is one platform that will always guarantee a large and eager audience. The TV Game show.

Author and short story writer Lynne Hackles had me chewing my fingers in anxiety for her when she appeared on *Deal or No Deal*. It wasn't just her close proximity to Noel Edmonds. It was the fact that she got through to the end and was faced with choosing between two boxes – one containing 10p and the other £75,000.

I'm pleased to tell you the tale has a happy ending. Lynne – who was sublimely calm throughout – walked away with the seventy-five grand, and earned a whole lot more money and publicity as a result.

If you've ever fancied having a go at a game show yourself, you'll be glad to know, Lynne says being a writer helped. Both in the filling out of the original application form and the many more questions, on her opinions and attitudes to life, she had to answer when she was invited to audition.

While those around me chewed the ends of their pens and gazed into the distance, I scribbled away happily. How many Writers' Circle exercises have been handed out over the years requiring me to 'write on the spot'? I treated this as if it was one of those exercises and hoped that my answers were entertaining.

At the next stage, sitting in front of a camera and told to talk about herself, Lynne says her work as a tutor and speaker came into its own. "In fact," she says, "the whole day could be related to writing experience."

The odds of being chosen to go on the show are probably far greater than those of getting a novel accepted by a mainstream publisher. I shortened those odds by supplying what the television company were looking for – just the same as doing market research for a story or article. I'd watched countless shows and read Noel Edmond's book, *Positively Happy*.

I played to my strengths giving sharp, concise and, I hope, witty answers to the questions asked and then, after I'd given it my best shot, I returned home to get on with other things, just as I do when one story is posted and another is begun.

After six weeks, she got her YES. "This was a much quicker response than can be expected from most magazine editors," she says wryly. "And it gave me almost as big a buzz as when, years ago, that first editor said he liked my story and wanted it."

Although no actual book titles were mentioned, they made much on the show of the fact that Lynne was a writer.

When I took out the two biggest sums in the first round, the Banker quipped that I had killed off my two main characters in the first chapter. I replied that I enjoyed twist-endings and spookily, my game ended with a very big twist.

Lynne watched the show in the local pub with friends. When she got home her answerphone was full. And in the coming weeks and months more money and sales resulted.

My website crashed because it received so many hits. Several magazines ran stories on my win and I sold several articles about it. Work came rolling in, especially when I said we'd spent the money on a motor home and would be travelling around the coast of Britain. I was asked to write about it and writers' groups from all areas asked me to speak or give workshops to them. *Deal Or No Deal* did far more than keep the bank manager happy.

Writers' Forum columnist and prolific womag short story writer Linda Lewis, too, found that her TV appearance reaped her more rewards than simply the money she won (though at £1350 that was very nice, thank you). Linda initially took on the challenge of a game show to tackle her shyness and, as she puts it, to "step outside my comfort zone".

She took courage in both hands and stepped as far away from comfort as you can get by braving Anne Robinson on *The Weakest Link.* Respect! Eh?

"I wasn't sure what would happen at the interview," she says, "whether I'd die of fright or not. I didn't. It was great fun."

Linda was filmed on Friday 13th – enough to make anyone twitch – and was understandably nervous.

Again, I was terrified, but it was the waiting around that scared me. From 10.45 until 2 p.m.we were kept busy with make up and wardrobe, and practicing saying our names (!). I kept running to the loo! Luckily once filming started I felt better and by round three, I was enjoying myself. I even had a chat with Anne – my, she's good at getting you to say things you really wish you hadn't.

Linda had told me I probably wouldn't recognise her because of all the slap they'd applied and the way her hair had been straightened. But I did – she looked terrific – and if she was shaking as much as she says she was, it certainly didn't show.

She came across as self-assured and smiley. Especially in view of the fact that her fellow contestants could barely answer a question between them. This meant she didn't grab as much cash as she could have done but she still won, has raised her profile, given herself a confidence boost and gained writing jobs through it since.

It was the then chairman Catherine Jones' idea to raise the profile of the RNA through TV.

Catherine took teams from the Romantic Novelists Association on to both *University Challenge* (I was deeply envious of her getting that close to the lovely Jeremy though immensely glad it wasn't me when I heard some of the questions) and *Eggheads*.

Judy Astley was one of the team members for the latter.

The idea was to get publicity for the RNA but the opportunity for personal publicity wasn't to be missed either as far as I was concerned. Always say yes, I reckon, however scary the gig. If you're a willing sort, you'll be asked again when other opportunities come up.

We had to stay overnight at a hotel on the A40 as we were first on the next day. Unfortunately there was another team there, men from Manchester and we got together with them and were all a bit silly over too much wine. So the next morning we were a tad under par. I think in hindsight "Don't Drink" is probably therefore rule one when you've got an 8 a.m. start.

Despite the slight morning-after-the-night-before feeling, Judy was fine after a dose of coffee and croissant in the green room and enjoyed herself.

The most fun bit was the one-to-one. You had to go beyond a screen that divided the studio and sit on a sweet homey cushion on a long bench, a few feet away from your opponent and Not Look At Them. I got lumbered with Sport, against a very grumpy sort called Chris. He wasn't at all pleased when I beat him.

There was one small fly in the ointment "having to say our ages along with our names. At least two of us lied."

The RNA was mentioned and talked about briefly on the show but although all the team managed to get in plugs for their books, these were all cut at the editing stage. Even their surnames weren't mentioned, so, as Judy says, you might think that publicity-wise on an individual basis, it wasn't that productive.

She was, however, surprised by just how many people had seen the programme.

A couple of years on I'm still meeting people who say, 'Oh I saw you on Eggheads...' One said she hadn't had a clue at the time who I was or what I wrote but she'd thought I looked good in the green cardi.

It wasn't their cardigans that caught the imagination of Jeremy Paxman when the Romantic Novelists hit the screens on *University Challenge*.

"We first encountered Mr Paxman when we were in the green room and he wandered in to gawp at us," says Catherine Jones, who writes as Kate Lace. 'So you're the Romantic Novelists,' he said. 'And none of you is wearing fishnets.' He sounded genuinely disappointed."

Catherine describes the whole experience as "exciting, exhilarating and completely scary". But worthwhile.

Of course it was all worth it in exchange for getting with in touching distance of Jeremy Paxman. I don't think he could believe that a team of romantic novelists would have cracked the really tough audition – and it was tough, hideous. Once we got into the studio he continued to be charming. Obviously we saw a different person from the one students and politicians get.

In retrospect it was the best fun ever and it was fantastic to make it through to the next round so we got to repeat it. Apart from meeting Paxo, the other 'best bit' was being made up by professional make-up artists; I really didn't want to take the slap off EVER. Those ladies really know how to make silk purses out of sows' ears.

Catherine, a retired army officer, went on with Anne Ashurst, Jenny Haddon and Steve Bowden – a Mastermind champion, Bank of England regulator and employee at GCHQ in their other, non-romantic fiction, lives.

They were very impressive and the aim of the exercise was undoubtedly achieved.

"Now whenever people (blokes usually) talk about lady novelists in a disparaging way," says Catherine with satisfaction, "the fact that the RNA got to the final, beating *Wisden* and *The Economist* en route, means I can usually shut them up..."

Being charitable

Sometimes, of course, one does things not to prove a point, or gain publicity, or even to sell books. But just because it is a nice and decent thing to do.

And those who believe that what goes around, comes around (in a good way, not in terms of come-uppance) may be interested to hear that whenever I have done something for charity the rewards have far outweighed the efforts I've put in and I've often carried on reaping the benefits for years.

I first met Hazel Cushion – the MD of Accent Press who is publishing this book – when she and Lesley Cookman were involved in fund-raising for Breast Cancer Campaign with the first of the *Sexy Shorts* short story anthologies all of which made money for charities.

Because I had contributed to the anthologies I took part in the Guildford Book Festival, which led to my presenting and interviewing for them which is a treat I enjoy every October and which has involved meeting lots of other, wonderful writers – some of whom have contributed to this book – that I just wouldn't have crossed paths with otherwise.

Standing on a box at Speakers Corner, yelling my lungs out, over the rumble of buses and the cries of hecklers was not something that felt like such a good idea when I was up there – especially when I forgot what I was talking about and the bloke at the back bellowed at me to "get off, you dyke" (charming) but doing that particular stunt for another charity gave me material for many a talk and cemented my friendship with the inspiring Rikki Arundel who helped me with the research for my third novel.

Supplying recipes for several charity cookbooks has taught me that I can in fact boil an egg, and the lovely people I've met when I've spoken at, been a compère for, or just donated some books to various fund-raising events, have always made it worthwhile.

Some writers get steamed up about other writers providing their words for nothing and I agree that in general you are not doing your fellow scribes any favours by churning out free copy willy-nilly, nor will you, perhaps, find yourself as valued as you might be (it is a sad fact of life that we tend to prize what we've paid hard cash for, over a freebie) and as a rule I don't do things for nothing unless there's a very good reason to.

I think raising money for important charities counts as one of those.

They loved me at speakers'
corner. 'Get off you dyke'
they cried.

Raffles & auctions

Which is why I must make mention of Anji Perkins. Anji is a woman of exceptional taste, who, at a Summer Ball to raise funds for Demelza House – the only children's hospice in the South East – bid for a signed copy of each of the books I've already published and a pledge to include her name in the next one.

I have given her a walk-on part in my current novel-in-progress but in case that gets eaten by a marauding billy goat or I get crushed by a bus, or the whole of the publishing industry grinds to a halt because we're all on twitter, I am going to flag her up here too.

Hello and thank you Anji! ☺

I am also going to type 'Marco Pierre White'. He didn't win a mention – I won *him*! In a raffle for the Journalists' Charity at a Women in Journalism Christmas party circa 2007. Which just goes to show that even brooding-looking chefs with allegedly filthy tempers (he seemed rather a sweetie to me) do a bit of good works too. In this case, offering themselves up to be interviewed over lunch or dinner at one of his establishments. (I am hoping it will also serve to remind him that we haven't done it yet.)

Which, I should make clear, is largely down to me not focussing on the matter and sorting it out. We have had several conversations by phone about the concept of meeting but, as yet, failed to arrange a date. But he was very nice the night I drew the lucky ticket, has been very nice since and I am looking forward to meeting him again when we do.

And that's got to be a long enough link in to this section...

Being nice

Being nice sounds obvious but you'd be surprised. "Don't, don't, don't – ever – be obnoxious," emphasises agent Carole Blake. "It is never forgotten. People talk, twitter, email: it's almost impossible to wipe out bad behaviour. If in doubt, think about ordinary rules of manners. It constantly amazes me that so many authors forget this."

I have to say, it amazes me too – that anyone wouldn't be polite and pleasant in their dealings with people they're depending on. But apparently sometimes they're not. Which is rather short-sighted.

You upset a bookseller, for example, at your peril. Phil Trenfield admits to removing all the books by one very well-known author and "putting them in the stockroom in a huff" after the female in question was "very diva-ish" and unfriendly and refused to sign a third of the books he had waiting for her because she had just had her nails done.

And he doesn't have anything very good to say, either, about the famous writer whose publicist later emailed to say that the great man would never come to Cardiff again because the carpet was shabby. "Like I should have re-carpeted for him?" asks Phil.

On the other hand he loves Carole Mathews and Catrin Collier – the latter won his heart by sending hand-written thank yous – and is full of praise for footballer Ryan Giggs who dealt good-naturedly with a queue of 600 fans when on a tight time schedule, and whose only request was for a glass of water.

You should always be good to fans, agrees Jill Mansell. "And always reply to messages from them. A disgruntled one can cause web havoc."

Jill Mansell also recommends being "gracious when people diss your books. Don't burst into tears or get into a fight!"

While actress and writer Helen Lederer believes in being equally nice to other writers. "I mean genuinely nice," she says. "It's a fraternity that can work for, or against you."

"Be polite, be attentive, take an interest in the people to whom you're talking or are helping you, no matter what their status," urges publisher Patrick Janson-Smith.

I don't know whether he's planning on writing any more books but if you want to see a real expert at this in action, then Terry Wogan is the man to watch.

It seemed as though half of Guildford had turned out when he came along to the festival to sign copies of *Mustn't Grumble* (Orion). Waterstones was packed. When he came down the stairs I was nearly knocked over by two old ladies. There was none of that po-faced "Name?" *Scribble.* "Thank you. Next," business going on here. Sir Tel looked genuinely pleased to see each new face, chatted, made jokes, posed for photos and gave every impression of someone who had unlimited time at his disposal.

I wanted to meet him in order to write about it but not being a great one for queues myself, I left and came back an hour and a half later to find the Wogan grin still intact. The adoration in the air was palpable. Two women actually curtsied.

A few yards away the same bloke who'd been lovingly gazing up at his idol when I left, "I've been listening to you since I was four ..." ("Your parents were very cruel," came the witty reply) was still there. "I could watch him all day ..." the bloke said.

TW had said at the beginning he would stay until everyone had been "satisfied" and he did. By the time I got to pose with him for a picture for my column, I'd got so caught up in it all I nearly curtsied myself, but managed to get a grip at the last minute and throw my arms around him instead. The girl wielding my camera had a bad case of camera shake so you can't see the alarm in his eyes but he stood his ground while I gushed about how good he'd been.

"It's my job," he said.

And it's ours too.

I held on tight so he couldn't get away

Be absolutely charming, no matter how people cock up. Smile, listen, be thrilled with anything from no hospitality at all, like somewhere to put your coat, to the table full of home-made canapés. Authors who grumble get a bad reputation

Katie Fforde, novelist

Serendipity

A job that can, on occasion, be made very much easier by a stroke of luck or fate.

I know the old quote about the harder one works, the luckier one gets (thank you Gary Player or Samuel Goldwyn depending on where you look it up) but there are times when one does just happen to be in the right place at the right time when the right person happens along (another reason to be smiley and agreeable as your default position because you won't always know they are the right person until later).

I was doing a signing in WH Smith Ashford once when a guy came in to buy a newspaper. I went into the full routine – this year's must-have, buy one for your wife, etc. – but he wasn't having any of it. If I want one, I can get your books a whole lot cheaper than that, he said.

It transpired his name was Ian Hall and he worked for a company called Waterside Books that supplied the onboard bookshops for all the cross-channel ferries as well as the shops in the docks and some cruise liners. Marvellous!

We had a bit of a chat and a laugh. He ordered my novels in, sold quite a few of them on vessels various and I signed my way from Dover to Calais and back on more than one occasion.

WH Smith was the setting too – this time in St Albans – when I met a lovely woman called Jean Hutton. I was promoting one of the *Sexy Shorts* books that time, but the manager had kindly ordered in a whole heap of both my novels too and was offering them on a three-for-two.

Jean came in, bought all three, took my phone number and booked me to speak at a charity lunch (and has invited me back since) where I sold a shedload more volumes. (And was given an orchid plant that has flowered for YEARS.)

Sometimes it's a short list for a prize or a book club selection that can come as a bolt from the blue and change your whole world. We are all familiar with the life-altering effects of the *Richard & Judy* Book Club with titles that had previously sold a few thousand copies rocketing into the bestseller lists, but that whole concept started in the States.

Carole Matthews saw her sales soar when her fifth book – *For Better, For Worse* (Headline) – was picked as a 'Ripa's Read' ("The most charming book yet. I adored it") on the USA television show *Live with Regis and Kelly* which was going out to 30 million Americans every morning. "It was right place, right time," says Carole. "It was the start of the whole chick-lit thing in the USA and Kelly Ripa swept in with a book club when Oprah had dropped hers."

Kelly Ripa was given the book by her producer who said something like 'we need to feature this, it's hilarious' and, fortunately for me, Kelly agreed. My publishers were given two days' notice of the announcement and, in that time, managed to print and ship 250,000 copies of the book. The announcement on the show went out that I was to be Kelly's favourite read for the month and a book that had been languishing quite happily on Amazon.com around 370,000 shot to number 3 by lunchtime of the same day. The book sold out in a week and went straight onto the USA Today best-seller list and the New York Times Extended List. It was like lightning striking my career and nothing you can do as an author can buy that luck. Kelly had been sent baskets of cookies, gold bracelets tucked in books – all manner of incentives to choose other authors' books – but, in the end, she simply picked a novel that made her laugh.

Carol also signed up with her US agent after a "a happy restaurant meeting of a friend who was working with her husband on game shows".

That is the wonderful thing about being in a game like this – however tired and dispirited you may get sometimes, however far your Writer's Bottom may spread or your books sales lag, there is always that tiny chance that overnight something will happen to turn everything on its head.

That possibility, however remote, is what makes this job exciting in a way that doesn't happen if you work in the local Building Society or Gas Showroom (even if you'd probably earn more there) and, for me, worthwhile.

Think about that when you feel it's all an uphill struggle.

We may not have the huge audience figures of the USA in this country but producer Amanda Ross – who brought us the *Richard & Judy* Book Club has brought a new TV Book Club back to our screens, hosted by such celebrities as Jo Brand and Gok Wan and as I write, Richard and Judy themselves have just announced a new book club of their own with WH Smith.

Being selected for either of the above or short-listed for a prize or featured in a national newspaper or on a major radio programme can happen when you least expect it.

But just in case it doesn't, it helps if we remain dogged.

Being determined

I'm aware that not everyone reading this will have published a book, or even written one. Or, indeed, will ever want to write one (sitting here at two in the morning, on my ever-expanding writer's bottom, suffering from a lack of sleep and a surfeit of chocolate, and the end STILL not in sight, I'm beginning to wonder if it isn't a little overrated myself).

You may want to be a different sort of writer we've heard of, altogether. If you aspire to be a poet or a playwright I can't help that much with the fine details – although all I've said about getting yourself out there will apply to you too. If you long to write film scripts or songwords I'm useless on that front as well.

But if freelance journalism is your bag I can tell you how I've built up a fat cuttings book. Or better still – I can let Kelly Rose Bradford talk about hers. It's fatter.

Like me, Kelly started out writing short stories for women's magazines. It was, as she says, "lovely, but it was never going to pay the mortgage".

In her hunt for more writing jobs she took to poring over the *Guardian*'s media supplement every Monday, and, one day in 1996, saw an ad for 'trivia writers wanted'. Kelly applied, not knowing exactly what being a trivia writer entailed, and for the next eighteen months or so wrote around 500 quiz questions a week for *Cosmo's Conundrum* quiz website.

"After a few weeks of doing it, I decided I was an expert on trivia, so I mailshotted every magazine offering my services as a quiz compiler. One responded (*Choice* magazine) and I have compiled their monthly quiz column ever since."

But really Kelly Rose wanted to be writing features, what she refers to as "stories about real people, interesting interviews with inspirational women, that sort of thing".

Her breakthrough came with 'real life' writing, when she came across a couple of stories she was able to sell to a weekly women's magazine.

Now comes the important bit of the story:

Also around this time I joined a fantastic networking group called Journobiz (www.journobiz.com) which was – and continues to be – a fabulous resource. I started networking like crazy and going to every PR event I was invited to (even if you didn't make any contacts you still got a free night of fizz & canapés, it was a win-win situation).

I joined the NUJ and WIJ. I invited established journalists for coffee and picked their brains. I started writing first-person pieces and capitalised on every bit of 'expertise' or interest I had. I had a baby – now a seven-year-old – who has been a constant source of inspiration through the years, from serious parenting articles, to light hearted first person pieces about negotiating birthday party one-one-upmanship and the playground mafia.

When he was two, I approached my local paid-for newspaper and asked if I could write a column about family life, taking in local stuff and my general news and views. They said yes. This lead on to doing local radio and taking on local copy-writing jobs as my name got around.

I used every opportunity to further publicise my work – every time I had a first-person piece in a national I emailed all the radio stations to see if they wanted to discuss it on air. Over a six-month period I posed nude for an artist, went organic, gave up my car for six weeks, spoke about my internet addiction and probably a ton of other stuff to boot and got booked to talk about it all on BBC Radio London. At around the same time, I confessed in the Daily Express to fancying Michael Portillo, something which was deemed so newsworthy the panel on Matthew Wright's Wright Stuff devoted a segment to discussing it.

I love this whole story but I shall just interject here to say that I saw Mr Portillo on the tube recently and actually Kelly's right – he is strangely attractive. But not very tall. I don't think he is anyway – he was sitting down at the time. I do like men to be of a certain height. Enough of that.

I like this story because it demonstrates just what can result from a concerted effort and the power of getting yourself out and about and noticed. Since I first met Kelly – we were in one of those *Sexy Shorts* anthologies together – she has gone from strength to strength and now pops up everywhere – a testament to the way she's made the right contacts and kept the pressure up.

She now writes on parenting and women's issues and does lots of first person pieces, regularly appearing in the *Daily Mail* and the *Daily Express*. Probably because she takes her own advice to "get your name out there and be brilliant at what you do – if you promise the earth to an editor, make damn well sure you can deliver it".

She still fancies Michael Portillo and says her key piece of advice for anyone wanting to make a full time career out of their writing is to "network like crazy".

I can only echo that.

NETWORK! NETWORK! NETWORK!

"I think networking is vastly over rated," says Suzanne Moore, columnist on the *Mail on Sunday*. "You can meet as many people as you like but in the end it comes down to whether editors like your work or not. Networking is really an excuse for writers to go and get drunk with other writers and pretend it's necessary. I have never got a job from being at a party. That doesn't mean you shouldn't go to parties. You should of course!"

I met Suzanne at a party. Although in fairness it wasn't a chance meeting. We were both there because we have a mutual friend in the *Metro* restaurant critic Marina O'Loughlin and she brought us together.

I first met Marina when she got in touch with me after reading one of my columns. It is through her introductions that I am thrilled to be quoting both India Knight and Trish Deseine in this book. The term 'Networking' can sound hackneyed and overused and doesn't seem at all right when you're talking about friends but that – basically – is the way these thing go.

At this same do where I first met Suzanne I also met some other friends of Marina's who happen to be neighbours of the novelist Maggie Alderson. I first got to know Maggie, by email, when I wrote to her after reading one of *her* columns, years ago, when she did fashion pieces for *The Times*.

Marina didn't know her at that point. And she didn't know me. Now we all know each other. So sometimes it's not really networking at all – it's just a small world.

Make friends and influence people Part Two

I don't think Networking is overrated. I think it's what makes things happen or at least helps them along.

I do totally know what Suzanne means about excuses to get drunk and of course she is absolutely right that ultimately whether you get a commission/a book deal/a shot at a slot will be down to whether your writing hits the spot with the relevant decision maker and not how many witticisms you've exchanged over the cheese straws.

BUT if that editor doesn't even know you exist, if he or she has never heard of you and your name is just one more amongst the 179 that week, who've been pitching articles and angling for book plugs, it's going to be that much harder to even get your work to that critical, appraisal stage.

So the basis I work on is that (sadly) I can't make anyone like the way I write – they either do or they don't – but I can, with a bit of effort and a fair wind bring about a situation by which, instead of hitting the delete button, they might just think, *Oh yes, her... the one with the funny hair that I talked to in the queue for the loo last night....I've got her card somewhere...*

Which is why I sometimes go to so many 'dos' I don't get any writing done (see section on learning to say no).

It was at one of these networking-type events that I first met Carole Stone, now the MD of YouGovStone and The Stone Club, the ultimate Queen of Networking, and author of *Networking: the art of making friends* (Vermilion) which is a good read. It was from Carole that I learned to be more organised about who I met and what I did as a result of that meeting.

"When you meet someone you'd like to see again," she advises, "take control and make sure you leave with their details and say you'll be in touch – don't just hand over your business card and wait for them to contact you."

When I first heard Carole speak she explained how she kept a database of all those she'd swapped cards with and debriefed herself after every outing – inputting who she'd met and anything pertinent about them. This is a good idea because you may think someone will be indelibly imprinted on your mind for ever but if you're anything like me it's very easy to come across someone's business card three months later and not have a clue who they are or even where you were introduced. Especially if wine had been taken!

Keeping a database

Carole uses a computer programme and I myself have started one using Microsoft's Access, (currently woefully in need of updating) but one computer crisis too many has taught me that, sometimes, paper and pen are best. As well as keeping details stored on my hard disk I use an old-fashioned index card system for anyone I don't want to lose. It is currently running at four plastic boxes each covering a quarter of the alphabet with each card containing all the contact details I have on each individual.

Of course these days it is much easier than it once was to 're-find' friends and acquaintances – there's twitter and Facebook and personal websites – but you cannot always re-establish a mobile phone number or a home address quickly so I take no chances.

I write anybody new on a card, back up my email address books regularly and keep a word document of all the numbers in my mobile phone too (those storage back-up things seem very complex, if anyone knows of a user-friendly one please let me know). The night I lost my mobile phone stands out in my memory as one of the most traumatic of all time – not only for the disappearance of a hundred plus numbers but the vision of some stranger surveying my drunken text messages.

Following up

When you do meet someone you'd like to develop a 'relationship' with, (this isn't dating advice – I am talking newspaper editors, agents, media gurus, the TV producer of the hot new book club, whoever it might be) I believe in striking while the iron is hot.

A quick "how lovely to meet you" email, with a low key reminder of any points of mutual interest will cement you in the recipient's mind if you do it the next day. If you leave it three months, they'll just think "Who?"

Something like:

Hello Fred

I enjoyed meeting you last night. As discussed, I'd love to write an article for **Teapot Times** *when my new book comes out. I'll contact you again in April...*

Should suffice. Or, if you didn't get as far as the nitty gritty:

Hello Fredricka

It was great to chat to you last night. Hope your hangover wasn't as shocking as mine. I was really interested to hear you were a producer on **Teapots FM**. *Perhaps I could talk to you in October when my new book,* **For the Love of a Good Spout,** *comes out....*

Most people usually respond I find, even if it's just with a couple of words (hopefully not including "off") and if you then keep that email, you can hit the reply button, when you do get in touch as promised.

This will act to subtly remind them that they've been in touch with you before, and act as an aide memoir of where and when.

This, by the way, is where having an unusual name helps. Being called Fortescue-Barrington-Smythe may be a mouthful when you're picking up the dry-cleaning, but it is more likely to stick in the minds of potential decision makers than 'Smith'.

I find most people remember they've heard of me before – in a way they probably wouldn't in quite the same way if I was just plain Jones.

So if you're a Tom, Dick or Harry (metaphorically speaking and no offence to any Richards, Thomases or Henrys reading this) then now might be the time to reinvent yourself as Luciana Luscious or Ferdinand Big-Boy, in the hope that it will still ring a bell in six months' time.

But whatever you're called, where do you go to meet these movers and shakers?

Where to go, what to join

As a minimum, I'd suggest, the Society of Authors, the Romantic Novelists Association (if you've got at least two people in your story and they've vaguely got the hots for each other) or the Crime Writers' Association (if you write – er – crime), some sort of journalists/press/media group (if you meet the criteria to join) and any other organisation you come across that has regular events and parties (I have just joined English PEN and am headed for their summer shindig).

Parties and dos

The main point of going to a party is to have a good time. And if you go along with that as your main objective then you very probably will. Anything else is a bonus.

However, I have to say that every time I have ever been to any party, gathering, conference, meeting, talk, drinks reception, or anything where more than half a dozen are gathered together, something good has come out of it. I've made a new contact or a new friend or been given an idea or discovered a fresh opportunity. Because if you talk to as many people as you can, it is very difficult for this not to happen.

Which is why there is little point splashing out on a new frock or jacket, paying to go there, and then spending the entire evening huddled in the corner with another new writer, comparing notes on how shy you are and how you wish you could get to write an article for *Buy My Book Monthly* when the features editor of that very magazine is standing a mere ten feet away.

You have to take your courage and business cards in both hands and go say hello. I know I keep saying it but – honestly – **the more you do it, the easier it becomes.** And I speak as someone who once upon a time could barely walk into a pub on her own and will now happily go to a party of hundreds where I know nobody but the host (thank you again Carole Stone).

Working the room

In fact, without wishing to sound too calculating, if you want to get maximum benefit from each outing – to make up for the travel costs, the angst about the jacket or the frock, the hangover and the three extra pounds you pile on from cramming canapés – you need to have a good look round and target who you want to talk to and make sure you do it.

How exactly do you strike up conversation with your chosen target? There are two tried and tested methods. One is to sidle up to the group where he or she is holding forth, and gradually shuffle your way into it, looking increasingly self-conscious, laugh loudly at his or her jokes and continue to nod and bob and hop from foot to foot until eventually they wonder who this simpleton is and smile doubtfully at you. You then say something arresting like, "Do you come here often?" Or, "Have you heard the one about the ferret and the fish-finger?"

Alternatively, you can simply wait for a suitable opportunity to catch his or her eye, smile, walk confidently towards them, hold out your hand, say, "Hello – I'm Fred." Making sure you do not actually elbow anyone else out of the way or interrupt in mid-flow. And apologising if there's any danger that you have. Do not then, of course, bang straight on about your books, your brilliant face for radio or the fact that you have had a long-held ambition to be photographed semi-dressed for the cover of their magazine.

Think up some other reason why you are thrilled to meet them – I love your magazine, I always enjoy hearing you on the radio, gosh what a gorgeous necklace and so on.

If you are lucky they will ask you what you do and then you can admit you are a writer. (Do not be downhearted if this is greeted with a sigh or a stifled yawn – features editors in particular get more than enough of us in their daily lives. Be extra sparkly to make up for it.)

There is a third way. Ask someone else to introduce you. I never mind doing this if requested. In fact I quite often offer to introduce new members of the RNA to The Fearsome One, when they're hesitating.

I see it as an essential baptism of fire. If they can get through five minutes under her gimlet gaze, they'll survive anything.

Suppose you don't know who anyone is? If you're lucky there'll be one thing that makes the whole process a lot simpler.

Wear the badge, Madge

There was a time when I felt daft wearing a name badge (especially when I forgot to take it off and was still wearing it on the tube) but I have now come full circle and much prefer the sort of dos where card and pin are proffered the moment you get through the door.

This is because a) I am rubbish at recognising faces from their byline picture/book jacket/TV show and b) because along with getting wrinkly knees and finding that menus need to be held at an arm-and-a-half's length to have a hope in hell of discerning the dish of the day, increased age brings the horrible realisation that one can no longer remember names like one once could.

Although badge-wearing means one does spend the entire evening looking at chests, it does mean you a) know exactly who everyone is (I once spent half an hour trying to impress someone I was convinced I'd seen on TV only to find that she'd just popped in to measure up for curtains) b) you know whether you've really met them before or you HAVE seen them on TV.

(The year I finally managed to procure an invite to the British Book Awards, I spotted a tall, blonde female smiling straight at me. I couldn't remember where we'd met, but knew I knew her, so I gave her a big grin back and mouthed "How are you?" and pulled a come-and-talk-to-me face. She smiled again and moved off. It was only when she appeared on stage to present the Play.com Non-fiction award with Ben Miller – someone was having a little ice-cream joke there – geddit? – that I realised it was Jerry Hall. Probably thinking, what is it with these women who want to pretend they know me?)

And c) it means when you forget what they are called only three minutes after you've been very clearly told their name, you only need glance back at their cleavage.

Many years ago, I met Jeffery Archer at the opening of a Haggis Factory in Glasgow. I noticed he called me – along with anyone else vaguely female – "love" which was clearly a ploy. And one I have tried to adopt myself.

However while one can get away with calling small children 'darling' on the first meeting, and I never find men mind it too much, one really needs to be on regular drinking terms with other adults of one's own sex before one can employ endearments only. (By which time, I hope, you know what they're called anyway.)

Even if you do manage to get through a whole evening calling everyone "sweetie" you're still going to break out into a sweat if called upon to do the introductions when someone else wanders up.

My husband once had a boss who used to recommend an imaginary stamp that would emblazon the name across the other's forehead and I have heard of a complicated system of association e.g. Brenda Big Teeth, Nobby No-legs or Terrance-the-Tattoo.

I'm not sure this would work for me and what do you do if they are non-descript, Doreen-mousey-hair-with-M&S-cardigan-and-boring-husband? Yolanda Yawn?

If they are important enough to you, you WILL remember their name, goes the thinking. (The guy, five years ago, who said I looked more gorgeous in real life than in the photo on my website, is called Alan ☺.)

The danger of canapés

Canapés are good because they stop you falling over; bad because they contain loads of calories and it's very easy, after several glasses of champagne to eat four mini-fish-and-chips without thinking.

I can only suggest if you go to a drinks party, hoover them up by all means – it will probably save you having a hangover in the morning – but don't go out to dinner as well.

Or if you do, ask for chopsticks. If the party was that good, you'll drop more than you eat.

Hangover cures

People often laugh at me at parties because I have a glass in each hand. One of them contains water and if you make an effort to drink lots of this as well as knocking back the vino, then it really does help you to stay sensible enough not to slur and ruin your networking chances, and also not to wake up feeling too ghastly.

If despite your best intentions you open your eyes groaning, I believe in Nurofen Plus and a fat girl's breakfast. Others go for orange juice or a raw egg (how that can possibly do anything apart from bring on projectile vomiting I do not know).

When I managed to blag my way into a press conference with Tracey Emin, I asked, in the absence of anything intelligent to say, for her favourite hangover cure. She said the best thing for her was being really happy.

So think back to all the contacts you made the night before, and how you're now a step closer to fame, fortune and the best-seller lists and you won't care about the fact that you're ready to throw up.

Being a party animal...

"There's no point being a writer and going to parties full of other writers," Simone Klass once said to me as we were sitting in a room chock full of the buggers. "You should go to events where you'll be the only one. Then you'll be a novelty and everyone will want to talk to you."

It was a good point and one I've never forgotten.

Writers' gatherings are great things to be at if you're after agents or publishers, want comradeship or to feel you're not the only one who's bonkers. But they won't necessarily lead to a boost in sales.

For while, of course, writers are readers too and in the main, a hugely supportive bunch – I certainly make a point of buying the books of my writer friends the moment they come out, as a gesture of solidarity, even if it's going to be many months before I reach that section of my teetering to-read pile (or years if the book in question is a Pseudo-erotic post-modern fantasy involving an alien with two heads) it still goes without saying that at a Society of Authors do or a Romantic Novelists Association party you are just one more coal in Newcastle.

And nobody will be desperately impressed that you've written a book because the guy in the corner's written 27 of them and sold more copies than you can shake a stick at.

So if you can embrace your inner party animal, now is the time to do so. Get yourself along to anything on offer. Charity receptions, fund-raisers, the birthday party of the weird bloke you went to school with who tracked you down on Facebook, the wedding you'd usually run a mile from, the opening of the new pie shop down the road. You never know who you'll meet and you may be surprised by how many of them are quite struck to meet a 'real' author.

Struck enough, one hopes, to order your latest when they get home.

But if you're shaking your head and the whole of this last section has brought you out in a rash, you are not alone.

Or not....

As you know, Lucy Mangan is a writer I've heard of and if you read the *Guardian* – or have come across her hilarious books – you'll have heard of her too.

When a reader called Mary Ann Marland from Grimsby wrote to me at *Writing Magazine* to say that although she'd started to get published she felt afraid to submit further work because it might mean having to socialise and for various reasons, she wasn't able to contemplate that, Lucy was the first person I thought of.

Her advice was robust. For the purposes of my agony aunt column, I took time to fillet this and intersperse it with my own soothing noises, but I will give it to you verbatim:

There is NO glamour or socialising to writing – or at least very little, and none at all if you don't want there to be. There is certainly no worry about it in connection with getting an agent or publisher – you just keep sending your work in by email and hoping for the best. And if you are both a brilliantly good writer and brilliantly lucky, one of them responds and you go to the office, have a chat and – all being well – sign a contract. I would have thought it was the perfect career for anyone who can only cope with the minimum of human interaction. I can't think of one that has less. Maybe pathologists or morticians but even they have to do a lot more standing up.

I added that even if you met a prospective agent or publisher in person, you wouldn't be advised to pin them into a corner and insist they listen while you recited your synopsis. You'd still approach them formally by letter or email.

As we've already said, it's ultimately going to boil down to whether they fall in love with your writing although I still cling on to the fact that if they do and have the choice between the much-loved writing of someone they've met and liked and the much-loved writing of someone they don't know from Adam – who-you-know always has the edge.

In the fairness of balance, however, I shall tell you that when I asked *Times* writer Carol Midgley if she'd got where she is today by meeting all the right people, her response was similar to Suzanne Moore's. "Networking has never really figured in my life," she says.

Carol arrived in London from Lancashire in 1991, "jelly-legged with terror". She'd previously been a reporter on various local papers in the north, when, knowing nobody but her boyfriend, she started doing news shifts on the *Daily Mail* and *Daily Mirror* which led to staff jobs on both in turn. She does however concede that when she wanted to move to *The Times,* she got an interview through a writer she knew there putting in a word with the news editor.

I have to say that my networking skills were zero. In those days – the mid 90s – you got to know people just by going to the journalist pubs after work and remaining there until closing time and then going for a curry. I don't recall many fashionable parties and I don't think I was EVER invited to a dinner party. But I think it's changed – I think who you know is probably more of an issue now. I'm not the best person to give tips on networking but people who are good at it always say that you should SMILE at all times and then people want to talk to you. But doesn't that make people look a bit mad?

The whole networking business does not make Lucy Mangan smile – madly or otherwise. Her further counsel to my *Writing Magazine* reader who worried her health would prevent extensive partying ran like this:

> I have no health complaints, I just hate a) people and b) my appearance so I am much happier indoors. Occasionally duty or desire means I go to a gathering of some kind. This never ends well, but I can always be proud of myself for making the effort. If I had a genuine excuse for going and sitting down in a corner at various points during the evening, I would seize it gladly.

Knowing how some readers take things literally – there was a minor rumpus on the letters page after I'd suggested that writing after a couple of hefty glasses of wine was worth a try – I was at pains to explain that Lucy was exaggerating and in fact looks great and is excellent company but I do know there are plenty of people out there who, like her, do not relish the prospect of a party in the same way as I do.

So take comfort from the fact that plenty of best-selling authors are rarely seen dancing till dawn and that there are many other ways of gathering potential readers to your literary bosom.

Building a readership

Jean Fullerton, as you may recall, is the novelist who writes Victorian family sagas set around the docks. When she was first published, she made a conscious effort to identify who her potential readers were and how she could reach them.

"The books I write may not reach the best-seller list but they are a very popular genre with devoted fans. Women who read sagas do so at a ferocious rate and are always looking for new books to read," she says.

Jean carried out some research and established that sagas are bought and read predominantly by women over the age of 40.

She then thought about which women in that group might like her books and where they might live.

> Like my own family, most of the old East End families who live where my stories are set were resettled after the Second World War in the new estates in places like

Barking, Dagenham, Basildon and beyond. As their children grew up and married they moved out further still into Essex. According to Essex County Council's own statistics, 1,340,000 people live in Essex and a huge number of them are baby boomers. Many are retired and have leisure time and money to buy books. If a quarter of them brought my books I'd be a very happy bunny.

Jean estimates that 4 out of 5 people living in Essex have East End ancestors and so they are potentially her readers. "Essex is the Cockney hinterland, as I like to call it, full of people with a personal interest in the area I write about and links to their own family's history."

Jean began by targeting the libraries in Essex to publicise her books, offering talks and events and found they were only too keen take her up on them.

By happy chance, it also transpired that Essex has the largest Women's Institute federation in the country. As she says, "So lo and behold, I had found a place where women with East End ancestry, aged 40 and upwards met on a regular basis." Thus her aforementioned speaking career was born.

Until Jean told me this, I had never thought about taking such a scientific approach but now I think it is terrifically good thinking.

Ask yourself, who is my *typical* reader. I have italicised typical because we all know that adults read children's fiction, straight read gay lit, 80 year olds sometimes enjoy the antics of teenagers and so on. For the purposes of this exercise think in generalities:

How old are they?

What sort of jobs might they do?

Where might they live?

How might they spend their leisure time?

And then the fifty thousand dollar question:

How can I reach them?

Scribble down any of the answers you can hazard a guess at now – right here

If you have concluded that your typical reader is an eleven-year old boy who likes adventure, you need to be offering your services to schools and sending out postcards to youth club leaders and the local scout master.

If you're aiming at 25-year-old women with a reasonable income, think how you can infiltrate the places they're to be found. Does the plush new gym chain have a place to leave postcards or a notice board? Can you chat up the owner of the trendiest wine bar in town? (When I co-owned a bar we had one of those free cards dispensers and it was surprising how often I refilled the section I'd commandeered as my own.)

Or to get to the fifty-plus male, brush up your speaking skills and get round the rotary clubs. Or find a company that organises corporate golf days and suggest that a signed copy of your book might make the perfect table gift.

Catherine Ryan Howard's book, *Mousetrapped*, is about the eighteen months she spent working in Disney World and she knew she needed to target other young people wanting to do the same. She got the job through a recruitment company specialising in US visas and Disney placements and so she started there.

> Shortly after publication I sent them a box of books for their staff and a stack of postcards, hoping they'd read the book, conclude that it might be helpful and pass out the postcards or leave them in the office where people could pick them up. I've no idea if they actually did this or not and it's impossible to measure sales from this area alone, but it couldn't hurt, right?

Right! It can never hurt. Because if just one person picks up your postcard and decides to read your book, who knows who else they will tell about it. Nothing I've suggested in this book can compare with the potency of word-of-mouth.

All we can do, is try everything in our power to kick start that process.

BURNING QUESTIONS &
COMMON CONCERNS

What shall I wear?

With all this talk of parties and getting out to meet your readers, your mind may, once again, be turning to matters sartorial. What to wear to a literary party, to meet your publisher for the first time, or to attend a book signing is something that keeps many an author awake at night.

"Dress well," advises publisher Patrick Janson-Smith, adding by way of explanation "appropriate to each occasion."

I couldn't begin to tell you what he means apart from to suggest you look as good and eye-catching as you can. But not to worry about it in the slightest because, as I have already suggested, if ever there was a time when the expression 'anything goes' comes into its own, its when you become a writer.

There is no group on earth with as diverse a dress sense. Put 50 accountants together and you will find 50 neat suits. At any gathering of authors you will see everything from T-shirt and jeans to floor-length chiffon with matching hat

Publishers have therefore long been braced to expect all sorts so, if you're off to meet yours, it simply depends what message you want to give.

Ancient skirt or trousers, cardigan gone at the elbows and run-down shoes indicate the need for a large advance.

Gucci handbag, Armani suit or Jimmy Choos demonstrate that you are above all that nasty lucre and care only for your art (or are an ex-model/WAG/Big Brother contestant ready to dish some dirt to help sales).

While arriving thematically attired shows you're ahead on the marketing campaign. (When Jill Hassall's *The World's Greatest Wedding Tips* was sold – now republished as *The Greatest Guide to your Dream Wedding* – her friends suggested she went forth in a plunge-necked, side-split, scarlet silk wedding dress, worn with killer heels, a long train and a couple of bridesmaids.)

I would suggest simply (and once more!) always wear something you feel fabulous in because then you have a fighting chance of looking that way too.

(Or something that shows off your magnificent cleavage – look what it did for Rosie Millard!)

My choice of dress depends very much on my mood so I can never decide what I want to wear until the very last minute. I therefore take at least three outfits with me if staying away while socialising/speaking. Typically this would be a Fat-day dress (insurance in case I wake up four pounds heavier – you'd be surprised how often that happens) a thinner-day dress (ever the optimist) and an embroidered tent in case neither are sufficient to cover my ever-expanding writers' backside. Plus a pair of jeans in case I just want to say, sod it.

But I have learned not to fret overly. For I now know two things. There will always be someone dressed even further up or down from whatever end of the spectrum I choose, and I will still look like a scruffy elephant if I get photographed anywhere near Joanna Trollope.

Joanna is lovely but much too slim & elegant to stand next to.. ☺

Photo by Roy Connelly

216

You might think, after all that, and in the face of such a variety of attire, that nobody would ever guess what you do. But short story writer Sue Houghton disagrees. She maintains there is definitely a writerly look which marks the authors out from the rest. "It's nothing to do with what they're wearing," she explains. "But the strange, far-away, glazed look in the eyes...."

I bought two frumpy suits from Jigsaw thinking this would make me look professional when in fact I looked like Miss Jean Brodie without the style.

Carol Midgley on becoming a journalist in London

Beauty tips and tricks

Never mind eyes, when I started asking other authors for their favourite beauty tips for those on the publicity trail, one word came up more than any other: **Teeth.**

"Get them whitened," said Judy Astley (who also offered the sage advice to always carry a toothbrush when on the publicity trail and to clean one's gnashers/check them for spinach, etc. before venturing in front of a TV camera).

I wouldn't be brave enough to have the laser treatment so popular these days because I've heard it leaves your teeth sensitive for a while and I can't tell you how much I hate that (this is the woman who takes Nurofen Plus and a stiff drink just to go the hygienist) but whitening kits work well – I've used the sort where you have a rubber mouth guard made and use little tubes of bleach stuff – and a sonic toothbrush with whitening toothpaste can work wonders.

"Get them seen to," counselled Linda Mitchelmore, "because when you're grinning broadly at these swanky events the gaps in your teeth will show in the pictures, especially when they are enlarged computer screen size!!"

I must admit I myself had a traditional black filling replaced with a white one when I kept spotting it every time I was photographed with my mouth opened indelicately wide – and Alison Penton Harper went further than that.

"Although I despair of our modern perfect-looks culture, I finally buckled at the age of 43 and had my teeth straightened," she confesses, explaining that her two front ones were "pretty wonky". She had always believed they lent her a "a certain quirky charm" until she found herself at a photo shoot for *Woman & Home* and overheard the test shots being discussed in hushed tones at the back of the studio.

"As an expert in earwigging other people's conversations, I caught a random phrase about '… teeth… shoot her head-on and we'll probably get away with it'.

A couple of weeks later, I took my Barclaycard to meet my new orthodontist, then wore train tracks for a year while she emptied my bank account."

I must say when I last saw Alison she did look pretty gorgeous but before you rush to have your own mouth braced to the hilt, she also offers this word of warning, "The downside was that I couldn't go anywhere near a camera (or a free lunch) for 12 months, and now that I have perfect fangs, nobody wants to interview me at the moment anyway."

I wasn't just thinking of you, dear reader, when I went canvassing for beauty advice. Having got up this morning, taken one look in the mirror and then spent half an hour on the internet looking for anti-wrinkle pillows, I am reminded once again how the rigours of a deadline can take their toll.

"I look old," I said gloomily to my son as he munched cereal and I sipped at Extract of Cherry, supposed to boost my collagen. "You are old," he replied comfortingly.

Faced with this encouragement and the knowledge that at some point, when the frantic typing's over, I'm actually going to have to get dressed again and take some of my own advice to scavenge for a readership (sorry – embark upon my publicity campaign) you can appreciate how I've been embracing the search for tips, tricks, and anything hailed as a quick cosmetic fix with a personal urgency. Since my own fount of wisdom on the looks front is limited and can can be summed up thus:

Drink lots of water
Get enough sleep
Have an eyelash tint
Don't rule out botox.

So I have just thrown the question open among my writing friends and colleagues – a sterling group, who can always be relied upon to drop their own work-in-progress like a hot potato for a chance to distract themselves with someone else's – hoping for a myriad of exotic potions and magical serums that have not yet reached my ears.

"Haemorrhoid cream," said Linda Mitchelmore briskly, "wonderful for sorting bags under the eyes."

Everybody else seemed to rely on hot baths and bracing walks which wasn't exactly what I was after. Past experience has taught me that both of these – depending on the time of year and water temperature – leave you either cold and red-faced or hot and red-faced but don't do much for crows feet.

Ignoring the witticisms about paper bags on heads and towels hung over the mirror, I am forced to accept that short of actual surgery, the best the collective intelligence can muster in this regard, comprises a large pair of sunglasses, lots of moisturiser and a heavy-duty concealer.

And perhaps acceptance that the root cause of one's sallow skin, spreading rear, and habit of blinking uncontrollably in sunlight is that the lifestyle of your average scribe, involving as it does, long hours spent on one's backside, squinting at a screen, chucking down chocolate and peanuts because it's quicker than lightly steaming a vegetable medley, and drinking unadulterated caffeine till one can decently hit the sherry, does not render one particularly wide-eyed and dewy.

Depending on your bank balance and principles you can accept this or consider something more radical.

Do I need a facelift?

I spent the first 40 years of my life saying I wouldn't dream of having any sort of 'work' done on my face (murmuring platitudes about letting one's character show, and other such nonsense) and have passed the last five wondering how I can decently re-mortgage the house without my husband finding out.

I used to be particularly vocal on the subject of botox – all that nasty poison being injected under your skin – ugh! Who would want an unnaturally smooth forehead anyway, and eyebrows you could no longer raise? When the phone call came offering me a free session in the interests of investigative journalism I hesitated for a nano second.

YES! I cried.

I knew I'd made the right decision when the photographer told me I looked tired. We all know that when you're the wrong side of 40 this means baggy-eyed and wrinkle-ridden. Bring on those needles.

It does hurt a little bit but I am a confirmed wimp so you probably wouldn't feel a thing and it does definitely smooth everything out even if it's odd not to be able to scowl in the way you used to.

Word of warning: having tried it once I can see how it could become compulsive. And it's not cheap. Worth it though if you've got something big coming up. Just be prepared to want it all over again when it starts to wear off. And to start thinking longingly of fillers, plumpers and lifters too....

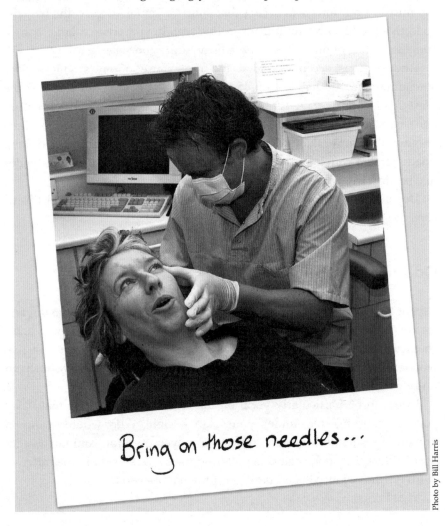

Bring on those needles...

Hair today, gone tomorrow

Even if your face is ravaged beyond repair and we've established it doesn't much matter what you wear, it's still good to go for one thing about your look that's going to be memorable – striking jewellery, fabulous shoes, funky handbags, wild ties – for which you can become known.

My signature seems to have evolved in the shape of my hair. Or as someone[17] said recently, "Where do you get your hair done darlin'? Traffic Lights 'R' Us?"

I take the view that anything that makes you stand out, is to be encouraged. I would favour wild hair, rainbow clothes or killer heels. But if you can't run to these you could take heed of my mate Tony Mulliken (thank you for that, sweetie) from Midas Publicity who advises helpfully, "be very pretty, very ugly, very thin or very fat."

Be very thin or ...

Losing weight

Talking of which, I don't know what possessed me to include this as a chapter heading. As I write this, I am close to deadline, swigging back wine, mainlining chilli peanuts and am beyond gross.

NB Chillis are supposed to raise your metabolism and cause you to burn more calories. I don't think it works when they're on nuts and you eat them by the packet.

I was going to talk about hold-it all-in garments and male girdles now. But I've rather lost heart. I'll just say if you're planning on being seen in public for one book – shortly after you've finished another – you might want to think about it...

Footnote 17: Thank you Eastcliff Richard, more of whom later

In the meantime, if the last few sections have had an overly female slant I shall now become thoroughly unisex and give you:

The internal combustion engine

I have to confess I have no idea what this really is. However, as I got several new and fervent male readers by explaining the offside rule in my first Wannabe book, I have decided to give it a mention. These days, everyone has cars that go and it's all done by computers (I gather), but in my youth I had a series of old bangers and became very adept at dealing with minor setbacks by variously whacking a solenoid with a hammer, spraying WD-40 about and fashioning new fan-belts from my stockings. I am still much better at analysing motor problems than my husband and can park better too.

Reverse parking

In fact, although I say it myself, I have been extraordinarily brilliant at this ever since a bloke called Chris Watkins took pity on my early hopeless manoeuvring and taught me about angles (having power steering does help too). If anyone would like to challenge me to a reverse parking competition for charity, (but preferably still featuring champagne and flowers for the victor), just call me up. I will win.

However, if you have no intention of venturing outdoors unless you have to and are of the Lucy Mangan persuasion "I can and do easily go eight days without leaving the house at all," then luckily, it is your era!

There's never been a better time to network and reach a readership without shifting your writer's bottom a single inch from the safety of your home.

Thanks to the enormous and ever-expanding power of The Internet...

THE INTERNET – PROS AND PROS

Today's authors have a huge advantage – a global market place on their doorstep. The internet gives you an opportunity to network with thousands of people who you could never dream of reaching without a massive marketing budget. Blogs and social networking offer free ways of reaching your target audience, an audience that not only consists of readers who might buy your book, but journalists hungry for a story, agents looking for the 'next big thing', publicity gurus, innovators and influencers.

Vanessa O'Loughlin, Director of Inkwell Writers Workshops and founder of www.writing.ie – the home of Irish Writing Online.

I must say straight away that when it comes to the internet and what they call viral marketing, I am no sort of expert. In fact it wasn't so very long ago I had to look the term up on Google just to see what it meant.

This is what I learned on wikipedia: *"The buzzwords viral marketing and viral advertising refer to marketing techniques that use pre-existing social networks to produce increases in brand awareness or to achieve other marketing objectives (such as product sales) through self-replicating viral processes, analogous to the spread of pathological and computer viruses."*

Which I took to mean – if you bang on about your books on twitter and Facebook often enough, someone might buy one.

(As long as you don't bore them so rigid that they block you, delete you, leave comments on blogs saying what a pain you are and post up the photograph of you asleep last Christmas with your head in the trifle).

Quite aside from my knowledge being rudimentary, the world of the web moves on so fast, that even if I were to attempt a master class on Twitter usage (generally amounting to: it may be good for networking but does not get books written!) or the power of streaming media via YouTube, by the time this book has hit the press all sorts of new features will have come along and all my witterings will be out of date.

So I am going to limit this section to a brief account of what I do, which isn't very exciting, and some examples of what other more internet-savvy writers have got up to – which might be.

If you need to know more, there are literally millions of words online on the subject of how to market yourself via the internet and thousands of books on the subject too.

It's worth finding out as much as you can because the thing about using the internet to spread the word about your books, yourself and anything else you're trying to promote, is that it's quick, it's cheap and if done properly reaches millions. With the world-wide web, the world – literally – is your oyster.

Websites

You need one.

The first thing any journalist, editor, researcher, producer or radio listener, who just caught your last sentence and wondered what you were going on about, is going to do when they have the faintest flicker of interest in you, is look you up on Google.

Your website is your shop window – giving a snapshot of who you are, what you do and why you're worth reading/interviewing/following up.

It's also a central place where ALL your information can be stored. Such as lists of your books, and how to buy them, links to Facebook, Twitter, YouTube or anywhere online you happen to be hanging out, articles you've written, how to contact you and what you look like.

The latter is quite important. Photographs make a website, bright and appealing. "Photographs are often underestimated," says Valerie Dwyer. "Considering that we decide about a person within about 3 seconds of seeing them, the right photograph is going to help you engage with your audience. People like to see who they are reading about. Think about when you read a newspaper or magazine. What's the first thing you look at? Words or pictures?"

As far as getting a website going is concerned, you can spend hundreds of pounds hiring a professional, or do it yourself with one of the many free or low-cost web-builders you'll find on the net.

However you go about it, get the best site you can manage/afford and take as much care writing/editing/tweaking the content as you would with any other piece of work. Have a look at other successful writers' sites to get an idea of what works. And put as much variety as you can on there. The more subjects you touch on, the more you'll pop up in search engines.

There are technical ways you can increase your hit rate too but I am not the woman to explain them to you. When researching this a couple of years ago I turned to Andy Harcombe, director of Web Net Marketing Ltd, who designed my own site.

"Think niche," he said. "The more niche your target keywords, the fewer competing sites and the more chance you'll have of being found." He then tried to explain Meta tags to me, which are – apparently – abstract or summary descriptions of the website or webpage and its contents, that are not displayed on a published page but are visible to search engines (programmed by someone who knows their html) and the comparative benefits of organic listings versus pay-per-click.

But I have to confess he lost me.

However, there is apparently a whole heap of information on such things on the web and if you use a professional to build your site he or she should be fully familiar with these terms and can advise you on how best to get noticed.

But there are other ways you can promote your site without specialist knowledge.

First, as I've said, keep bunging in the topics. "If you have an extra interest," says Lynne Connolly, "put it on. My site started as a place to show off my dolls' houses."

Sue Moorcroft used to get extra hits because her site made much mention of Malta – the setting for her first novel and her "favourite place in the world".

I get traffic, because my website has a page entitled 'Bugger the Diet'.

(And I'd probably get even more by calling it 'lose three stone in five days while eating crisps' but I'm still working on that one.)

While Sue Houghton over at www.suehoughton.co.uk, who is a contributor to the *Sexy Shorts* range of short story collections, says it is amazing how many hits the word 'Sexy' gets!

Sue also suggests including a site meter so you can trace who's visited your site and which pages are attracting the most interest, then you can build on those areas.

Sue Moorcroft – an assiduous self-publicist after my own heart – recommends contributing to blogs or forums that already get lots of hits, e.g. discussion boards on national newspapers or the blogs of more famous authors, and always signing off with your web address. "You do run the risk that they'll delete the URL but most of them don't bother," she says.

This is really good advice – if you can say something fascinating or controversial enough, readers may well want to find out more about you.

Sue puts her web address on everything she possibly can – letterheads, bookmarks, flyers, invoices, cards, emails, etc. – as I do.

If you get anything published anywhere from the parish magazine to a national glossy, always ask for your web address to be put at the bottom.

If you've got a new site, email everyone in your address book and inform them – begging for a link to it if they have one too (which you will then of course reciprocate).

Once you get the visitors, you need to keep them coming back and telling others too – as we've said ad infinitum, nothing works like word of mouth.

Romance Queen Kate Walker at www.kate-walker.com, gets tens of thousands of visitors to her site from 111 countries.

"The important thing is to keep it up to date," she says. "Keep adding in new things, even if little changes."

Many writers encourage visitors to sign up for a newsletter and this is an excellent idea, too.

Newsletters

On www.trishaashley.com you can sign up to receive Trisha's Skint Old Northern Woman newsletter. "And yes, there are some SON Men, too!" she says. Trisha explains:

The newsletter was born several years ago as a kind of thank-you to my core group of faithful readers, a way of giving something back for their support. I felt this was important, because I had a couple of years when my books were only available in expensive library hardbacks and yet still they bought them – and not only that, but in many instances, then paid to have them shipped out to the USA, Australia, New Zealand, South Africa… And the great thing about Severn House library editions is that my books are now in many libraries in all those countries, too, which has led to even more readers and SONW members...it snowballs. Now my books are available as Avon HarperCollins paperbacks and much more easily available, so that means even more SONW joining in.

Agent Carole Blake also believes in newsletters, or anything like this that offers 'added value' or special content, so that fans feel they are getting something extra. So much better, she says, than 'hard sell' messages on twitter or Facebook.

Valerie Dwyer agrees. "When people appreciate you, you need to appreciate them in return. If you're publishing your own newsletter, you can let your fans know when you are launching new work or invite them to events, which you'll encourage them to share with their own networks, which spreads the word exponentially!"

Trisha has found her network of fans has certainly expanded. "A newsletter is a two-way thing," she says, "and you get back loads of lovely mail. We all share a sense of humour: I have the biggest group of friends in the world and it is still growing."

I don't do a newsletter – yet – but I do have regular live chats with my readers on the Wannabeawriter website and this too has led to real friendship. There is a core group who chat most Sunday mornings and at the time of writing we are shortly going to meet for our fifth lunch (if anyone wants to come to the sixth see www.wannabeawriter.co.uk for the details).

To blog or not to blog

My mate Kevin Machin who's a bit of a nerd (I mean this in the nicest possible way, Kev), and responsible for the whizzy new Wannabe site that I hope will be up and running by the time you're reading this, tells me that blogging as a verb originally derived from the noun blog which was an abbreviation of 'web log', the term used in the early days when a blog was little more than a personal diary.

Now, they have become big business. While some people still just blog about what they had for breakfast, others have found an individual slant or quirky take on life that has led to millions of readers following their every word.

"Blogging," says Kev, "is possibly the most versatile way for a writer to network on the web. Once you start blogging, you'll start to connect with a large number of fellow bloggers. Before you know it, you'll be having difficulty keeping up with everything. Blogging can consume a huge amount of time, if you allow it to."

This is why I don't do a blog yet either – frankly I have enough trouble finding the hours to do the work I'm paid to do – but those that do, swear by them. And uplifting cases of blogs bringing widespread fame and spawning lucrative publishing deals are now commonplace. Indeed, companies like *The Friday Project* exist solely to search for the best of the talent on the web and develop it into books.

At the very least, if you're good at it – and you should be, you're a writer – it will almost certainly bring you a heap more followers and fans.

Lynne Connolly suggests joining "a big blog" if you can't face the work of setting on up on your own. "You get all the advantages of people hitting it for the big names and finding you." But Catherine Ryan Howard maintains that starting a blog is simple business.

"You can host a free, easy-to-use blog on Wordpress.com; their templates look really professional. I also paid $15 for my own domain name – www.catherineryanhoward.com instead of www.catherineryanhoward.wordpress.com.

The most successful blogs often have a particular theme and Catherine used blogging to generate interest in her self-published *Mousetrapped*:

> I blogged about every aspect of the self-printing experience, all the headaches and stress-fests along the way. This not only introduced people to my writing but it also generated a bit of a buzz; people knew the book was coming out and they were interested to see how it turned out after my tribulations. Also, it gave me something to blog about – I didn't have to rack my brains every week for something to write.

Hazel Gaynor had been made redundant when she joined Vanessa O' Loughlin's 'Inkwell Web Wise Workshop', hoping to start a new career as a writer. Vanessa told me:

> She found out how to create a blog, thought about her niche and developed her brand, taking every opportunity to write, both her blog www.hotcross-

mum.blogspot.com and a novel. Now she's blogging for *Hello* Magazine, was listed in *The Independent* top 50 Mummy blogs, was interviewed on Irish National TV, is writing for the *Irish Independent* and has found an agent for her book.

Wow!

So, if you're going to blog – if one who's never done it can make so bold – once again do think about your angle. Rather than just cataloguing how many cups of coffee you've had and the colour of your new slippers, think of a persona or subject matter.

Whether it's fatherofthirteenbrats or motheronthegin, granny-withattitude or Mybodilyfunctions.com (perhaps not the last one, I'm a tad squeamish), try to think of an area where you're going to have plenty to say and it hasn't been done to death.

Take as your inspiration, perhaps *Wife in the North*, the blog turned best-selling tome by Judith O'Reilly or something like *Shit My Dad Says*, the brainchild of Justin Halpern, which started life as a twitter feed and is now a book, a TV show (and probably by the time this book hits the shelves, a blockbusting film, screen saver and video game with matching mugs and T-shirts).

(If something has suddenly sprung to mind write it down here NOW)

Be daring, be bold, and if you really want to have a bit of fun and let it all hang out, you could always try:

Anonymous blogging

If you want to add a little mystique to your blog or you're afraid of what others might think, you can do it anonymously or adopt a fictional persona. Then you can have all the excitement of 'coming out' when the time is right.

Brooke Magnanti became *Belle de Jour* for her blog about life as a call girl – and is now famous for the five books and three television series that have resulted.

If you have a Twitter account or read *The Bookseller* you may have come across the hilarious 'Miss Daisy Frost' a literary agent with 'The Edward Cecil Literary Agency' who began the blog because "it was time to tell the world what publishing is really all about" and who offers such gems as "to be honest, publishers are rubbish at negotiation" and "surely no agent would commit career suicide by 'fessing up to drug-use and going a.w.o.l. Oh no – we leave that sort of behaviour to editors every time."

By dint of much exhaustive stalking of Miss Frost, I was able to glean some exclusive insights into her role as an agent and some valuable advice for all of you which is going to fill another page nicely. (We shall ignore her reference to me as "Jane Whenindoubtgeteveryoneelsetowriteyourbook-foryou-Jones")

> My writers are expected to whore themselves around to every opportunity put to them – from library events in Barnsley to arena-sized residency at the O2. These days it isn't enough to write a good book – you need to tell the world about it at every opportunity. Of course if any really juicy opportunities come my way like, say, an invitation for one of my clients to appear on *Newsnight* or the *Today* programme then I immediately tell the producer that my client is far too busy but that they have insisted that I appear instead. Even better if there is a fee attached. My ego and my bank-balance both expanding at once. Kerching!

Asked for her top dos and don'ts she was – eventually – also forthcoming:

> DO – always tell the press and any writing groups you talk to about how you were discovered sleeping in a doorway somewhere under a copy of your manuscript and that your brilliant agent, Miss Daisy Frost, plucked you from penury and that

you are now living in a flat-fronted Georgian house in Holland Park with a statue of your agent in the garden.

DON'T tell anyone what you are really earning as a writer – always add 100,000 pounds to the real figure.

Miss Daisy's reputation has spread so far that she has even been mentioned in an editorial by the Literary Editor of *The Times*, Erica Wagner, and as I write *"I am the real Miss Daisy Frost"* badges" are changing hands at a vast price (I am so glad she sent me mine when they were still two a penny). A fat book deal, brokered by herself, presumably, must be just around the corner.

For a sample of this compelling blog that ticks all the boxes, see http://missdaisyfrost.blogspot.com

Totally different but just as funny is the Eastcliff Richard blog, started by a DFL (Down from London) in Ramsgate when he moved to the seaside back in 2005 and began living on the East Cliff...

For his blog *"Squeezing the news pimple on the arse of Thanet"*, he has reinvented himself "as a naive parvenu, a fading celeb and champagne socialist millionaire-about-town," with walk-on parts for his security man Fat Kev, his agent Bev, and 'my factotum Mr Ceaucescu' (no relation). He tells it like this:

> Being a writer by trade, I could knock off a quick blog post in my coffee break. As I don't ordinarily do humour, it also gave me a chance to indulge myself in another style of writing. Initially, the only audience I really wanted to amuse was myself. But the blog soon attracted attention. It was one of only two in Thanet at the time (now there are hundreds), the other being run by a rather pompous Tory councillor-in-waiting. So I began taking the micky out of him, and then our Tory council. Another good reason for remaining anonymous.

And he does go to quite some lengths to keep his identity hidden. I first met 'Richard' when I wanted to write about him for my *Isle of Thanet Gazette* column and having become mates with him since, have been amused to discover the extremes he went to, to disguise his true appearance at that first meeting.

It has obviously made him some enemies and the local council are none too pleased, but the blog gets thousands of visitors, has made the top 500 on the wikio list and been an internet pick in the *Guardian*, and ECR has only been threatened with libel action four times! (Happily he has an old chum who is one of the country's top media lawyers.)

I asked him for his pros and cons of doing things under a pseudonym.

1) If you fancy being controversial, you can more or less say what you want (within the laws of libel). Ordinarily I'm a rather shy and retiring chap, so it gives me the freedom to experiment and get it wrong without having to take the criticism too much to heart. People slag me off (I've lost count of the number of times I've been called a paedophile), it's the nature of blogging. But they're not slagging me off, they're slagging the character off, so I can live with it.

2) The mystique can create a whole following in itself. Soon after I began, one of the local papers ran a 'grass-him-up' phone line. You couldn't buy that sort of publicity. People were gagging to know who I was, with all kinds of theories being touted about. As the truth would be rather mundane, I prefer to keep the mystery going, rather like Morse's first name.

And the cons?

3) One of the pitfalls of creating a fictional character who writes about the real world is that sometimes the two can get horribly blurred. Clearly there's a lot of the 'real me' in Eastcliff Richard. But he often says outrageous things that I wouldn't dream of espousing even in my drunkest moments. Then the 'real me' comes into contact with the people the 'fictional me' has slated, and actually quite likes them. Consequently my list of targets has been diminishing over the years.

4) Don't, whatever you do, think that being anonymous can help you with libel. There are ways of tracking you down, and, as we all know, the UK has the most convenient libel laws on the planet for those doing the suing. It might put them off if they have to spend a heap of dosh finding you first, but if they're serious they will, and then they'll take your house. Remember, it's the only law on the statute book which assumes the defendant is guilty until said defendant has mortgaged his or her arse proving otherwise, and even then he or she will probably lose.

5) By far the biggest con is that my experiment in anonymous blogging has never paid off. I can't 'monetize' (to use an awful Americanism – it means place ads on it), as I'd need to give my host Blogger my real bank account details. I've done one or two bits of investigative journalism based on it, but they've been low- or no-paid. I do a strip for the local paper based on it, but they don't pay a bean.

I always hoped I'd be spotted for a Belle de Jour-style book deal. But that hasn't happened either. Sniff.

Ah well, it might happen yet – in the meantime, entertain yourselves here too www.eastcliffrichard.blogspot.com

Going on a blog tour

Kate Walker had a 'blog party' to celebrate the publication of her 50th title – *The Sicilian's Red-Hot Revenge* (Harlequin Mills & Boon), inviting various other authors to contribute and offering signed copies of their novels as prizes in a competition. It was great fun, word spread and it was hugely successful in bringing us all new readers.

Nicola Morgan went a step further and went on a 'blog tour'. I'd never heard of one of these, but it sounds a fabulous idea.

As an award-winning author for teenagers and a blogger for writers wanting to become published (see www.helpineedapublisher.blogspot.com), Nicola has written over ninety books including many story and maths volumes for use in schools and for home-learning. When it comes to her twelve "proper full-length ones," she says she approaches each book's promotion differently.

For Wasted, a blog tour sprang to mind for two main reasons. First, as a blogger and internet nut myself, blogs were comfortable territory for me; I already had contacts amongst bloggers and Twitterers; and I'd already decided to set up a blog especially for the book (though that's not necessary for a tour). Second, I already had lots of ways of contacting schools, where my existing readers mostly were, and wanted to open up a wider conversation. One point against a blog tour is that it's not the best way to reach schools, because school computer servers usually block access to blogs...

My part-time assistant, Catherine, identified relevant bloggers who might be interested and she set up a diary of about 20 blogs I'd visit on different days. They could either interview me or ask me to write on a particular topic, and probably half chose each. My publishers sent each blogger a free copy of Wasted well in advance. They all wanted to review it, which we had not asked for, and most put their reviews on their blogs separately from the actual date of my "visit", so that doubled the exposure. Then, once I'd written all the material, it was simply a matter of making sure I visited the blogs at the right time to add and reply to comments. We also all added the links to Twitter and did what we could to drive traffic to all the blogs.

Did it work? I don't know how to measure it but it felt very positive. It certainly generated many 5-star reviews on Amazon, because most of the reviewers added their reviews there – this was not something we asked for but was obviously wonderful. I think the benefits came because the bloggers did like the book so much and said so, a lot, and used their own networks to pass it on. They really talked about it and I know that Wasted was bought by many people who very likely would never have heard about it. They, in turn, mentioned it on Twitter or their own blogs. But it's early days as I write this (the tour still hasn't finished) and I have no idea about the long-term impact. It was fun, though, and I'd do it again, though I might spread the visits out more.

The main benefits to this type of promotion are: it's free; you meet more people and make contacts that could have big effects; you reach new readers; you don't have to leave your desk but can do everything at a time to suit you. (I was even moving house in the middle of all this!) I know I had help, but this was a big tour and complicated, and it would be perfectly possible to manage a less intensive one without it.

I think this is a really inspiring tale and I love the idea of doing something like that. Take a look at Nicola's www.talkaboutwasted.blogspot.com to get a bit more of a flavour of how she works.

I don't know about you but I'm convinced, and I think we can conclude that blogging is A Good Thing. Just beware – if you are yet unpublished – of becoming one of those bloggers who writes 2000 words a day on their blog about how they wished they had time to write a novel!

NB If you are as technical as I am not, and the above has been all too waffly and you're crying out for some hard jargon, Kev has made one of his nerdy tables, summarising the "main components of blogging" (wot?) just for you:

Component	Description	Purpose
Account / Profile	Most, if not all blogging facilities need you to have a log-in account in order to post articles and to leave comments on other blogs. Some allow anonymous blogging but these are becoming rare due to attacks by spammers and other annoyances.	Your log-in account allows you to have a personal blogging profile. As with Facebook, you can make some of the information in your profile public and keep the rest of it a secret. It is up to you to decide how extrovert or introvert you want to appear.
Blog	Each account can have one or more blogs associated with it. This effectively means that you can "own" several blogs, if you want to. Some blogs can be set up as group blogs, shared by several contributors, for example: to collaborate on projects or subjects of interest.	The blog is essentially a repository for all of your articles (posts). They are usually arranged in reverse-chronological order, i.e. latest first, making it easy to keep up with new things. The content and subject matter are entirely up to the owner(s) of the blog.
Comment	Nearly all blogging facilities allow other bloggers to make comments on the articles posted there, though this option can be disabled if required.	This is where all the networking comes in. You leave comments on other people's blogs and they come and leave comments on yours. This is how your circle of blog friends will increase.
Side-bar / Gadgets	A popular, though optional feature where you have a second display column running vertically parallel to your articles. This column, or side-bar as it's known, contains a number of gadgets (sometimes called widgets). There are a huge variety of gadgets available from the blog service provider and from third parties. You can even write your own if you're a JavaScript nutter like me.	Gadgets can have all kinds of purposes and functionality, too numerous to list here. For example, a popular gadget is known as the **blog roll** – a list of hyperlinks to other blogs that you want to endorse and encourage other people to visit. These obviously assist the process of networking. Gadgets can be informational, practical, fun, financial and many other things.

Facebook

I am beginning to think that in the same way that I believe that everyone in the world is intrinsically either a cat or a dog person (irrespective of whether they keep both or neither) so it is the same with Facebook and Twitter. We might do both but our heart belongs to one or the other.

I adore Twitter.

I do Facebook but I don't do it properly. I never quite understand its intricacies – there are walls, and messages and postings and thumbs up and down that all seem unnecessarily complex – and just say yes to everyone.

So if you want to be my friend on Facebook – do come on down. Unless you have particularly mad eyes or list your hobbies as stalking and chewing on kittens (I am a cat person) I'll accept you.

And even if you do have strange attributes, you might still get away with it because if I'm busy I don't even bother to read the profiles, just hit the confirm button.

I can do this because I don't share anything particularly personal, don't put up photos of myself (tho there are plenty up there because others have – thank you, pals, so much for the ones where I look a chump!) and only really go on there at all when someone speaks to me and I get an email alert to say so.

OR when I have something I would like to impart to as many people as I can get hold of, e.g. I have a new book out.

This isn't terribly subtle and I really should make an effort to get to know how to work it all a bit better. I did manage to start a group once – Tomato tops are scary to Arachnophobes – and it gathered 116 members, but I have never really got to grips with all the finer points of what else one can do.

My main problem with Facebook is that I have an aversion to asking anyone to please be my friend in case it makes me look needy and I tend to get confused between friend requests and friend suggestions when I've had too much wine and then feel a bit of a dick. (If anyone knows how to 'undo' a friend request you've made by mistake, please tell me now.)

For those of you who are a little more switched on and will appreciate what she's talking about, I offer you Catherine Ryan Howard's take on Facebook instead.

Facebook isn't anyway near as useful as Twitter (at least, I haven't found it to be) but it's free and every little helps; you may as well use it. Establish a fan page (or 'community page' as FB recently started calling them) for either you as a writer or a specific book of yours. People will then 'like' your page, becoming a fan.

As soon as you set it up, tell all your existing, People You Know in Real Life Facebook friends to hurry over there and click the 'Like' button. You'll get an instant fan base and avoid the humiliation of having seven fans for a fortnight.

The main benefit of having a Facebook page is that you can update your fans/people you're related to in real time. When you update your status, all fans will see it in the home page when they log in. You can also send email updates to all fans with one click. You can also upload photos and videos, invite people to review your book and set up events.

For the tech-savvy, Facebook has an application called FBML which is like HTML but just for Facebook. It gives you more freedom over the appearance and content. You can use it to put a Paypal button on your page, enabling you to sell direct from there also. On my page,[18] I have a Paypal button and links to Amazon.

Get yourself a Facebook page, not an account. You'll need the second to get the first, but after that, focus on the page. People will be more inclined to become a fan of a page or a book than 'friend' a total stranger, and you want to keep all your content public. Also, FB limits 'friends' to 5,000. Well, we can dream, can't we??!!

If, like me, you are now boggling slightly, let us see how Facebook can work in real practical terms.

When Victoria Connelly's first UK novel, *Molly's Millions* (Allison & Busby), was published, she used what she calls "the truly amazing networking opportunities of Facebook" to swell the numbers at her launch party.

Up until then, I'd only been published in Germany where it was hard for me to visit and see my books in the shops so I wanted to celebrate in style with a launch at Jarrolds in my hometown of Norwich. I got in touch with some of my old school friends via Facebook and loads of them turned up on the night to support me.

It was amazing to see my novel in a UK bookshop at last but it was my dear friends – whom I hadn't seen for over 20 years – that really made it a night to remember. They all bought lots of copies of my book – enough to make Molly's Millions the number two best-seller in Jarrolds that week – catapulting me ahead of John Le Carre, Maeve Binchy and Stephanie Meyer.

Footnote 18: Catherine's page is http://www.facebook.com/mousetrappedbook.

I think this is lovely. But if you'd rather get back to the nerdy bits, Kevin has made you a table about this too!

Feature	Description	Advantages	Disadvantages
Status	Each status update says what your current state of being or thoughts are. A bit like Twitter Tweets in their nature.	Probably the easiest thing to change and update in Facebook. Other users can reply to specific status updates and the context is maintained. The simplest and most obvious advantage over Twitter, in my view.	The persistence of status updates is relatively short, so you shouldn't put information of any real importance there. In any case, Facebook will reset your status if it's been unchanged for several days.
Wall	A kind of electronic chalk-board where people can post text, videos, pictures, hyperlinks and other media.	They are easy to use and everyone has their own wall on their user profile pages. A rich set of multi-media can be attached to wall postings.	It's a kind of "file and forget" system, in that no context is maintained. Older posts drop off the bottom of the wall. This means that information on the wall has no real longevity.
Groups	A group is a forum for like-minded users to share their thoughts and discussions about a particular subject. You can also put photos and videos there.	Groups have a wall but also a discussion board, which is a collection of topics and their subsequent replies from users discussing these topics. These have better context retention and longevity than walls.	Many, many groups have a very transient and/or frivolous theme behind them. Consequently there are a huge number of groups on Facebook that have ended up effectively defunct.
Fan Pages	Fan pages are a mini-platform where individuals, groups, societies, or even specific products can be promoted. They are similar in nature to personal profiles, but designed with marketing in mind, rather than just social networking.	Ideal for writers to put themselves "out there" in a manner that's 100% controlled by themselves.	There's no real restriction on who can create fan pages. For this reason, they are akin in some ways to self-published books. Fan pages can be about great writers and their books, or equally about some jumped-up quacks trying to sell their snake oil.

Twitter

I prefer Twitter to Facebook because you don't have to ask anyone to love you, you just tweet away and hopefully, others, off their own bat, decide to follow you and keep up with your inane outpourings.

You are also limited to 140 characters per utterance so you don't lose your life there – in theory. Although in practice it is quite easy to get up at 6.a.m find it is now 11.10 am and all you have achieved so far is a lengthy exchange of witticisms about flowerpots with a food writer from Surbiton who you don't know from Adam.

I won't go into tortured explanations of how it all works, because if you haven't found out by now, you soon will have done – it is a constant source of wonder that any books are still being published at all, for every other writer, agent and publisher seems to be on Twitter too.

I joined because The Fearsome One had been going on about how I should be writing a blog – "give writing tips or something" (I now do this too, see http://twitter.com/UWannabeawriter) – and appeared unimpressed with my whining that I wrote four regular columns already and would rather have a lie-down.

And because I kept hearing about other people having 5,000 followers, I was feeling vaguely left out and wanted to see how many I'd get.

The answer turned out to be three. I joined on Tuesday and by Wednesday could still only count my sister, Kev – who is naturally spot-welded to his keyboard 24/7 – and, interestingly, someone I'd never heard of. How she knew I was there is one of life's little mysteries.

I have a few more than that now. Twitter – find me at http://twitter.com/JaneWenhamJones is my new solitaire, and while I shall leave you to find out for yourself what an RT is and how to shorten urls and use twitpic, I will share with you the lessons I have learned.

1) **Don't get stressed** if you can't keep up. In the beginning, I thought I had to read every single tweet and it was taking all day. Then @marinametro (Marina O'Loughlin) put me right with something she'd got from @rhodri (Rhodri Marsden). Namely, you treat it like a cocktail party. You pop in, chat to a few people (work the room, if you like!) and pop out again. You don't expect to be privy to every conversation that happened before you got there or to continue to

know what's being said after you left. I had a lot more time after she told me this.

2) **Don't be cynical.** There's always plenty in the press about how we don't form proper relationships any more but spend our whole time on networking sites and emailing people we met in dubious-sounding chat rooms, but taking a less jaundiced view reaps rewards. I have at least a dozen honest-to-god, flesh-and-blood, hug-hello-and-go-out-to-lunch-with pals whom I first hooked up with on the internet

3) **Don't tweet after wine.** Once upon 4 a.m. brought: Omigod what did I say? Now it's: Oh my God, what did I tweet? (The answer can be sobering)

4) **Don't tweet too much:** 1000 tweets at an average of 20 words a tweet is... a quarter of a novel.....

5) **Or too little** – do engage with other people and comment on what they're saying, rather than giving hourly bulletins on what's in your sandwich

6) **But do let your personality shine through** (even if, like mine, it invariably involves toast and marmite). As Suzanne Moore says, "You can use Twitter to build a brand but on the whole it doesn't work unless you have a feel for it which is why so many politicians are rubbish at it. Tweeting 'I went to a constituency meeting in Bedfordshire' hardly gives you a glimpse of someone's inner soul."

7) **Don't keep on about your books** – it's bad form and boring

8) **Do remember it's public** (unless you have protected your tweets). @katiefforde summed it up thus, "I kind of want to use twitter like a diary, and express my innermost thoughts. But then Google will make them look really silly." (And if a prospective publisher/agent takes a peek you might also make yourself look off-puttingly barking.)

9) **Don't panic.** If you do wake sweating, you can a) hastily delete any ill-advised confessions b) comfort yourself with the fact that if everyone's following point 1) not many will have seen it.

10) **Overall verdict:** very easy to make a prat of yourself but all so fast-moving it will soon be forgotten

Twitter is also incredibly useful as an instant source of information on anything you care to name. Whether you want to solve a crossword clue or find out where you can buy a left-handed egg whisk, there will always be someone, at any hour of day or night, who knows.

As a journalist, you can also get an immediate feel for what everyone's thinking – about a particular unfolding event or story, and hear about it as it happens.

"Increasingly it is valuable as a news source," says columnist Suzanne Moore. "No exclusive lasts longer than 3 minutes because of twitter."

It's also great for research. While writing this, I wondered about my sudden theory that it would be the cat people who felt passionate about twitter and those of the canine persuasion who preferred Facebook.

One question thrown out on my twitter page and I quickly had over a hundred responses. They all pretty much loved Twitter – well they would, wouldn't they – but I am pleased to say the Cat-lovers had the edge.

(I also got twenty new followers, just by posing this conundrum, though I rapidly lost a couple when I said I didn't think much of dogs licking their testicles and then wanting to do the same to my face.)

And if you are wondering what any of this has to do with publicising yourself as a writer, I shall leave you with Catherine Ryan Howard again:

"Twitter is the single best thing I ever did in terms of publicising this book and my career as a writer. I would say 90% of people who've bought my book heard of it directly or indirectly via Twitter and it helped me get an agent."

Can't ask much more than that!

YouTube

But if your ambitions do run further, then these days its not just the written word that can promote you as a writer.

My only dalliance with YouTube is a short, (mercifully anonymous) film of me dancing on a table at Writers' Holiday in Caerleon (thank you Simon Whaley – you're a pal!).

But other writers have found more creative uses for the video-sharing website. Lorelei Mathias won a Book Marketing Society Award back in 2008 when the 'book trailer' for her novel *Step on it, Cupid* (Little Black Dress) was the first of its kind in the UK.

The novelty of what Lorelei had done – see it on www.youtube.com/watch?v=4a1-ITF7wb8 – led to her writing an article for *The Bookseller*, giving a talk at the London Book Fair on viral marketing, and even getting a mention on the *Today* Programme.

The former publishing marketer wrote a TV-style trailer ad for the novel which she produced "on a shoestring budget" after persuading various people "to help out for free, or very cheaply". These included production staff and actor Sarah Smart of *At Home with the Braithwaites* fame. The trailer was posted on YouTube and was complemented by a MySpace page set up especially for the heroine of the novel, Amelie.

Lorelei explains, "Once the fictional Amelie joined various online chatrooms and the trailer was "seeded" – i.e. links were emailed to friends,

My only dalliance with YouTube is a video of me dancing on the table...

Photo by Bill Harris

family and colleagues – things took off. Traffic to Amelie's MySpace page increased, while on YouTube the trailer had 280 plays in the first hour."

At the time of writing, that figure has risen to nearly 7,500, attracting viewers from all over the world. "It certainly helped sales," says Lorelei, "but that's not the only benefit of viral marketing; it's more about generating awareness, talkability and that old elixir of publishing, word of mouth."

Nutritionist Zoë Harcombe, has also exploited the potential of YouTube to promote her book *The Harcombe Diet* (Accent Press). It was her husband Andy (he of the website design) who had the idea of Zoë talking to camera. "He plonked me in front of it," says Zoë, "and I realised I can talk for Wales."

Zoë has recorded 40 videos – "They don't need editing," she says, "I don't pause" – and has had over 70,000 views so far with many of her recordings being shared on sites all over the world. Andy also encouraged her to start tweeting and set up a Facebook page which generated over 1000 fans in a few months. Later they started their own forum on www.theharcombedietclub.com. Members of the Diet Club share their weight loss stories and get help and advice from 'super fans'.

Zoë puts huge amounts of energy into what she does. "We blog, we link sites, we do all the stuff that makes your web presence as valuable as possible. From 2004-2009 I personally answered every email from people who wrote to me and it was only when the sales went so mad, that I, with huge reluctance, put an auto response on saying I was no longer able to personally reply". She still tries to check as many messages as she can and also offers personal consultations and a quick query phone surgery.

Zoë has been repaid for her efforts with a massive increase in sales and her 'Harcombe Diet Club' continues to expand.

Other things you can do online

Join forums/make comments
If you are the author of a non-fiction book, try searching the net for a forum or blog on the subject. There will be one – or dozens – for sure.

Post comments (leaving your web address underneath) and try joining in any live chats that are happening.

Also get involved by offering the owner a couple of copies of your book – one for them (they may review it) and one to give away as a prize.

You can do this yourself too.

Hold contests/ give away freebies

Kate Walker holds regular contests and offers two larger prizes – the 'Beach Bag of Books' and the 'Christmas Stocking Stuffed with Books'.

Books are donated by friends who then get a write-up and a weblink. "They'll then mention it on their own sites," explains Kate, "and send people over to my website as a result – it's reciprocal and circular."

The indomitable Catherine Ryan Howard held "a coffee giveaway" to launch her new blog.

> I went to some local coffee roasters here in Cork and asked them politely for 3 bags of their signature blend coffee. This was the perfect prize because it was a) small and therefore cheap and easy to mail to any destination worldwide, b) from Cork, like me and c) it was coffee, my #1 Twitter topic. My new blog was called Catherine, Caffeinated.
>
> I persuaded them to give me the coffee for free by doing the numbers, very optimistically: I had 400 Twitter followers at the time. To enter the competition, they had to 'Retweet' or repost one of my tweets about the coffee, which would include the brand name. 'Conservatively speaking' I said, each of these people would have, say, 200 followers. 400 x 200 = 80,000 people who would potentially see Cork Coffee Roasters flash up on screen the day of the blog launch/contest.
>
> Was this true? Who knows. But I got my coffee, the contest was a success and in the first month alone, my brand new blog got nearly 2,000 hits (500 on the day of the contest). Not too shabby...

I think it is absolutely bloody marvellous. I am thinking of hiring Catherine to run a give-away for this book. I am thinking chocolate. Or wine….
Catherine also gives away an appendix to her *Mousetrapped*, called *The Sane Person's Guide to Walt Disney World*, in the form of a free e-book. Which, as she says, is only "a fancy word for an MS Word document saved as a PDF". The way it works is simple:

"At the back of the book is a blurb about it and readers are invited to head to my website to download their free copy, thus bringing them to my blog/site."

Easy eh?

Set up Google alerts

An easy way to keep your finger on the pulse, is to set up Google alerts (you will be directed how to do this if you just visit the Google home page and see their list of options).

You can use alerts two ways. You can put in your own name and/or the title of your book so you're informed every time there's a new mention of either or someone is rude about you.

Or you can set it up for your subject area. Zoë Harcombe has alerts for 'obesity' for example, (and this may well be my own specialisation too if I don't finish this book soon). You'll then know where people are discussing, say teapots for example, and you can pop along and leave a comment yourself – with "author of *Loving Sex through Leaf Infusions*" casually typed underneath!

NB I have recently been introduced to something similar called **Social Mention Alerts** (www.socialmention.com). These can be slightly hit and miss. So far I've been informed of mentions of David Wenham, Ms Alison Joan Wenham, DICK & JANE and Rashida Jones as well as being pointed towards a couple of blogs where someone has been talking about me. I wouldn't have known about the latter without this facility so, since it's quick and free, why not give that a try too?

Be professional

Kev suggested I make this point. As he puts it:

For most people you network with over the web, all that they know about you will be derived from your tweets, posted articles, profiles, web pages and comments. For this reason it is important to maintain a high level of professionalism in everything that you write. You may not yet be published and writing may not yet be your main source of income, but that can change in the future. When it does, you would not wish to be on record as having said something you then regret. In the worst case scenario, a lack of professionalism may land you in legal trouble.

These are Kev's recommendations:

1) **Keep high standards:** Make sure all of your articles, comments and pages are of a high quality. Apply the same level of rigour as you would to the novel you're writing. Check all spelling and punctuation at the very least.

2) **Use the media:** Don't just write plain text all of the time. Make your articles more interesting by utilising the media available to you. Why not include pictures or diagrams with your text. Put in plenty of hyperlinks to related material – this will save space and can avoid forcing your visitors to read large chunks of reproduced text.

3) **Cite your sources:** If you're reporting information or facts, then please remember to quote your references if it is not your original work. Many writers are (usually unjustly) paranoid about plagiarism, so don't fuel their angst by neglecting to cite their work if you use it.

4) **"Don't feed the trolls":** You may encounter individuals who, deliberately or otherwise, make rude and/or inflammatory remarks. It's a good idea not to respond straight away (or at all in some cases). Think things through before replying.

5) **Stay polite:** In other words, don't develop troll-like attributes yourself. Try to remain polite and courteous at all times. It is usually best to say positive things or nothing at all, rather than negative things.

And here are a couple of my own:

Be tough

If I may just add a word to Kevin's point about trolls, try and keep a sense of perspective if someone is rude about you.

It can be hurtful if someone makes personal or spiteful comments about you – I have read about my "grotty books", quite inaccurate surmises about my politics and the view that it would take several beers and a whisky chaser before anyone could find me attractive, to name but a few – but it is best to consider that the perpetrators are saying an awful lot more about themselves than they are about you.

If they've actually got something really wrong you may want to politely correct it: Zoë Harcombe, for example, says, "I would jump in if someone described my book as low cal – but I'll put up with almost anything else!"

If you do want to put the record straight, Zoë does it like this:

"Always go in as yourself with your full name, and be as gracious in correcting errors and as positive as you can – even when you've been horribly, unfairly misrepresented. You then 'win' the high ground and people can judge on two sides – not just one biased view. But mostly – I just let the news spread and hope people try the diet for themselves!"

I think this is good advice when dealing in anything presented as fact – if for example, someone wrote that your book "contains explicit language and gratuitous violence" and actually it's the rather sweet tale of a six-year-old and her pet rabbit – but if it is just your average dollop of subjective abuse, I should rise above it.

Hold as your mantra the old quote attributed to everyone from Benjamin Disraeli to Katharine Hepburn:

Never complain, never explain

In other words, do not reply, do not justify yourself and treat rudeness with the contempt it deserves.

So to the person who has just referred to me as "facially challenged", I'll just say that if sitting at your computer was the most exciting thing you could find to do on a Saturday night while I was out being wined and dined, I expect you are pretty ugly and revolting-looking too...

And finally... Be disciplined

Any twitter and email friends reading this (thank you!) may now be taking a sharp intake of breath at my gall and hypocrisy, but do remember that if you're a writer, you're going to need to write some time, too.

If the little tour of the internet you do each morning just as a warm-up, to ease you into the day – I personally do emails, twitter, Amazon ratings, Waterstone stocks, second twitter account, hits on website and my four favourite blogs as a bare minimum – is beginning to last till lunchtime, heed this final bit of advice.

Know that router you've got? The one that handles your broadband connection? There's a switch on it. *You always can turn it off.*[19]

Footnote 19: I know, I know. I wouldn't dream of it either...

Tomorrow's chip wrapping? Unfortunately not...

In the good old days when fried fish came in newspaper, instead of sweaty polystyrene boxes and the net was something you put over your curlers at night, there was always the famous comfort that any embarrassments in the news would only be so much wrapping for your chips the next day. Not any more!

Now articles appear online as well as in newsprint and the indiscretion you shared with that nice journalist after he'd bought you the sixth gin can stay there pretty much indefinitely.

As Valerie Dwyer warned me darkly, "Experts say that whatever gets on to the internet will remain there forever, even if it's hidden, so be careful what legacy you leave!"

I can't really be worrying about my legacy but I am a little more careful these days to give a bit of thought to what's churning round the web while I'm still alive.

It was back in 2005 that I answered an internet interview question by saying, "If streaking down Oxford Street would result in a million sales I'd seriously consider it." All these years on, I still get offers to take my kit off (it would be art, I was assured by the photographer who wanted me to pose naked on Margate beach) and I continue to be asked if it remains true (answer: yes, probably, although God help the tourists).

So it is probably wise to give yourself plenty of time to answer questions sent to you by email rather than just dashing off the first thing that occurs to you, which, as I know to my cost, might seem very droll at 10 p.m. after half a bottle of Pinot Grigio but not quite so side-splittng when you're faced with it on your screen a week later and it gets thrown up every time you're googled.

The same goes for what you say in interviews by phone or in person that might end up online. If you're not sure how to answer something, say so, and ask to come back to it at the end or promise to email your answer later that day.

Although all of this depends on how much you care about your dafter statements coming back to haunt you (I don't mind about Oxford Street at all) and whether you believe in:

NO SUCH THING AS BAD PUBLICITY?

"There's no such thing as bad publicity with the sole caveat of being a paedophile," says Kelvin Mackenzie. "It's the only exception. Otherwise, fill your boots!"

I'm not sure I would go quite that far myself. I know what Kelvin means – he spent some time holding forth about Jeffrey Archer, pointing out that even ending up in the slammer needn't affect your book sales – and I realise that as a society we are largely unshockable these days. However, I get put off reading the books of those who sound arrogant, or unpleasant in interview or who have done or said something that makes me uncomfortable, and I'm sure I'm not alone.

Quite aside from one's personal proclivities anything that makes your book seem a sham, or you a hypocrite, is not likely to boost the takings.

The *Ultimate Guide to Being a Perfect Wife and Mother* is not likely to sell in shedloads if it transpires its author has been shagging her plumber for the last decade and keeps her children in the broom cupboard.

Nor will *How to Make a Million and Find Lifelong Passion* if an exposé shows it was written by a penniless male virgin.

And one of the reasons I wouldn't want to write a proper diet book (visitors to my website will see I have long hankered to pen a jokey one) is because the pressure to weigh eight stone and avoid being snapped with a burger hanging from your mouth would be overwhelming.

But these are extreme examples. When one is starting out (one hopes) on the road to fame, I would say the vast, vast majority of the publicity you receive can only help things along. Which is why my motto always used to be:

Never say no

I hate those self-help books that basically say the same thing over and over again – don't eat carbs, love yourself, it's all your parents' fault – just varying the words slightly, every single chapter until you're close to screaming, YOU'VE TOLD ME THAT ALREADY and ramming your head in a bucket, so I shall keep this resumé very short.

If you wanna be heard of, embrace whatever opportunity fetches up. Sign, speak, party, be interviewed, teach, talk, blog, donate, contribute and turn up smiling.

If you get one extra reader, he or she may tell one more. If you make one contact it could lead to something else. Think pyramid, think snowball, think of the free wine.

Never say die

Not everything you do or try will be a success – some people will ignore your overtures, or give you a sniffy response. You may turn up to do a talk to fifty and find three people waiting for you, all looking as it they'd have rather stayed at home and watched the shopping channel. You may feel disheartened and that it's a lot of work for little reward.

I was touched by this affirmation, that my friend Lynne Hackles sent me when I was feeling miserable and disheartened myself (I think she was sent it by www.tut.com – she likes all that the-universe-loves-you stuff) (And if you do too, you can sign up on the site to receive a whole lot more of where this came from.)

However long your dreams take to come true, no matter how prickly, thorny, or bumpy the path; and whether or not you even remember these words, if you stay the course, I can promise you this:

1) *They will come true.*
2) *You'll recall the entire journey with fondness.*
3) *You're going to miss shopping in complete anonymity.*

In other words, don't give in, keep your spirits up and your headscarf and dark glasses to the ready.

Good lines when things go wrong

And until then…

"If things go wrong, you step up! It's all about the way you handle it," says Simone Klass.

"When something funny or humiliating happens to you," says Jill Mansell, "make a note of it and use it in talks. I keep mine in a notebook."

This is a very good approach to take. Because things will go wrong for sure. But hopefully, even if you don't laugh about it later, you'll at least look back with a wry smile.

My worst moments have been when speaking – the time that I was supposed to speak at nine in the evening and was eventually called on at half past eleven when everyone in the room – including me, almost – was drunk and the heart-stopping occasions when I have totally forgotten what I'm talking about.

This happened when I was interviewing Julian Clary in front of a packed theatre in Guildford. I asked him a question with such a long intro that I completely lost where I was going.

There was nothing for it but to come clean and say so. The same evening I also rather ran out of material. I had prepared lots of questions but had been over-optimistic about how long his answers would take (JC had been on the interview circuit for week and had them all down to a fine pithy art).

I was sweating but I managed to cobble a few extra queries together and was saved by his agreeing to read (which he did most entertainingly) and take lots of questions from the audience. And the appearance of Valerie the dog – back from her walk with one of the theatre staff – on stage, distracted everyone from my ineptitude and won their hearts.

And Valerie the dog came too....

Sheila Norton, author of eight novels speaks of her "miserable failures to promote myself" including a signing where she was so confident of selling heaps of books that she offered to donate half the profits to charity, "and then sold precisely 4 copies" and a book signing where the only copy of the book she sold was to the bookshop manager, and the shop closed down soon afterwards.

(Which reminds me that if this sort of thing has happened to you, or even if it hasn't, do look at the painfully funny **"Signing in the Waldenbooks" by Parnell Hall** on YouTube – which I'm sure will resonate with anyone who has ever done a signing of any sort.)

Another friend, who has begged to remain nameless, tells a great story of giving a talk in a bookshop to a huge circle of empty chairs with just the one elderly gentleman sitting in the front row, who not only fell asleep with his mouth open but dribbled to boot.

And I've also heard tell of a writer turning up at bookshop for the signing of her chick-lit novel to be faced with a huge pile of ... the Bible.

Melanie Whitehouse made a faux pas on Southern Counties Radio, when she assumed the interviewer was gay "he was camp as a nine bob note" and found out later that she'd upset him by turning him down for a drink while they were on the air. "I thought he was taking the mick."

While Sue Houghton describes her "uber embarrassing incident" as the time the local press turned up to interview about her contribution to one of the *Sexy Shorts* charity books.

"They were much more interested in my day job – I owned and worked in a butcher's shop with my husband and they seemed to think it immensely funny that I was up to my armpits in sausages during the day and wrote at night."

Well she *was* writing sexy stories…

Sue continues the tale:

"A photographer turned up at the shop and insisted I pose in full butcher's garb with meat cleaver in one hand and pen in the other. The photo appeared the following week with a half-page spread about how I get all the juicy gossip from my customers then turn them into erotic stories! I'm still getting jibes about it!"

However, remember we're Never Saying Die? Sue goes on –

"BUT the up-side was, I got to go on Radio Sheffield to talk about the charity range, then more newspapers picked up on it and ran the story, so there was yet more publicity. I guess being a butcher is my USP!"

That's the spirit! Remember it's not only publicity but grist to the mill. Everything you go through can become material. In other words:

How to justify everything you do?

Tell yourself you'll write about it one day…

But…

Learning to say no

For all I've said about this harsh world of commercial enterprise that bookselling has become, and how every disastrous cloud may still have a silver lining (even if it takes five years to make itself apparent) there comes a time when the word 'no' has to enter your vocabulary.

Once upon a time, as you will have gathered, I said YES even if it meant travelling all day to appear for three minutes on a little-known satellite channel with six viewers, only to find that just as one had opened one's mouth, and long before there was any mention of things literary, it was the advert break and the teenage producer was thanking me very much and ushering the next sucker in.

Then I was taken on by The Fearsome One, who lost no time in pointing out that part of my job as a novelist was to actually buckle down and write a novel.

She made me practise saying, "I'll get back to you", and insisted I write it on a post-it note (next to her other instructions) and stick it somewhere prominent!

I spent a week practising it into the empty telephone receiver, achieving what I liked to think was a note of quiet authority, which I planned to accompany with the rustling of diary pages to show what a packed schedule I had and how I could not possibly make snap decisions.

The next call to come was the one about appearing on *The Wright Stuff* on Channel Five. I was ready. I took a deep breath. "YES," I shrieked.

Why? There wasn't a book plug opportunity in sight. As I've already told you, I was required to hold forth on the joys of motherhood – or in my case, ten ways to get them to watch a DVD, instead. I looked ghastly; there was reference to my being a novelist but no actual book titles. There was not an upsurge in sales.

I have a fifty/fifty success rate now with getting "I'll get back to you" out before saying YES as a knee jerk reaction. Because – and this is a genuine

word of warning – my career as a writer (as opposed to half-baked media tart) would have probably benefited from a little less hob-nobbing and a little more applying fingers to keyboard. (And that's not to send emails or go on twitter either.)

In order to ensure that I occasionally produce another book, I have had to develop a small ability to employ:

Taste and discernment

There can be various reasons to turn something down and I admire people who think through all the ramifications every time and make their decisions accordingly.

Sometimes the end result really doesn't justify the effort and energy you'll need to expend – e.g. driving from Land's End to the far reaches of the frozen North in order to address three men and a dog in a library in the middle of December on the same night as the final of *X Factor*. When you're not even being paid.

You may consider other propositions to be on the tacky side. JoJo Moyes turned down a feature that would have involved her performing burlesque, and talking about her love life. "The opportunities for humiliation were too great – and I decided that if people won't read my books without me wearing a purple corset then I'm in the wrong job anyway."

Or just too damn personal – there's no point doing anything if it's going to make you feel you can't look the local newsagent in the eye.

Even I've said "no thanks" to a couple of features that meant spilling the beans about sexual encounters, including one that included tracking down ex-boyfriends (save me!) and a 'documentary' that would have involved me being monitored to see what sort of things turned me on (Can you imagine? How embarrassing if it turned out to be gerbils or rubber gloves).

I'm a pretty open and honest, heart-on-sleeve sort of woman but after the nauseating "our eyes locked across a crowded room" feature, I'd be very dubious about exposing too much emotional stuff, especially if I couldn't control things by writing it myself.

"One sure way to secure inches is to bleed all over the page," says Alison Penton Harper. "Being a comedy-writing clinical depressive, my publicist has tried to nudge me towards this angle several times, but I came to the firm conclusion that I'm just not interested in spatchcocking my unhinged condition across the pages of *Heat* magazine. Besides, I like to kid myself that nobody actually knows I'm deranged, although I suspect my family might have something to say about that."

Sometimes it's not about being reluctant to bare your soul but hard maths. Marco Pierre White, he told me, in one our conversations about the moveable feast, doesn't do interviews with the *Guardian* for example.

"They're not my diners – it's too expensive for them." (He wouldn't do the red tops, either, he said.) Why spend his time and energy and use up a story for, say, the *Observer* when it wouldn't make any difference to his business?

"*The Times* does, the *Telegraph* does. And the *Daily Mail*. But I turn down 95% of what I'm offered." Except, he added, where his TV contract obligates him not to.

Suzanne Moore, also says no. Particularly to television.

I have done TV in the past and do the odd bit if it appeals. It only works for me if I care about the subject and have some measure of control, i.e. I don't want words put in my mouth as words is what I do. There is little live TV where you can say what you think or TV where you can write your own script. If you accept it's a collaborative process that can be fine and if you don't mind being packaged in a certain way it can work. If you are an awkward control freak, and I think most writers are, think carefully about it.

The whole business of where to draw the line is also going to differ hugely according to your personality and how far down the primrose path to fame you've made it so far.

Obviously Marco and Suzanne don't need the publicity like I do. The more sought after you become, the more you can be choosy.

The more sought after you become, the more weirdos you're going to attract too....

Nutters & weirdos

Joanne Harris's secretary, Anne, keeps a special file marked 'Mad People'. Joanne happily lists some of them for me:

A man who stalked me for years, believing that I was an incarnation of the Virgin Mary; Occultists asking me to join their coven; a man who swore blind he knew me, as he'd been a lodger of my mother's when I was at university and had recognized my picture on the piano (my mother has never taken lodgers and doesn't own a piano, but he was most insistent); various American evangelists, high on verbiage, low on charisma, who seem to believe that I am the Antichrist's sister.

I do like "high on verbiage" and, with no offence intended to our cousins across the pond – this does seem to be a trait displayed by a certain sort of US correspondent...

Below is an unedited, verbatim extract (yes there was more) from an email sent to me by one Alvin of Michigan.

i slowed down for a look at your pictures showing your nose closer to mouth than eyes indicating more passionate than opinionated though i have to consider that only prima facie evidence since the titles of your books indicate a definite socialite butterfly considering herself somewhat more trendy than her hair but yet with the glow of an inner soul not fully hid behind the cover of the sarcasmic judge of all thats good and decent and you are right i have never read a single line of any of your books...

What he'd been on, apart from my website, is anyone's guess.

At least Michigan is a fair distance from Broadstairs and I didn't have to worry about Alvin attempting to pop round for tea.

Unlike the time when I replied (obviously unwisely) to one "fan" (one of the "Alfred Hitchcocks" as we might like to call them) to explain that the reason I was sadly unable to take up his kind offer to meet him for drinks and the study of his six unpublished manuscripts, was that I would be at a book launch at that very time.

Imagine how taken aback I was to receive another email proudly telling me that he'd given yahoo a good bashing and now knew where the event was! No, he wasn't gazing lovingly from the pavement opposite when I got there, but it sure made my hair stand on end.

As it did when he then started delving into the bowels of Genes Reunited and speculating as to who my second cousins might be (fortunately he was way off-beam on that one!).

258

I have always accepted that you get the odd loonie turning up to book-signings and talks (and poor Leona Lewis got punched by one) but have only personally experienced the sort who are clutching their own 300,000 word, leather-bound and totally incomprehensible manuscript, and claiming that they'd have written *The De Vinci Code* but the publishers stole their idea.

Or the kind that stare at you throughout, appearing increasingly disappointed and disgruntled until you think they *might* punch you, until it transpires that they've got the wrong week and were expecting Joanna Trollope.

All part of the rich fabric of our delightfully diverse book-reading society, one might think, and at least they keep their clothes on.

But not necessarily. I am hugely grateful to the Art Historian Sir Roy Strong for this wonderful account of the time he was in the Topping & Company bookshop in Bath to talk about his *A Little History of the English Country Church* (Jonathan Cape).

Just before he went on, a woman approached him to ask if he minded if her daughter drew him while he spoke. Sir Roy agreed, even though he thought the younger woman looked a little odd (it was the shaved head and bowler hat with scarf around it that did it).

But instead of sketching, the young lady in question waited until the author had been introduced, got up from her chair turned round and bent over and then lifted up her skirt to present to Sir Roy what he describes as a "naked, no-knickered bottom" and then calmly sat down again.

I am pleased to report that Sir Roy did not bat an eyelid, the rest of the audience sat in silence and the lecture continued unscathed. That is the sort of response that makes Britain great.

He did feel a little apprehensive later.

"She never sketched me," says Sir Roy, "but, at the close, when I was signing books, hovered closer and closer towards me. She made me feel quite nervous and I chose a moment to sharply move off and go to the bookshop manageress and say, keep that woman away from me! The mother made no attempt to apologise for her daughter's behaviour. The bookshop said that she would be struck off their list!"

Anyone would find such behaviour unnerving, because you never know if you're dealing with someone who's a harmless eccentric or their bizarre behaviour – and you don't get much more bizarre than flashing your backside in the middle of a shop – is an indication of something more alarming.

However, I've told these tales because they amuse me. I'd truly hate to worry anyone. You might get the odd strange email or bonkers member of an audience and obviously it is wise to take the normal, sensible precautions when communing with strangers.

But most people who contact me are absolutely lovely – I am endlessly touched by the way readers will take the trouble to write and say they've enjoyed a book or article – and as I've already said, I have met, and made real friends of, quite a few of them.

And talking of friends – and fans, and family come to that (if you want to see bonkers…), my original plan for this book consisted of an entire section entitled **HASSLES & HAZARDS,** taking in other drawbacks the writer craving recognition might encounter along the way.

There was a section called **Highlights & Limelight** too and **ten things you mustn't forget** (God knows what they were[20]) and an introspective entitled **Common Misconceptions** (in which I was going to explain how the hapless author is so often misjudged).

But unfortunately I have exceeded my word count already and need to draw to some sort of conclusion. So I shall save the above for my third tome in the series –

Wannabe a Writer Who Stays Sane?

(Hot tips for doo-lally scribes and everything else she forgot to say last time)

To be published some time in the future if my publishers will forgive me for missing another deadline... (A question I am asking myself right now.)

But before I sign off, I realise, that having read this far, you may have a question for me....

Footnote 20: One of them was: don't forget to write too.

SHOULD I JUST HIRE A PR?

OK so you've read the book – thank you ☺ – or at least flicked through as far as here. If after all that, you're throwing up your hands and thinking bugger that, wouldn't it just be easier to hire a publicist to do it all for me? – I can only say, Yes – if you've got the finances, why not do just that!

There are plenty of arguments that say the practised PR will do a better job than us – if only because they do it all the time and have the contacts already in place.

As Simone Klass puts it, "Yes of course you could do it yourself. Just like cutting your own hair, mending your shoes and fixing your teeth. PR is a profession."

Tony Mulliken, Chairman of Midas Public Relations, who works with many big-name authors, finds that even they don't always get a huge amount of time from their publisher's in-house team.

"Out of house means you get lots of TLC and time with the publicist."

It was this thought that led Zoë Harcombe to invest in some PR. Zoë had left the corporate world to see if she could make her "passion and hobby" – researching and writing about obesity, her living, and went for a "no fee/no strings meeting" with a top PR company, to see if they could help her

"I was just stunned at how well and quickly they grasped what was different about where I'm coming from," she says.

She signed up and began a tireless PR campaign including "walk the pavement" days and writing countless articles for a wide variety of publications.

My account Manager – Jess – would set up a day in London at the magazine and newspapers houses and we would traipse around London with goodie bags with the diet and recipe book in and a bio on me and a brief on the book. We would turn up at Nat Mags or Northcliffe House and sit in reception with all the models with their portfolios and the beauty reps with their products. I would then have 2-3 minutes to do the 'elevator pitch' on how *The Harcombe Diet* was different, and what we could do for their magazine and readers.

Zoë's account manager had the experience and knowledge to know when to offer an exclusive, when to pitch one magazine against another and how Zoë could get maximum column inches from each idea. The results were impressive.

Zoë got masses of coverage (see http://theharcombe-diet.com/mediapage/), saw sales of *The Harcombe Diet* rocket and ended 2009 with the number one slot on Amazon.

It hasn't been cheap – Zoë estimates she has spent around £50,000 so far. Has that given a good return?

> Not pound for pound anywhere close! But what it has done is get the diet known to many people who would not previously have known about it and those people are starting to spread the word. I may never know if it comes close to even breaking even over the coming year but it's been an invaluable experience and, if you've got some money you're prepared to not see again and you really believe in your product, I would say go for it.

Peter James takes a different tack. And in the balance of fairness, I am including his experiences too even if it renders the whole of the rest of this book redundant (thanks Mate ☺)

> When my first novel, *Dead Letter Drop* (a bad spy thriller I now keep out of print!) came out, in 1981, I was bitterly disappointed not to see it on sale in most shops, nor to get many reviews. So I decided when my second *Atom Bomb Angel* (equally bad, also kept out of print by me!) came out a year later, I decided to hire a publicist.
>
> I spent my entire advance of £3,000 hiring a young Tony Mulliken to organize a nationwide tour. He did it brilliantly, and I was on the road for nearly a month with a packed schedule every day. Imagine my disappointment to find the books were still on sale in only very few shops and that the total hardback subscription was a meagre 1,800 copies – mostly to libraries!
>
> It wasn't until 1988 when Victor Gollancz (now part of Orion) published my supernatural chiller *Possession* to a massive fanfare of publicity, free sample chapters given out, a huge marketing campaign and a huge publcity campaign, which propelled the book to No 2 in the *Sunday Times* in its first week and subsequently to No 1 on several lists, that I realized what the secret of "wanting to be a writer we have

heard of" really is: **Best-sellers are decided in-house, long before the book is ever published.**

This is even more true today with the dominance of the supermarket chains and Amazon. Very simply if you are not in the supermarkets and you are not getting a heavy promotion on Amazon, you will need a near miracle to make the best-seller lists. And you will only be in the supermarkets if your publisher pushes the book hard and offers a massive marketing spend to them.

Which is why, on an earlier page, you may recall Peter entreating us to take our publishers out to lunch.

I feel both Zoë's and Peter's experiences are equally valid. Were I to win the lottery tonight and find myself with untold millions I would hire a PR company for sure, just because it's jolly hard work doing it all yourself and I'd sometimes love someone else to make the phone calls and do a bit of the endless door-knocking.

But I'd also, if I were setting my heart on a place on the best-seller lists, try to buy my way into some three-for-twos. Because there is no doubt that the job of promoting ourselves becomes a whole lot easier when one's books are piled high in the bookstores, splashed across the airports and are the first thing you trip over when you do the weekly supermarket run.

Peter's point about one's publishers is a good one.

Summing up, if you've got the money, why not buy some help. If you haven't, just remember nobody ever said it would be easy. And all the best things are worth waiting for. Books do appear from nowhere, from small publishers with no marketing budget, and become sensations. Not often, but often enough to make it worthwhile to have a try.

Nothing will ever be as potent as word of mouth. But you still have to reach the first person so they can pass it on. Anything is possible. If I didn't believe that I would never have written this book.

JOIN MY WAITING LIST

NB: When I'm too old and mad to write any more books I am going to become a PR myself. I will be famed for the staggering array of diamonds from past lovers encrusted upon my gnarled fingers and the fact that I still sport hair extensions in pink and blue.

I will have a small and select list of clients whom I shall terrify and a waiting list that goes back years. I will fix like no-one has ever fixed and impressionable young editors will quake before my gimlet eyes. Think Max Clifford meets Ann Widdecombe crossed with Cruella de Ville.

I shall have my own table at the Ivy Club, a suite at the Savoy and a young male secretary whom I summon by banging my stick. There will be rumours that I was once a beauty, my parties – attended by grateful newspaper moguls and TV executives – will be legendary and it will be well-known that it's no use phoning me after 3 p.m. because I shall always be drunk on gin.

If you want to put your name down – email me now.
jane@janewenham-jones.com

And then, my lovelies, read what the rest of 'em have to say…

WANNABE A WRITER WE'VE HEARD OF?

What They Say...

Long ago, in the dawn of time, when Harry Potter was the hot new sensation, JK Rowling said to me, "The *Daily Mail* is ruining my life" and I replied, "Only if you let it"...The thing modern writers should always remember is that we are not extras for *Sex and The City*, we are WRITERS, and thus not required to look like Cheryl Cole or behave like Lady Gaga. Journalists may not know – or may pretend not to know – the difference, but we should never forget it. Our communication with our audience is through the page, not through the stage. So, by all means buy killer heels to wear on telly if you crave them – but only wear them if you can walk in them. It's your head and what's inside it that counts...leave what's outside it to those who can't write...

Joanna Trollope, novelist.

Do whatever it takes to publicise your book. Allow your publishers to offer you for interviews on local radio stations; go to book festivals and fairs; give talks to book clubs; offer to do signings in book shops (a signed book is a sold book). If there is a newspaper feature article to be gleaned from your book, offer to write it. Books don't sell themselves and the author can do a lot to help things along. Be proud of your book and all your hard work in writing it, don't be boastful but don't hide your light either.

Richard Madeley, author and broadcaster

My kind of author!

Patrick Janson-Smith, Publisher, Blue Door, Harper Collins

Don't think about that! Go to university and do an English literature degree. That's what I say to people who tell me they want to be an artist. I say, don't think about being famous, learn to paint, learn to draw. There are no short cuts. If you want to write, then f***ing write. Write every day and be really well-read.

Tracey Emin, artist and writer

Don't try too hard and don't try to be someone you're not. On the other hand don't be too shy and humble either. People take you at face value in these frenetic times. Writing a book is no mean feat; getting it published even more so.

Remember that and hold your head high.

Don't let yourself get discouraged. If a programme turns you down it could well be because they've covered a similar subject on the show within the last few weeks.

Radio and TV shows would rather have an amusing talker than someone who has written a marvellous book but can't string two sentences together.

Sue Cook, author, TV and radio presenter

Be prepared to prostitute yourself

Kelvin MacKenzie, columnist and broadcaster

First I'd say, ditch the wish to be 'heard of' initially and instead aim to 'write well'. The first should follow the latter. The old-fashioned qualities of manners cannot be underestimated either: thank those who help (Maeve Binchy's habit of hand written postcards to everyone in bookshops she'd met made her a legend). There's a very, very fine line between being effective and being obnoxious or smug. But Brits most often err on the side of caution so I think many could well be a little more pushy without losing friends!

Carole Blake, literary agent

If I was being flippant and looking at it with my publicist's hat on I would say that while you are waiting for that exciting offer from an agent you should also take up some extreme sports, have a life-threatening illness, get your heart tragically broken, go on some exotic holidays for research, take up tantric sex, make friends with as many journalists and TV and film people as you can find, blackmail a huge literary name in some way so that they have to give you an awesome quote for your forthcoming book jacket, start an achingly cool blog about something like' what your friends say down the pub', 'what your dad says on the loo', 'what you overheard on the No 73 bus' (its always the 73 cos all meedja types live in Stoke Newington) and finally read every newspaper and magazine every day for months as well as watching loads of telly and listening to loads of radio so that you get very good at seeing how they work and will be able to pitch beautifully your consummate skill in feature writing and being a scintillating interviewee (or ask your ever-fabulous publicist to do it for you!).

Caitlin Raynor, Head of Publicity for The Headline Publishing Group

Most people are polite and charming. Just occasionally they aren't. So a thick skin is required!

Charles Collingwood, author and "Brian" in *The Archers*

Read. Read everyone. Read everyone and everything. Don't imitate, just let it swirl around inside you. By some mysteriously alchemical process, exposure to and then inward digestion of other voices allows you to find your own. I don't know how. If I did, I'd write a book about it.

Lucy Mangan, author and columnist

Never forget that you're promoting a "brand" – you – rather than any specific book. No promotion effort can be directly linked to x number of book sales.

Lynne Connolly, novelist

Don't underestimate how the public, shiny, performing aspects of being a writer – whether it's an interview by phone for the local paper or a Hay Festival appearance – can throw your quiet, shy, introverted self off-balance for ages, both before and after. Whether you love it or hate it, that side of being an author is all about outwards, not inwards, and the shift between the two can be very uncomfortable. Give yourself time and forgive yourself.

Emma Darwin, novelist

Nothing is too sad, bad, mad or personal for the researchers to leap on with cries of glee. As long as you stay in control and make sure that what goes "out there" is what you want everyone to know then "come out" with pride. Sell your story to the plethora of "true story" magazines. Contact the women's pages of the national newspapers and your local telly/radio stations – they're all desperate for something different – and the fact that you're a writer will already convince them that you're some sort of minor celeb and slightly insane and therefore worth a punt.

Christina Jones, novelist

Write the best book you possibly can. Fight to make sure the cover is brilliant.

Then be as creative as you can in finding places to plug it.

Teresa Chris, literary agent

Treat yourself to some new stuff – clothes, make-up, hairdo and that kind of thing. Whether or not it helps with the publicity I have no idea, but it's the best excuse you'll have in a long time.

Alison Penton Harper, novelist

With publishing houses slashing their publicity budgets, it is wise for authors who want to establish themselves as household names to have a personal marketing plan. So get a clear vision of your brand, your product and your readers. Then get out there and reach them. I am convinced that word of mouth is absolutely the best way to establish a solid fan base and ultimately increase your sales.

Jean Fullerton, novelist

Use every life experience – whether your own or someone's – to your advantage. See a story in anything and everything. And have no shame; offer yourself as a rent-a-gob, case study or commenter on anything and everything.

Kelly Rose Bradford, freelance journalist.

When you're a tiny minnow in a very big pool, you have to learn to roll with the punches – if you will forgive the mixed metaphor!

Stanley Johnson, journalist, author and environmentalist
(Father of Boris)

It's all very well writing an exquisite novel that deserves to be a massive best-seller, but it isn't going to happen if you sit there on your bottom thinking "Why isn't everybody raving about my book?" You need to get out there and make people aware that your book exists. Do whatever needs doing, and abandon any concept of dignity. Go to every single literary festival you're asked to, even if you're only going to be addressing a couple of nans in an otherwise empty church hall. Do every single regional radio interview, every cable TV show you've never heard of, every signing in random bookshops in the back of beyond. Obviously, do *Today* and *Newsnight* as well, if they ask you. But don't be snooty about what you say yes to – every appearance anywhere translates into sales and into people remembering you. And put some welly into it – I've seen incredibly famous authors address the aforementioned two nans in a church hall and basically woo them into lifelong fandom. Never appear embarrassed or bored; give the impression that there is nothing on earth you'd rather be doing.

India Knight, author and columnist

I would never give any sort of advice on writing to anyone who said "wanna". In fact I doubt I'd talk to them at all.

Giles Coren, author and journalist

Unless it's hugely inconvenient, take any opportunity to appear on radio or TV. Even if it's a small station you've never heard of, consider it as good practice for when 'the big one' comes along. You'd be surprised who may be listening – stuff gets repeated, can go up online, can be heard by other journalists and producers who are looking for lively contributors to their own programmes. I was certainly not afraid to filch ideas like this when I was at the BBC!

Tom Maddocks, Course Director, Media Training Associates

Be patient. Work at it.

Richard Charkin, Executive Director, Bloomsbury Publishing plc

Have an angle. No one's interested in how many qualifications you've got or where you went to university. What they want to know is what it is about you that makes you different from everybody else. For me, even though I'd done many different things during my career, the one thing most journalists focused on was the fact that I had been an agony uncle for a teenage girls magazine. They loved it. For other writers it could be the fact that prior to getting published they were doing seemingly ordinary jobs and are now best-selling authors on their way to the high life and so the journalist gets a neatly packaged rags to riches tale.

Mike Gayle, novelist

Be a pain in the arse. Come up with lots of ideas and drive your publicity company and the publisher nuts – they will only complain and hold a grudge if you are a failure!

Tony Mulliken, Chairman Midas Publicity

Never try to go on a diet whilst touring. Pack small, and take hand luggage only if you can. The rest will only get lost anyway.

Approach touring as a survival holiday, not a fashion parade. Warm sweater, emergency med-kit, multi-purpose utility belt, etc. Think Lara Croft, not Carrie Bradshaw…

Joanne Harris, novelist

Write every day, and try to write a little by hand. Use the internet to locate research documents but turn it off while you are writing, or even better, write on a computer without the internet enabled.

Most importantly of all (for me at least) – if there is no-one to set you a deadline, such as an agent or editor, then set one for yourself, and try your best to stick to it.

Kate Williams, author, historian and broadcaster

Then never, *ever* worry about whether anyone will hear of you.

Erica Wagner, Literary Editor, *The Times*

If you want to be a writer people have heard of, of course I'd suggest the obvious things: you need to work hard (a book a year helps), have great ideas, come up with killer titles, and preferably write brilliantly. Do also trust that your publisher is working hard on your book – they'll have fallen in love with it, *and* paid you for it, so you can probably believe they want the book to succeed as much as you do. If you're worrying that not enough is being done to market and publicise your book, then maybe it's time to be proactive? Offer to do whatever you can to help them market and publicise your book – be this merrily going to a Library event in Skegness, or signing up to Twitter and Facebook, so you can talk to your fans directly. And finally, I'd also suggest you start collecting four-leaf clovers, horseshoes and rabbit's feet, because at the end of the day, a little bit of luck can go a very long way…'

Isobel Akenhead, Senior Commissioning Editor, Women's Fiction & Digital, Hodder & Stoughton.

Write a blog. It's like stripping in a shop window. The more you bare, the more they'll stare!

Richard Eastcliff, media mogul, writer & producer

Sometimes, you have to hang your balls out there. What's true of the leaps of faith required to write your book is also true of selling it after publication. Put yourself *out* there. You will also need good shoes. Don't forget that you have a *readership,* not just *people who buy your books.* You can write things and they will read them. You don't have to wait until your next book before the two of you have this relationship again. Be yourself, but be professional. Think about everything you do and how it comes across. Act confident, even if you feel the opposite. Don't cheap out when buying sunglasses. Use Twitter, use Facebook, write a blog. Be kind and appreciative to everyone who works behind you in the trade. Do not become an arsehole.

Ben Johncock, novelist, freelance writer and blogger for *The Bookseller.*

Ignore the power of dedicated PR at your peril. It is easy to rely on the publisher's PR person but unless you have scored the ultimate dream publishing deal and they are willing to invest a lot of time and money promoting your book, you end up with diddly squat. You will need to look at your book as a business and invest in it accordingly. Be prepared to hire a PR company. Get active on Twitter, start a Facebook page and set up a GoogleAlert. Avoid posting silly tittle-tattle and concentrate on telling everyone where they can buy it, how it's doing on Amazon, where you have appeared press wise with links. Be prepared to do local radio even if it's very late at night or early in the morning. Don't expect to be automatically offered national coverage. Local radio or local press are invaluable and any PR worth their salt will work hard to get you in the local press around the country.

Sylvia Tidy-Harris – Managing Director womenspeakers.co.uk

Be prepared to have direct eye contact with publisher/agent/editor, suggesting complete belief in your own produce. Make sure your spin is unique but timely (nothing is unique or timely but selling it as such works). Embellish any mutual contact and above all say you are a fan of their work. Wikepedia is a wonderful self-promotion tool. All good vibes to you.

Helen Lederer, writer, performer, actress.

1) If you are over forty and it's not *Vogue,* do your own hair and make-up.
2) Never, ever agree to have a photographer snap you in a 'lighthearted' or humorous pose. I once ended up in a bath with my dog and a dead lobster (hair looked good though).
3) In interviews, JOURNALISTS ARE NOT YOUR FRIENDS.
4) In interviews, your interviewer will have already decided 75% of what he will write about you before you have met
5) For food writers, it is always worthwhile inviting the journalist chez vous with lots of food prepared. Cakes, preferably. And NEVER alcohol unless that's your special thing.
6) Sometimes, the person interviewing you will be one of your idols. Instead of stuttering and spluttering inanities for half and hour, tell him. At worst he will be flattered, at best disarmed and everyone can relax.
7) If you are still terrified going into your third TV appearance and the director's eyes go all glassy as soon as you open your mouth, STOP. Do radio.
8) Never, ever get annoyed with store staff at a book signing if no one turns up. It's not their fault, it's your publisher's publicist's fault. And yours for being boring or just not famous enough. ALWAYS invite a close friend as back up. If no one comes, do not prolong the agony. Get out quick and go straight to the bar.
9) ALWAYS thank the store/venue afterwards. Directly or via your publicist.
10) Do not make political/feminist/controversial comments in your speeches or presentations, however tempting. It's ungrateful and party-pooping. Talking about sex, however, especially for food writers, is always welcome.

Trish Deseine, international cookbook author, recipe and features writer for French *ELLE*.

Be nice to everyone you meet on the publicity trail – you never know when they'll end up running the company and will be in charge of stocking your books or will be way above you in the best-seller charts and you'll want a quote from them!

Carole Matthews, novelist

Get a really sexy author photo done, rip off a Jane Austen novel, modernise it and throw in some gratuitous mentions of Cheryl Cole and Twitter and you can't fail.

Follow @missdaisyfrost at every opportunity and read my blog www.missdaisyfrost.com

'Miss Daisy Frost', literary agent (allegedly)

If you can tie your book to a piece of news, however tenuous the link, then do. That way you can talk your way on to local and national radio to promote your book, as well as having the possibility of having the story picked up by television news producers, who often scour the papers and radio shows for stories and guests. From there it is a short step to being considered something of an expert commentator in that field and getting repeat calls to appear or comment, usually with some kind of opportunity to push your work or, shock-horror, even get paid. Think about how the supermarkets or big brands feed stories to the media and see if you can think of something similar on a budget.

Iain Aitch, author and journalist

Once you get published there will be lots of photographs so get your teeth whitened and the best haircut and colour you can afford.

Judy Astley, novelist

Be prepared to work to publicise your book. The big shock to a first time novelist is to discover that writing really is only the half of it. You need to be able to 'sell' it to sales teams within your publishers, to talk about it enthusiastically in public (it took me at least one book to stop being self-deprecating about my writing – publishers HATE that!) and to think up unusual ways that you might be able to get it into newspapers and magazines.

Don't be precious, accept that not everybody is going to be fascinated, and know that unless you are in that lucky one per cent your book is likely to get a lot less publicity than you think it perhaps should.

Jojo Moyes, novelist

Spend money on getting a good blow-dry but check out the hairdresser first on a dry run. Wear something you feel comfortable in. Glam is all very well but not if the discomfort reaches your face. Invest in one of those slinky underwear jobs that iron out your body. Carry a spare copy of your latest book at all times so you can bung it in a photograph if you happen to be snapped.

Sophie King, novelist & journalist

Prepare for the worst; writing is hard, receiving criticism is hard, getting an agent is hard, getting published is hard.

Lisa Jewell, novelist

Be as proactive as possible. Don't simply assume your publisher is doing all the work for you!

Emma Lee-Potter, journalist & novelist

1) Have absolutely no shame. Apart from accredited geniuses, the writers who are the most rabid shmoozers are the ones you're likely to have heard of.
2) Use social media to pimp your work mercilessly. Everyone else does it.
3) Drop names of high-fliers in your field at every opportunity.
4) Even if you don't know them, get said high-flyers to blurb your work. Flattery is very useful in these cases.
5) Have a high-profile fight with someone: your sub-editor (a la Giles Coren); your publishers (make sure there's a hack about); your wife (Hanif Kureishi); your children (Julie Myerson).
6) Pose naked in a surprising place: *The Spectator*, say, or Westminster Cathedral.
7) Make sure your launch party is properly catered. Book launches are notorious for serving indifferent plonk and limp canapés. Greedy people will remember yours if the fare is properly deluxe.
8) Work really hard for ten years with a modicum of success and then discover you're ten years older than the schmoozers and liggers who are getting all the limelight. Go back to point one and start again, this time with some ATTITUDE.

Marina O'Loughlin, restaurant critic & columnist

You'd hope there was some truth in the cream coming to the top

John Hegley, poet

When my first book was coming out it occurred to me that the three most useful things I could do for it on publication day were: say something outrageous, take my clothes off in public, or die. Since I haven't done any of those things yet, my advice to myself, and therefore others, is: just write the best damned books you can.

Nicola Morgan, award-winning author of teenage fiction

If you write something controversial you're more likely to get noticed but don't be controversial JUST to get noticed. It stands out a mile.

Carol Midgley, columnist and feature writer

I remember sitting in a local radio studio early on a Saturday morning, answering questions about a book I'd written while the presenter stared at me with blank contempt. His voice was excited and jolly, as if he'd just stepped off a funfair ride, so it was odd to watch it spool out of this bored, careworn, sneering face. I found the contrast unnerving, and my answers got shorter and shorter. Later I wrote a novel featuring a scene where the protagonist, a writer, experiences something similar, but nobody asked me to go on the radio and talk about that one. My advice is, bring a notepad. Even if you don't write anything on it, you'll still have something to stare down at while you speak. Eye contact on the radio isn't necessary. For all I know it's frowned upon.

Tim Dowling, author and journalist

Make yourself interesting to look at.

Sir Roy Strong, writer, broadcaster and art historian

The world really doesn't need more mediocrity. You will get published if you stand out and if you make editors' lives easy. If an editor asks for 600 words then don't expect them to clear the entire magazine for your 10,000 word dissertation. It helps if you are writing opinion pieces as I do, to have some. Don't fake it as it shows. Have some politics. Have some passion. Prepare to be disliked.

Suzanne Moore, columnist

Never say no to an interview.

Carole Stone, Managing Director YouGovStone

Be shameless. And be in it for the long haul. You can still generate publicity a year or two down the line. You just have to come up with a new marketing strategy (and not lose interest).

Melanie Whitehouse, author and journalist

Never make any assumptions about how much the publicity department of your publishers will do for you. This is because they are overwhelmed with huge piles of books to promote each month and if your masterpiece isn't one of the key titles, you simply won't be in the front of their minds. It's nothing personal.

So even if they seem to be looking after you – publicists are generally charming people in my experience, or they wouldn't be good at the job – it's still worth following up every lead of your own.

Analyse your book from a features editor's point of view. What topics are in it which would make a good article? Also think about what kind of magazine or newspaper section they would be appropriate for.

Volunteer to write these articles yourself. It makes publications look good to have published authors writing for them and they are more likely to commission the piece.

Maggie Alderson, novelist & journalist

Decide what your goals are and develop your brand. Think about your name, your profile, and be consistent across everything. Look for opportunities where you can offer your expertise, get articles published, affiliate with already successful businesses or products to promote yourself, look for 'win win' opportunities where you will both benefit – remember the theory that buyers need to see a product mentioned in 3 different places before they buy. Think of 10 points about yourself that people may be surprised to know and use them. Get a blog, get on Twitter. Blog regularly and visit other blogs. Find interesting people on Twitter and see who they are following, and follow too. As a writer you are creative, bring that creativity to your marketing campaign, market yourself, build your profile and sell sell sell!

Vanessa O'Loughlin, Director of Inkwell Writers Workshops,
founder of www.writing.ie

Get a fatwa put on you. You'll get loads of publicity, your own armed body guards, and gorgeous women will all want to marry you. There is nothing sexier than a dishevelled intellectual half balding writer with a fatwa.

Sleep with me. It might not be good, but it'll give you something award-winning to write about.

Stop wearing corduroy.

Next time you open your mouth, eat a fresh mint.

Shazia Mirza, writer and comedienne

Organise lots of events. The upside is everyone knows your name. (The downside is people forget you also write books :-))
Jan Jones, conference and party organiser, Romantic Novelists Association

As chair of the RNA, and a member for a very long time, my best tip is to join us. You'll get support from other writers – we're a very friendly bunch – you'll meet agents if you come to the parties and conferences and you'll hear of new publishing opportunities via the local chapters and the newsgroup. And – worst case scenario – even if it doesn't further your career, you will have a lot of fun! That said, I can't think of a single member whose career hasn't benefited by joining.
Katie Fforde, novelist and Chair of the Romantic Novelists' Association

Concentrate your efforts on the key sales, marketing and PR people in your publishing house. Remember they will be publishing several hundred books a year and will only be able to focus on a few. Most of their list will slip beneath their radar. So, don't focus all your energy getting your local bookshops to agree to support you – they will, but they are only going to sell a handful of copies and that will be nice but it won't achieve your goal. Focus your energy on getting your publisher enthused about you and your book – and your future books.

Peter James, novelist

Endear yourself to your publishers! At a Pan Macmillan sales conference I inadvertently (honest) switched on the porn channel and, not realising, went for a bath. Of course it turned up on the bill. The publishers paid but the teasing never stopped. I've often wondered if they hadn't watched it too...

Anita Burgh, novelist

Demonstrate your passion.

Simone Klass, personal advocate

Answer your fan mail. People have taken time out of their busy lives to write and tell you they love your books: sheer good manners should mean you get back to them as soon as you can. But you would be surprised how many times they say 'thank you for answering, I wrote to so-and-so and they never did.' But if they just made my day a great one by saying something nice, I really want to tell them so.

Trisha Ashley, novelist

Some things you probably **shouldn't** do:

1) Be annoying. If all that's in your Tweet stream is 'BUY MY BOOK OK? PLEASE RT!' you'll be talking to yourself pretty soon.

2) Be dishonest. For example, I self-published because it's the New Publishing – all agents are in bed with publishers and they only want to publish Katie Price and Martine McCutcheon. Down with them! Plus I wanted more control and to keep more of the royalties, instead of some Evil Agent stealing most of them from me loosely translates to: Despite eleven years of querying and offerings of my first born, no one would publish me. Doing this also falls into the annoying category.

3) Sit back and relax. When you do that, your books will stop selling.

4) Pay for reviews. They're really expensive, they don't necessarily translate into sales and you can get them for free by approaching bloggers.

5) Follow any 'advice' that encourages you to buy your own book.

6) Be impatient. Not everyone is going to rush out and buy your book on the day of publication. Also, this may surprise you, but your friends aren't going to like it if you ring them up every day and say, 'Have you bought it yet?' (And then, after they do, ring them up every day and say, 'Have you read it yet?') How many times have you thought to yourself, 'I must buy that book...' and then left it languishing on your Amazon Wish List. Answer: 398 times. I know this because that's what's currently on mine!

7) Assume (or even hope.?) you're going to get rich. YOU ARE NOT.

Unless you wrote Chicken Soup for the Soul or something. Aim to cover your costs and keep yourself in ink cartridges.

8) Rely on your friends/relatives. It's been my experience that the people you were sure would buy the book don't (or don't for a while) and people you never thought in a million years would part with cash in exchange for your ramblings are the first in the queue.

Finally, I would like to offer this tit bit of advice to self-published authors:

When you self-publish, you can have as many pages as you want. When you can have as many pages as you want, you can have as many names in the Acknowledgements as you want. If someone finds out their name is in the Acknowledgements, they will buy the book.
I'm just sayin'…

Catherine Ryan Howard, self-published author I've heard of

Change your name by deed poll to Philip Roth

Sam Leith, author and journalist

The Bookseller magazine has been the 'book trade bible' for over 150 years. If it's big news in publishing we cover it and the industry reads it. The magazine has a 40,000+ readership and our website close to a million page impressions per month.

If you want to make an impact with booksellers & librarians across the UK who are the frontline to influencing book buyers, then you could do worse than getting your name into *The Bookseller*.

So hunt out our editorial team often found at industry parties, London & Frankfurt Book Fair, but in general where the action is.

Sam Missingham, Head of Audience Development, *The Bookseller*

I would say to any writer who wanted to be successful, you need to think of your book as your own perfect little business which needs constant imaginative care and attention. The one thing you must not do is think that your role is over when the last full stop is written. It's only just begun. You should get yourself well acquainted with your publisher's plans, and then set up your own activities alongside them. Obsessively pursue every single opportunity to promote your book. Think like an

American: don't be embarrassed about putting an ad for your book as the signature of your emails. Host coffee mornings. If your book has a scene with a coffee bar, go to your local coffee bar and pretend that you based it on theirs, and ask if they'll sell copies. No-one actually finds it offensive to hear a writer talk about their book, so think every day about ways in which you can do that. There is absolutely no limit to the amount of positive things you can do to help raise sales of your book, and the truly successful books are the ones that, through word of mouth, reach the fabled tipping point. Don't pester your publisher with ideas: he will think they are all rubbish, and will only pretend to carry them out. But remember that your publisher is also trying his best to sell as many copies as you, he just thinks differently about how to do it. So don't go on at him (unless he really is rubbish) and try to think of your publicity work as complimentary rather than competitive. You are really in a commercial partnership, so try and do your best to contribute.

Simon Petherick, publisher, Beautiful Books

ALWAYS have something with you, business cards, flyers, post-it notes, with your most important details: name, email; website; phone; blogs. You never know who you'll be bumping into. Not expensive, you can easily design and print your own. And do use both sides, the back can list some of your works and a little photo will always help sell you!

Valerie Dwyer, writer, coach and mentor

1) ON TOUR: It is important to be a hit with book sellers and people who may buy your book, so in order to stand out don't be like every other self-obsessed writer and talk about yourself. You'll be remembered for being a good listener (very rare!) and being interested in THEM (unheard of!). Like lovers, they need to be seduced, and the surest way to do that is to be totally fascinated by them, their lives and especially their opinions. Book tours are mines of funny characters, so pick away for your next book.

2) GIVING TALKS: At literary lunches and dinners people come to drink wine, have a good meal and wear their best dresses. They don't come to be bored rigid by you giving a dreary talk about how many words you write a day. They want to be entertained. So be brave and talk off the cuff (reading a script sends them straight to sleep) about all the

funny things that inspired your characters – the ex lovers you put in for revenge is always a winner. Be irreverent, risqué, self -deprecating and above all funny. Publishers don't mention the fact that you have to be an actor as well as a writer, but you do and you have to be good.

3) COLUMN INCHES: If you have been raped, beaten up by a drunken husband, adopted by Madonna or Angelina, divorced, betrayed, are bulimic, anorexic or suicidal, or if you have slept with Wayne Rooney or David Beckham, you will be loved by the press and asked to write your story every time you have a new book out. If you haven't you might consider inventing something – otherwise there's very little chance you will get anything published in the newspapers, ever.

Santa Montefiore, novelist

If you are female, simply follow in the footsteps of Jordan. If you're male, it's harder. If you're handsome enough, get off with a movie star. If not, do something great, daring, stupid or dramatic – like sailing across the Atlantic naked or hang-gliding from Nelson's column. Otherwise, just go on *X Factor* and get five minutes of fame at least.

Paul McMullan, celebrity news photographer

and I say?

Go for it!

Thanks for reading
and all best

USEFUL INFO

Things to Join

English PEN
www.englishpen.org.
"A registered charity, working to promote literature and human rights."
A jolly good cause obviously, and events, talks, parties…

Romantic Novelists Association
www.rna-uk.org
"Promotes romantic fiction and represents writers, agents, editors and other publishing professionals."
If you're as yet unpublished, a veritable hotbed of people you should know – check out The New Writers' Scheme. Good parties for all – take your milk thistle tablets[21]

Society of Authors
www.societyofauthors.org
"Serves the interests of professional writers, helping members with any query relating to the business of writing."
Talks, panels, gatherings. Excellent source of information and support.

Women in Journalism
www.womeninjournalism.co.uk
"A networking, campaigning, training and social organisation for women journalists who work across all the written media."
Fab parties – usually with goodie bags. ☺ Useful place to hobnob with features editors and freelance journalists

---

Footnote 21: Very good for the liver

The Media Society

www.themediasociety.co.uk

"Unique in bringing people together who work in all parts of the media."
Networking events, speakers and media contacts.
Can't tell you much more – not joined yet.

National Union Of Journalists

www.nuj.org.uk

"An active, campaigning organisation seeking to improve the pay and
conditions of our members and working to protect and promote media
freedom, professionalism and ethical standards in all media."
Useful outfit to be part of if you want to make your name as a hack …

Things to read

The Bookseller

www.thebookseller.com

"Daily news and comment about the book business."
Keep up with what's what, who's who and read some amusing blogs.

The Writer's Handbook

www.thewritershandbook.com

"A wealth of indispensable resources for the writer and publishing
professional."
Contact details for newspapers, magazines, agents, editors …

Writers' and Artists' Yearbook

www.writersandartists.co.uk

"Helps writers make it into print and to develop their career.
As above – a useful directory.

Words with JAM

www.wordswithjam.co.uk

"Free online magazine designed for writers (and readers), something a
little different …"
Looks good and I've been in it! ☺

Writer's News
www.writersnews.co.uk
Useful for picking up on new publications that may be looking for contributions and keeping up with who's editing what.

Writing Magazine
www.writersnews.co.uk
"the best British how-to writing publication."
I am the agony aunt ...bring me your woes ... ☺

Woman's Weekly Fiction Special
Check out "Just Jane". ☺

Booktime
(Free magazine, published by distributors, Bertrams and available through independent bookshops) check out the inside back cover (do you feel a bit of a theme coming on here?)

Sites to visit

Goodreads
www.goodreads.com
"Free website for book lovers".
Reviewing and discussion site for readers where authors can set up their own profiles, arrange give-aways and lots more ...

Journo Biz Forums
www.journobiz.com
"Online community and discussion forum for freelance, staff and student journalists."
Great for networking and media opportunities.

Response Source
www.responsesource.com
"Independent resource for PRs and Journalists."
Lots of media opportunities here.

Romance Angels Network
Search them out on **www.facebook.com**
"Network where you will find practical help, support, critique groups and forums for the unpublished Romantic Novelist."
Daft as brushes but if you want to be king or queen of romance there's masses of information here.

Find a TV Expert
www.findatvexpert.com
"An online database of new and existing TV experts, designed to introduce & promote the professionals to the programme makers."
If you're an expert, have a look …

Literary Festivals
www.literaryfestivals.co.uk/festivalslist
A comprehensive list of all the literary festivals taking place in the United Kingdom.
If you've got a new book coming out … (or even if you haven't).

Radio Now
http://www.radio-now.co.uk
Find all the radio stations in any area in the UK.
Marvellous!

Social Networking

Facebook
www.facebook.com

My Space
www.myspace.com

Twitter
http://twitter.com

Keeping tabs on contacts

Linked In
http://www.linkedin.com

Plaxo
http://www.plaxo.com

Useful Online Tools

Google alerts
www.google.com/alerts
"Email updates of the latest relevant Google results based on your choice of query or topic."
Find out what they're all saying about you ...

Social Mention
www.socialmention.com
"A social media search engine that searches user-generated content such as blogs."
Same sort of idea but not as comprehensive. Worth a try.

Self-publishing

Word Press
www.wordpress.com
Blog tool and publishing platform. (NB see Catherine Ryan Howard)

If in London ...
London Book Fair
www.londonbookfair.co.uk
"The opportunity to meet with over 23,000 publishing professionals, from 112 countries, over 3 days at a key time in the publishing calendar."
Wear flat shoes ...

If in Ireland …
www.writing.ie
"The home of Irish writing online."

Me

www.janewenham-jones.com

A bit more of me …
www.wannabeawriter.co.uk

And if you're not thoroughly sick of me by now, finally –
http://twitter.com/JaneWenhamJones
http://twitter.com/UWannabeawriter

INDEX

Index of Contributors, companies, names dropped or mentioned (And if you wanna find out a bit more about them, how you can do just that.)

Aitch, Iain 274
www.iainaitch.com
Akenhead, Isobel 271
http://twitter.com/isobelakenhead
Albion Bookshop 79
Alderson, Maggie 277, 202
www.maggiealderson.com
Archer, Jeffrey 208, 250
www.jeffreyarcher.co.uk
Arkell, Steve 17
www.retina-productions.co.uk
Armani* 215
www.EmporioArmani.com
Arundel, Rikki 193
www.rikkiarundel.com
Asda 46, 113
www.asda.co.uk
Ashley, Trisha 60-1, 226-7, 279
www.trishaashley.com
Ashurst, Anne 192
www.millsandboon.co.uk/authors/
SaraCraven
Aslet, Clive 185
www.cliveaslet.com
Astley, Judy 87, 105, 130, 191, 217, 274
www.judyastley.com

Barnes, Julian 167
www.julianbarnes.com
Barnes and Noble 82

www.barnesandnoble.com
Barrett-Lee, Lynne 9, 100, 133, 155
www.lynnebarrett-lee.com
Bates, Matt 81, 301
www.whsmith.co.uk
Batten, Neil 19-20
www.waterstones.com
Beautiful Books 62-4, 281
Beckham, David 140, 282
Beer, Alice 140
www.alicebeer.co.uk
Benn, Tony 105
www.tonybenn.com
Bennett, Alan 166
www.faber.co.uk/author/alan-bennett
Best 183
www.bestmagazine.co.uk
Binchy, Maeve 237, 267
Blake, Carole 4, 10, 12-13, 39, 174, 195, 227, 267
www.blakefriedmann.co.uk/agents/
caroleblake
Blessed, Brian 107
Bloomsbury 60, 270
www.bloomsbury.com
Books a Million 82
www.booksamillion.com
Books Etc. 75
Bookseller, The 105, 230, 242, 272, 280, 284
www.thebookseller.com

Borders 70
Bowden, Steve 192
Boyt, Susie 107
www.susieboyt.com
Bradford, Kelly Rose 200-1, 269
www.krbradford.co.uk
Bragg, Melvyn 105
www.hodder.co.uk/authors
Brand, Jo 199
www.tvbookclub.co.uk
Breast Cancer Campaign 193, 100
www.breastcancercampaign.org
Brookesmith, Peter 27-8
www.firecrest-fiction.com
Brown, Gordon 43, 52
www.gordonbrown.com
Buerk, Michael 85
www.randomhouse.co.uk/catalog/author
Bulgari 187
www.bulgari.com
Burgh, Anita 98, 278
www.anitaburgh.com
Burton's Foods 188
www.burtonsfoods.com
Byatt, A.S 105
www.asbyatt.com
Bylines Calendar 171
www.bylinescalendar.com
Bywater, Michael 185
http://twitter.com/mbywater

Cadbury Chocolate Fingers* 87
www.burtonsfoods.com
Cameron, Valerie A.R.P.S 19
piggys.paradise@btinternet.com
Campbell, Glen 135-6
www.bbc.co.uk/programmes/insideout

Carmichael, Christine 59
http://twitter.com/romanceangels
Carré, John le 237
Cartland, Dame Barbara 17-18, 79
Celebrity Bird Watch 109
Charkin, Richard 60, 270
www.bloomsbury.com
Cheek, Mavis 85
www.faber.co.uk/author/mavis-cheek
Choice Magazine 200
www.choicemag.co.uk
Choos, Jimmy* 215
www.jimmychoo.com
Chris, Teresa 269
teresachris@litagency.co.uk
Clary, Julian 2, 252-3
www.julianclary.co.uk
Clary, Valerie 2, 252-3
Clarins* 130
uk.clarins.com
Clarkson, Jeremy 129
www.jeremyclarkson.co.uk
Collier, Catrin 195
www.catrincollier.co.uk
Collingwood, Charles 97, 268
www.bbc.co.uk/radio4/archers
Connelly, Victoria 105-6, 237
www.victoriaconnelly.com
Connolly, Lynne 225, 228, 268
www.lynneconnolly.com
Cook, Sue 121-3, 125, 267
www.suecook.com
Cooke, Rachel 177
*www.guardian.co.uk/profile/
rachelcooke*
Cookman, Lesley 186, 193
www.lesleycookman.co.uk

Cooper, Jilly 2, 85, 105
www.jillycooper.co.uk
Coren, Giles 43, 270, 273
http://twitter.com/gilescoren
Cork Evening Echo 83
Cornwell, Patricia 123
www.patriciacornwell.com
Country Life 185
www.countrylife.co.uk/magazine
Cowell, Simon 7, 44
www.simoncowell.org
Crampton, Robert 88, 159, 162-3, 178
www.thetimes.co.uk
Crowe, Russell 133
Cushion, Hazel Hazel 52, 94-5, 143, 193, 301
www.accentpress.co.uk

Daily Express 183, 188, 201
www.express.co.uk
Daily Mail 163, 167, 177, 201, 211, 257, 266
www.dailymail.co.uk
Daily Telegraph 84, 86, 177, 257
www.telegraph.co.uk
Dankworth, John 107
www.quarternotes.com
Darwin, Emma 12, 58, 120, 160, 268
www.emmadarwin.com
Davies, Ray 107
Davis, Bette 22
Davison, Emily 173
de Jour, Belle 230, 233
http://belledejour-uk.blogspot.com
de Ville, Cruella 265

Deal or No Deal 188
www.dealornodeal.co.uk
Demelza House Hospice 194
www.demelza.org.uk
Dench, Dame Judy 152
Deseine, Trish 202, 273
http://twitter.com/trishdeseine
Desert Island Discs 177
www.bbc.co.uk/programmes/b006qnmr
Dettori, Frankie 147
www.frankiedettori.co.uk
Devon Life 66
http://devon.greatbritishlife.co.uk/magazines
Diana, Princess of Wales 17
Disraeli, Benjamin 247
Doughty, Louise 86
www.louisedoughty.com
Dowling, Tim 276
www.guardian.co.uk/profile/timdowling
Drivetime 176
www.bbc.co.uk/radio2/shows
Duncan, Sarah 29, 91-2, 139
www.sarahduncan.co.uk
Dwyer, Valerie 172, 224, 227, 249, 281
www.mywonderfullifecoach.co.uk

Earl, Laura 123, 126
www.bbc.co.uk/kent
Eastcliff, Richard 221, 231-2, 272
http://eastcliffrichard.blogspot.com
EastEnders 66
www.bbc.co.uk/eastenders
Economist, The 192
www.economist.com

Edinburgh University Press 86
www.euppublishing.com
Edmonds, Noel 188
www.dealornodeal.co.uk
Edward Cecil Literary Agency 230
www.edwardcecilagency.com
Eggheads 191-2
www.bbc.co.uk/programmes/b006z736
Emin, Tracey 209, 266
www.tracey-emin.co.uk
Everest, Elaine 99, 159
www.elaineeverest.co.uk

Fabes, Lyn-Marie 143, 145
Falke, Tracy 143
http://twitter.com/tracy_falke
Family Circle 129
www.familycircle.com
Fearsome One, The 11-12, 14, 25, 29
Fforde, Desmond 63
Fforde, Katie 63, 92, 197, 278
www.katiefforde.com
Financial Times 133
www.ft.com/home/uk
Finnigan, Judy 23, 85, 154, 198-9
http://judyfinnigan.blogspot.com
Fiorato, Marina 62-4
www.marinafiorato.com
Floris 64
www.florislondon.com
Forsyth, Bruce 52
Forsyth, Frederick 85
www.booksattransworld.co.uk/frederick forsyth
Foyle, Shelagh 64
www.florislondon.com

Friday Project, The 228
www.harpercollins.co.uk
Frost, Miss Daisy 230-1, 274
www.missdaisyfrost.blogspot.com
Fry, Stephen 105
www.stephenfry.com
Fullerton, Jean 47, 159-60, 212-3, 269
www.jeanfullerton.com

Garland, Judy 107
Gayle, Mike 270
www.mikegayle.co.uk
Gayler, Paul 53
www.paulgayler.com
Gaynor, Hazel 228-9
http://twitter.com/hotcrossmum
Giggs, Ryan 195
www.ryangiggs.cc
Goddard, Robert 123
www.robertgoddardbooks.co.uk
Goethe 173
Goldwyn, Samuel 197
Goodman DFC, Flt. Lt. Michelle
Gornall, Jonathan 178
www.penguin.co.uk
Grant, Russell 117
www.russellgrant.com
Greaves, Jon 136
www.bbc.co.uk/programmes/ insideout
Green & Black's* 164, 187
www.greenandblacksdirect.com
Grey-Thompson, Dame Tanni 53
www.tanni.co.uk
Grisham, John 100
www.jgrisham.com

Guardian, The 176, 200, 210, 232, 257
www.guardian.co.uk
Guildford Book Festival 165, 167-8, 193, 196, 252
www.guildfordbookfestival.co.uk
Hackles, Lynne 188-91, 251
www.lynnehackles.com
Haddon, Jenny 192
www.jennyhaddon.com
Hall, Ian 198
www.watersidebooks.com
Halpern, Justin 229
http://twitter.com/
shitmydadsays
Harcombe, Andy 225, 243
www.webnetmarketing.ltd.uk
Harcombe, Zoë 243, 245-7, 262-4
www. theharcombediet.com
Harper Collins 58, 94, 170, 266
www.harpercollins.co.uk
Harriott, Ainsley 155
www.ainsley-harriott.co.uk
Harris, Joanne 257-8, 271
www.joanne-harris.co.uk
Hassall, Jill 215
www.greatest guides.com
Hayward, Sue 183
www.suehaywardmedia.com
Heath, Edward 167
Hegley, John 275
www.johnhegley.co.uk
Hello Magazine 229
www.hellomagazine.com
Hepburn, Katharine 247
Hom, Ken 107
www.kenhom.com

Houghton, Sue Sue 217, 225, 254
www.suehoughton.co.uk
Hume, Mick 24, 178
www.spiked-online.com
Hutton, Jean 198

Independent, The 183, 229
www.independent.co.uk
Inside Out 135, 139
www.bbc.co.uk/insideout
Ireson, Annie 76, 78
www.annieye.blogspot.com
Irish Independent 229
www.independent.ie
Isle of Thanet Gazette 54, 132, 180, 186, 231
www.thisiskent.co.uk/thanet

James, Peter 95-6, 187-8, 263-4, 278
www.peterjames.com
Janson-Smith, Patrick 4, 94, 170, 196, 215, 266
http://twitter.com/deadspy
Jason, Sir David 52, 53
Jewell, Lisa 26, 275
www.lisa-jewell.co.uk
Johncock, Ben 272
http://twitter.com/benjohncock
Johnson, Stanley
www.stanleyjohnson.com
Jones, Catherine 191-2
www.katelace.co.uk
Jones, Christina 109-10, 268
www.christinajones.co.uk
Jones, Jan 278
www.jan-jones.co.uk

Just For Starters 147

Kaplan, Juliette 65
www.juliettekaplan.com
Keating, HRF 184
Keeble DSC, Lieutenant Donald 53
Keith, Bernie 128
www.bbc.co.uk/northamptonshire
Keith, Penelope 12
Kelly, Grace 133
Kelly, Ross 140, 147
Kent on Sunday 52
www.kentonsunday.co.uk
Kettle Chips* 65, 187
www.kettlefoods.co.uk
Kilroy-Silk, Robert 24, 110, 137,
139, 143, 144
King, Sophie 127, 275
www.sophieking.info
King, William Benjamin Basil 173
King, Stephen 90-1
www.stephenking.com
Kinsella, Sophie 21
www.sophiekinsella.co.uk
Klass, Simone 40-1, 67, 117-8, 177,
209, 252, 262, 279
www.simoneklass.com
Knight, Bernard 86
http://authors.simonandschuster.co.uk/
bernard-knight
Knight, India 202, 270
http://indiaknight.posterous.com
Kyle, Jeremy 65, 119
www.itv.com/lifestyle/jeremykyle

La Senza 29
www.lasenza.co.uk

Lace, Kate 192
www.katelace.co.uk
Lalique 63
www.rlaliqueglass.com
Latham, Martin 78, 105-8, 166-7
www.waterstonescanterbury.
co.uk
Laura Ashley 130
www.lauraashley.com
Lawson, Nigella 105
www.nigella.com
Leaper, Paul 176
www.bbc.co.uk/kent
Lederer, Helen 165, 168, 196, 272
www.helenlederer.co.uk
Lee-Potter, Emma 157, 163-4, 275
www.emmaleepotter.co.uk
Lee-Potter, Lynda 163
Leith, Sam 84-7, 280
http://twitter.com/questingvole
Lewis, Leona 259
www.leonalewismusic.co.uk
Lewis, Linda 190-1
www.akacatherinehoward.weebly.com
Loose Lips 139, 152
Lynn, Dame Vera 53

Machin, Kevin 227
www.kevinmachin.pwp.blueyonder.
co.uk
MacGregor, Ewen 53
MacKenzie, Fiona 90
www.petsitters.co.uk
MacKenzie, Kelvin 109, 114, 116,
127, 133, 174-5, 251, 267
Macmillan Publishers 10, 154, 278
www.macmillan.com

Maddocks, Tom 118, 121, 122, 270
www.mediatrainingassociates.co.uk
Madeley, Richard 166, 168, 267
http://twitter.com/richardm56
www.richardandjudy.co.uk
Magnanti, Brooke 230
http://twitter.com/belledejour_uk
Mail on Sunday 202
Mangan, Lucy 12, 165, 210, 212,
222, 268
www.guardian.co.uk/profile/
lucymangan
Mansell, Jill 94, 128, 196, 252
www.jillmansell.co.uk
Marland, Mary Ann 210
Marsden, Rhodri 239
http://twitter.com/RHODRI
Marsh, Pat 123
www.patmarsh.com
Matthews, Carole 187, 198, 273
www.carolematthews.com
Mathias, Lorelei 241-3
www.loreleimathias.com
Mayne, Sadie 24
McCallum, Trevor 148
Red Door Television Ltd.
McCarthy, Maria 133, 175
www.mariamccarthy.co.uk
McKinley, Tamara 61
www.tamaramckinley.co.uk
McMullan, Paul 41, 282
Merton, Paul 124
www.paulmerton.com
Metro 202
www.metro.co.uk
Meyer, Stephenie 237
www.stepheniemeyer.com

Midas Public Relations 40, 221,
263, 271
www.midaspr.co.uk
Midgley, Carol 132, 211, 217, 276
www.thetimes.co.uk/tto/opinion/
columnists/carolmidgley
Midweek 124
Millard, Rosie 48, 183, 216
www.rosiemillard.com
Miller, Fenella 163
www.fenellajmiller.co.uk
Millington, Mil 165, 178
www.mil-millington.com
Mirza, Shazia 278
www.shazia-mirza.com
Missingham, Sam 280
www.thebookseller.com
Mitchelmore, Linda 66, 217, 219
lindaoccombe@tiscali.co.uk
Monbiot, George 185
www.monbiot.com
Montefiore, Santa 282
www.santamontefioreauthor.com
Moon, Lady Sarah 154
Moorcroft, Sue 116, 128, 225, 226
www.suemoorcroft.com
Moore, Suzanne 202, 211, 240,
241, 257, 276
http://twitter.com/SuzanneMoore197
Morgan, Nicola 233, 276
www.nicolamorgan.com
Morgan, Piers, 174
www.officialpiersmorgan.com
Mossiman, Anton 53
www.mosimann.com
Moyes, JoJo 87, 111, 256, 274
www.jojomoyes.com

Mulliken, Tony 40, 221, 262, 263, 271
www.midaspr.co.uk
Murby, Anna 117
My Weekly 37, 61, 111
www.dcthomson.co.uk

Naughtie, James 122
http://news.bbc.co.uk/today
New Writer, The 38
www.thenewwriter.com
New York Times 199
www.nytimes.com
News at Ten 17
Newsnight 110, 157, 230, 270
news.bbc.co.uk/1/hi/programmes/newsnight
Norton, Sheila 253
www.sheilanorton.co.uk
Nurofen* 68, 187, 209, 217
www.nurofen.co.uk

Observer, The 177, 257
http://observer.guardian.co.uk
O'Loughlin, Marina 202, 239, 275
http://twitter.com/MarinaMetro
O'Loughlin, Vanessa 223, 277
www.inkwellwriters.ie
Only Fools and Horses 139
Open Book 124
www.bbc.co.uk/programmes/b006qp6p
O'Reilly, Judith 229
www.wifeinthenorth.com

Pallenberg, Anita 130
Pankhurst, Emmeline 173
Parker, Shelley E 101

Parkinson, Michael 2
www.michaelparkinson.tv
Patch, Private Harry 53
Paxman, Jeremy 116, 120, 192
www.bbc.co.uk/pressoffice/biographies/biogs/news/jeremypaxman
Payne, Lisa 133
www.missmaybe.com
Pearce, Mike 54, 132, 180, 181
Penton Harper, Alison 36, 131, 154, 217, 256, 269
http://twitter.com/alisonph
Perkins, Anji 194
Petherick, Simon 62, 64, 281
www.beautiful-books.co.uk
Pilcher, Rosamunde 98
www.hodder.co.uk/authors
AuthorID=2178
Pinot Grigio* 249
Player, Gary 197
www.garyplayer.com
Prescott, John 113
http://twitter.com/johnprescott
Prince Charles 17
www.princeofwales.gov.uk
Private Eye 27
www.private-eye.co.uk
Psychologies 50
www.psychologies.co.uk
Pullen, Sqn Leader Jon 53
Pycraft, Glenis 167
www.guildfordbookfestival.co.uk

Randall, Penelope Jane 29
Rankin, Ian 2, 85
www.ianrankin.net
Rantzen, Esther 144

Raynor, Caitlin 268
http://twitter.com/bookywookydooda
Redgrave, Sir Steve 53
www.steveredgrave.com
Reed, Jo 19
http://joreed.co.uk
Rigg MC, Captain Dave 53
Ripa, Kelly 198
bventertainment.go.com/tv/buenavista/
regisandkelly
Robinson, Anne 178, 190
www.bbc.co.uk/programmes/
weakestlink
Romantic Novelists Association
81, 163, 191, 192, 205, 210, 278
www.rna-uk.org
Ross, Amanda 199
www.cactustv.co.uk
Rotary Club 73, 159, 214
www.ribi.com
Ryan Howard, Catherine 82-3,
214, 228, 236, 241, 244, 279-80
www.catherineryanhoward.com

Samson, Alan 85
www.orionbooks.co.uk
Scarlet Magazine 50, 183
Seeber, Claire 15
www.claireseeber.com
Sharpe, Adrian 188
Sky TV 142, 150, 152
Smart, Sarah 242
Smith, Rebecca 180
www.thisiskent.co.uk
Society of Authors 11, 84, 205, 210
www.societyofauthors.org
Spencer, Raine 17

Springett, Ulli 141
www.piatkus.co.uk
Stone, Carole 203, 206, 276
www.yougovstone.com
Strong, Sir Roy 259, 276
www.thelaskettgardens.co.uk
Sun, The 24, 109, 116, 135, 139,
175, 178
www.thesun.co.uk
Sunday Times 48, 58, 129, 183,
263
www.thesundaytimes.co.uk
Swanwick Writers' Summer
School 169
www.swanwickwritersschool.co.uk

Tesco 58
www.tesco.com
Thanet Times 182
www.thisiskent.co.uk/thanet
The Author 84
www.societyofauthors.org/author
The Good Day Show 142
The Heaven and Earth Show 147
The Politics Show 139, 143
*news.bbc.co.uk/1/hi/programmes/politics_*
show
The Salon 146, 147
The Weakest Link 190
www.bbc.co.uk/programmes/
weakestlink
The Wright Stuff 144, 255
www.five.tv/thewrightstuffonfive
Thomas, Pamela 167
www.guildfordbookfestival.co.uk
Tidy-Harris, Sylvia 272
www.womenspeakers.co.uk

Tobin, Tony 155
www.tonytobinrestaurants.co.uk
Today Programme 230, 242
news.bbc.co.uk/today
Transworld Publishers 11, 24, 29,
51
www.booksattransworld.co.uk
Trenfield, Phil 100, 195
www.myspace.com/philtrenfield
Trisha 24
www.trishatv.com
Trojan Condoms 178, 179
www.trojancondoms.com
Trollope, Joanna 216, 259, 266
www.joannatrollope.com
Turner, Brian 53
www.brianturneronline.co.uk
Turner, Janice 175
www.timesonline.co.uk

University Challenge 191, 192
www.bbc.co.uk/programmes/b006t6l0
Ursell, Amanda 48
www.amandaursell.com
USA Today 199
www.usatoday.com

Varney, Reg 2
Vickery, Phil 155
www.vickery.tv
Vine, Jeremy 177, 185-6
www.bbc.co.uk/radio2/shows/
jeremy-vine
Vokos, Marina 51

Wagner, Erica 86-7, 231, 271
www.ericawagner.co.uk

Wan, Gok 199
http://twitter.com/therealgokwan
Waitrose* 148, 187
www.waitrose.com
Walker, Kate 226, 233, 244
www.kate-walker.com
Warnett, John 128, 176
www.bbc.co.uk/kent
Waterstone, Sir Tim 105
Waterstone's 19, 77, 78, 79, 105,
106, 107, 184
www.waterstones.com
Watkins, Chris 222
Web Net Marketing Ltd 225
www.webnetmarketing.ltd.uk
Webb, Vanessa 75
Vanessa's Books
Vanessa@vrwebb.fsnet.co.uk
Weldon, Fay 177, 187
www.corvus-books.co.uk
Wener, Louise 178
www.louisewener.co.uk
WH Smith 81, 100, 198, 199
Whaley, Simon 241
www.simonwhaley.co.uk
White, Marco Pierre 194, 257
www.marcopierrewhite.org
Whitehouse, Melanie 109, 253, 277
www.melaniewhitehouse.com
WI 213
www.thewi.org.uk
Wickham, Madeleine 21
www.sophiekinsella.co.uk
Widdecombe, Ann 52-3, 116, 265
www.annwiddecombe.com
Williams, Kate 157, 271
www.kate-williams.com

Winfrey, Oprah 198
www.oprah.com
Wisden 192
www.wisden.com
Wisdom, Norman 105
www.normanwisdom.co.uk
Wogan, Sir Terry Terry 2, 196, 197
www.terrywogan.com
Woman & Home 218
www.womanandhome.com
Woman's Hour 124, 176
www.bbc.co.uk/radio4/features/womans-hour
Woman's Own 48
www.ipcmedia.com/brands/womansown
Woman's Weekly 37, 111, 285
www.ipcmedia.com/brands/womansweekly
Women in Journalism 194, 283
www.womeninjournalism.co.uk
Wood, Jo 130

Worrall-Thompson, Antony 53
www.awtonline.co.uk
Writers' Forum 190
www.writers-forum.com
Writers' Holiday 29, 241
www.writersholiday.net
Writing Magazine 19, 38, 104, 112, 210, 212, 285
www.writersnews.co.uk
X Factor 1, 113, 256, 282

Your Cat 111
www.yourcat.co.uk

Zemmel, Andrea 124, 125, 138, 148
Zigmond, Sally 98
http://sallyzigmondsbookblog.blogspot.com

*free samples gratefully received, product placement deals negotiable.

WANNABE A WRITER WE'VE HEARD OF?
Blurb-writing Competition

Closing Date 30th April 2011
Judging Panel includes
Matthew Bates – Book Buyer for WH Smith Travel
Hazel Cushion – Managing Director of Accent Press Ltd
Jane Wenham- Jones

To enter: Write a contemporary back-cover blurb for one of these classics and win lunch with a top book-buyer. Choose from:
The Age of Innocence by Edith Wharton
To Kill a Mockingbird by Harper Lee
Oliver Twist by Charles Dickens

Blurbs should be no more than 125 words and in a contemporary style as if these books were to be published for the first time today. For example modern blurb for *Pride and Prejudice* by Jane Austen, might read:

> Lizzie Bennett's mum is hell-bent on getting her daughter down the aisle and doesn't much care who she marries as long as it's soon. When the neighbours throw a huge party, she insists Lizzie and her sisters go along…

The best blurb for each book will win a year's subscription to *Writing Magazine* and *Writers' News*. The overall winner will be taken to lunch at a top London restaurant with Matt Bates from WH Smith Travel, Hazel Cushion from Accent Press Ltd and author and journalist Jane Wenham-Jones. Permission will be sought to publish the short-listed and winning entries on www.wannabeawriter.co.uk and the winner will be featured in *Writers' News*.

1) Entrants are invited to write a contemporary blurb for one of the three classics listed (maximum 125 words). Entries should be the original, unpublished work of the author.

2) Entries should be in English, typed and double-spaced on one side of the paper only.

3) The author's name should not appear on the blurb. Please attach an official entry form (no photocopies please) which can be taken from the back of *Wannabe a Writer We've Heard Of* or downloaded from www.wannabeawriter.co.uk

4) Only one entry per person

5) Entries cannot be returned

6) The judges decision will be final and no correspondence can be entered into.

7) Entries which fail to conform to these requirements may be disqualified

8) No cash prize alternative to the prizes will be offered.

9) All entries must be received no later than 30th April 2011

10) Entries should be posted to

Write a Blurb Competition
Wannabe a Writer We've Heard Of
Accent Press Ltd
The Old School, Upper High Street, Bedlinog, CF46 6RY.

Hand-delivered entries will NOT be accepted.
Copyright remains with the author but permission will be requested to display winning and short-listed entries on www.wannabeawriter.co.uk

The short list will be posted on www.wannabeawriter.co.uk by 30th June 2011 and the final winners by 30th July 2011. *The Writers' News* and *Writing Magazine* subscription will commence from the August 2011 issues. If you are a current subscriber you will be granted a year's free subscription renewal. The Winner's Lunch will be held at a time to suit all participants before the end of 2011.

THE NEW WANNABE WEBSITE

We hope you've enjoyed *Wannabe a Writer We've Heard Of?*

If you have a comment or query or simply want to get networking straight away, please visit:

www.wannabeawriter.co.uk

A one-stop resource and networking centre for writers at all stages of the journey to publication and fame!

The newly re-launched site includes message boards, forums, competition news, critique groups, online chat and "In the Guest Room" a blog spot featuring visiting agents, publishers and best-selling authors. Join up and meet other like-minded scribes, for encouragement, information and to keep up with the latest literary gossip.

Hope to see you online very soon!

jane wj xx

CONTACTS LIST

Name: ....

Title ....

Email address ....

Telephone ....

Info ....

....

Name: ....

Title ....

Email address ....

Telephone ....

Info ....

....

Name: ....

Title ....

Email address ....

Telephone ....

Info ....

....

Name: ....

Title ....

Email address ....

Telephone ....

Info ....

....

Name: ....

Title ....

Email address ....

Telephone ....

Info ....

....

Name: ....

Title ....

Email address ....

Telephone ....

Info ....

....

Name: ....

Title ....

Email address ....

Telephone ....

Info ....

....

Name: ....

Title ....

Email address ....

Telephone ....

Info ....

....

Notes

Notes

Notes

Notes

Notes

Notes

Notes

ALSO BY JANE WENHAM-JONES

Perfect Alibis

Jane Wenham-Jones

*"Throughly enjoyable and full of deft,
sparky humour"* – Jill Mansell

Stephanie – bored housewife and disillusioned mother – wants a job, and Madeleine's recruitment company appears to be the ideal place to go. Except that PA's isn't quite what it seems.

Far from providing companies with Personal Assistants, the agency offers Perfect Alibis to unfaithful women. And as Stephanie soon discovers, there are lots of them about!

Founder member Patsy is a serial philanderer and there could even be a dark side to her best friend Millie. For the well-heeled ladies of Edenhurst, PA's is a ticket to risk-free adultery.

When Stephanie's first love, Troy, returns to town even she is tempted. But her life is soon in turmoil, and that's before the tabloids get involved….

ISBN 9781905170852
£6.99

One Glass Is Never Enough

Jane Wenham-Jones

*"Delightfully sparkling, like champagne,
with the deep undertones of a fine claret."*

Three women, one bar and three different reasons for buying it. Single mother Sarah needs a home for her children; Claire's an ambitious business woman. For wealthy Gaynor, Greens Wine Bar is just one more amusement. Or is it?

On the surface, Gaynor has it all – money, looks, a beautiful home in the picturesque seaside town of Broadstairs, and Victor – her generous, successful husband. But while Sarah longs for love and Claire is making money, Gaynor wants answers. Why is Victor behaving strangely and who does he see on his frequent trips away? What's behind the threatening phone-calls? As the bar takes off, Gaynor's life starts to fall apart.

Into her turmoil comes Sam – strong and silent with a hidden past. Theirs is an unlikely friendship but then nobody is quite what they seem in this tale of love, loss and betrayal set against the middle-class dream of owning a wine bar. As Gaynor's confusion grows, events unfold that will change all of their lives forever...

ISBN 9781905170104
£6.99

Wannabe a Writer?

Jane Wenham-Jones

Foreword by Katie Fforde

This hilarious, informative guide to getting into print is a must-have for anyone who's ever thought they've got a book in them.

Drawing on her own experiences as a novelist and journalist, Writing Magazine's agony aunt Jane Wenham-Jones takes you through the minefield of the writing process, giving advice on everything from how to avoid Writers' Bottom to what to wear to your launch party.

Including hot tips from authors, agents and publishers at the sharp end of the industry, *Wannabe a Writer?* tells you everything you ever wanted to know about the book world – and a few things you didn't...

Contributors include writers Frederick Forsyth, Ian Rankin, Jilly Cooper and Jill Mansell and publishers Harper Collins, Hodder Headline and Simon & Schuster as well as leading journalists and agents.

ISBN 9781905170814
£9.99

Wannabe a Writer We've Heard Of?
Blurb-writing Competition

ENTRY FORM

Name:. . . . .

Address . . . .

. . . .

. . . .

. . . .

Email:. . . . .

Phone number . . . .

Classic chosen. . . . .
(Please choose from **ONE** of the following: *The Age of Innocence* by Edith
Wharton; *To Kill a Mockingbird* by Harper Lee; *Oliver Twist* by Charles
Dickens)

Number of words.(maximum 125) . . . .

**Please attach your blurb to this form. The entrant's name should NOT
appear on the manuscript.**

For full rules and address to send entries to, please see p301 or visit
www.wannabeawriter.co.uk

About the Author

Jane Wenham-Jones is an author and journalist. Her short stories and articles have appeared in a wide range of magazines and national newspapers and she has contributed to several anthologies including the successful *Sexy Shorts* charity collections and *Loves Me, Loves Me Not*, published by Mira Books to celebrate 50 years of the Romantic Novelists' Association.

She writes a regular column for her local paper, the *Isle of Thanet Gazette*, monthly pieces for both *Booktime* and *Woman's Weekly Fiction Special* and is the "agony aunt" for *Writing Magazine*. She has also published three novels.

A witty and articulate speaker, Jane gives talks and workshops and is regularly booked as after-dinner entertainment. She has appeared on many radio and TV shows and has presented for the BBC. She lives by the sea in Broadstairs, Kent

Also by Jane Wenham-Jones

Raising the Roof
Perfect Alibis
One Glass Is Never Enough
Wannbabe a Writer?

Photo by Bill Harris

Visit Jane's website at www.janewenham-jones.com